Birth of a Worldview

EXPLORATIONS

Lynn Davidman, Gillian Lindt, Charles H. Long,
John P. Reeder Jr., Ninian Smart, John F. Wilson,
and Robert Wuthnow, *Advisory Board*

*Birth of a Worldview: Early Christianity
in Its Jewish and Pagan Context*, Robert Doran

FORTHCOMING

*Politics and Religion
in the Contemporary United States*,
Robert Booth Fowler and Allen D. Hertzke

*The Book, the Church, and the Bishop:
Conflict and Consensus Building in the Early
Christian Church*, Peter Iver Kaufman

Images of Jesus, L. Michael White

Ancient Israelite Religion, Saul Olyan

Religious Ethos and the Rise of the Latino Movement,
Anthony Stevens-Arroyo and Ana María Díaz-Stevens

New Religions as Global Cultures,
Karla Poewe and Irving Hexham

Birth of
a Worldview

Early Christianity in
Its Jewish and Pagan Context

Robert Doran

AMHERST COLLEGE

Westview Press

BOULDER • SAN FRANCISCO • OXFORD

Explorations

Copyright © 1995 by Westview Press, Inc.

Published in 1995 in the United States of America by Westview Press, Inc., 5500 Central Avenue, Boulder, Colorado 80301-2877, and in the United Kingdom by Westview Press, 12 Hid's Copse Road, Cumnor Hill, Oxford OX2 9JJ

Library of Congress Cataloging-in-Publication Data
Doran, Robert, 1940–
  Birth of a worldview : early Christianity in its Jewish and Pagan context / Robert Doran.
      p.   cm. — (Explorations)
  Includes bibliographical references and index.
    ISBN 0-8133-8745-0 (hc.) — ISBN 0-8133-8746-9 (pbk.)
    1. Church history—Primitive and early church, ca. 30–600.
2. Theology—History—Early church, ca. 30–600.   3. Christianity and other religions—Judaism.   4. Judaism—Relations—Christianity.
5. Christianity and other religions—Roman.   6. Rome—Religion.
I. Title.   II. Series: Explorations (Boulder, Colo.)
BR166.D67   1995
270.1—dc20   94-39072
                                                                          CIP

Printed and bound in the United States of America

The paper used in this publication meets the requirements of the American National Standard for Permanence of Paper for Printed Library Materials z39.48-1984.

10   9   8   7   6   5   4   3   2   1

Contents

Acknowledgments

I want to thank my students at Amherst College for pressuring me to explain why these debates of the early church occupied so many minds and why they were so important. I also want to thank Elizabeth A. Clark for encouraging me in the early stages of the project. I am particularly grateful to Derek Krueger and L. Michael White for their close reading and detailed comments. Amherst College generously provided funds for the preparation of the manuscript, Diane Beck expertly typed it, and Susan Krautkremer was most helpful in telling me where I needed to say more. Spencer Carr of Westview Press was extremely supportive. Finally, thanks as always to my wife, Susan Niditch, who convinced me I could do it and was there when I thought I couldn't.

Robert Doran

Time Line

Roman Emperors	Persons and Events
Augustus, emperor, 27 B.C.E.–14 C.E.	Philo of Alexandria, ca. 20 B.C.E.–50 C.E.
	Birth of Jesus, ca. 6 B.C.E.
Tiberius, emperor, 14–37 C.E.	Josephus, ca. 35–100 C.E.
Gaius Caligula, emperor, 37–41	Paul, conversion, ca. 35
Claudius, emperor, 41–54	Seneca, fl., 40–65
	Letters of Paul, ca. 50–64
Nero, emperor, 54–68	Persecution of Christians at Rome, 64 (traditional date of martyrdom of Peter and Paul)
	First Jewish war, 66–74
Four emperors, 68–69	
Vespasian, emperor, 69–79	Destruction of Temple in Jerusalem, 70
	Synoptic Gospels, ca. 70–85
Titus, emperor, 79–81	Epictetus, fl., 80–120
Domitian, emperor, 81–96	Gospel of John, ca. 95
	Persecution by Domitian, 95
	Book of Revelation, ca. 95
Nerva, emperor, 96–98	
Trajan, emperor, 98–117	Pliny's correspondence with Trajan, 112–113
	Ignatius of antioch, martyred before 117
	Jewish revolts in Cyrenaica, Egypt, Cyprus, and Mesopotamia, 115–117
Hadrian, emperor, 117–138	Justin Martyr, fl., 130–165
	Second Jewish war, revolt of bar Kosiba, 132–135
	Basilides, fl., 132–135
	Marcion, fl., 140–161
	Valentinus, fl., 140–160
	Aristides, Apologist fl., 145
	Martyrdom of Polycarp, ca. 156
	Melito of Sardis, fl., 160–180

Antoninus Pius, emperor, 138–161

Marcus Aurelius, emperor, 161–180

Galen, fl., 160–200

Ptolemy, *Letter to Flora*, ca. 165

Montanist movement in Phrygia, ca. 172

Tatian, fl., 175–180

Pogrom of Christians at Lyons, 177

Celsus, *On True Reason,* 178

Irenaeus, bishop of Lyons, ca. 178–202

Commodus, emperor, 180–192

Scillitan martyrs, 180

Origen, ca. 185–254

Clement of Alexandria, fl., 190–215

Civil war, 193

Severan dynasty, 193–235

Monarchian controversies in Rome, ca. 190–220 (Noetus, the Theodoti, Praxeas)

Bardaisan, fl., 190–222

Tertullian, fl., 195–220

Persecutions in North Africa (Perpetua and Felicitas), Rome, Alexandria, Antioch, and Corinth, 202–206

Mishnah compiled, 200–220

Cyprian, ca. 200–258

Plotinus, ca. 205–270

Hippolytus at Rome, fl., 210–236

Further persecutions in Carthage, 211–213

Mani, founder of Manichaeism, 216–276

Sabellius, fl., ca. 220

Maximinus, emperor, 235–238

Christian church at Dura-Europos, ca. 232

Gordian III, emperor, 238–244

Porphyry, ca. 241–301

Philip the Arab, emperor, 244–249

Iamblichus, ca. 245–330

Frescoes of the Jewish synagogue at Dura-Europos, 244–245

The Sardis synagogue, mid-3rd century

Decius, emperor, 249–251	General order to sacrifice throughout the provinces, 250
Gallus, emperor, 252–253	Lactantius, ca. 250–325
Valerian, emperor, 253–260	Anthony the monk, ca. 251–356
Gallienus, emperor, 260–268	Eusebius of Caesarea, ca. 260–339
Claudius Gothicus, emperor, 268–270	Paul of Samosata, bishop of Antioch, ca. 260–268
Aurelian, emperor, 270–275	
Tacitus, emperor, 275–276	
Probus, emperor, 276–282	
Carus, emperor, 282–283	Manichees active in Egypt and Syria, 280–300
Carinus, emperor, 283–285	
Diocletian, emperor, 284–305	Anti-Manichaean measures by Roman government, 297
Empire divided into east and west, 293–303	Christians in army forced to resign, 298–302
	Athanasius of Alexandria, ca. 300–373
	Great persecution, beginning February 23, 303
Constantine hailed as Augustus, 306	Ephrem the Syrian, ca. 306–373
Constantine's defeat of Maxentius at Battle of Milvian Bridge, 312	Edict of Toleration by Galerius, 311
	Ulfilas, ca. 311-383
	Donatist schism begins, 311–312
	Edict of Milan, grant of universal toleration, 313
	Apollinaris of Laodicea, ca. 315–392
	Hilary of Poitiers, ca. 315–367
	Arian controversy, ca. 318
Constantine, sole emperor, 324–337	Council of Nicea, 325
	Gregory Nazianzus, ca. 323–389
	Basil of Caesarea, 330–379
	Gregory of Nyssa, ca. 335–395
Constantius II, emperor, 337–361	Aphrahat, fl., 337–345
	Ambrose of Milan, ca. 339–397
	Dedication Council of Antioch, 341
	Melania the Elder, ca. 342–410
	Jerome, ca. 347–419/420
	John Chrysostom, ca. 347–407
Julian the Apostate, emperor, 361–363	Theodore of Mopsuestia, ca. 350–428

Jovian, emperor, 363–364

Valentinian I, emperor in the west, 364–375

Valens, emperor in the east, 364–378

Gratian and Valentinian II, emperors in the west, 375–383 and 375–392, respectively

Maximus, emperor in the west, 383–388

Theodosius I, emperor in the east, 379–395

Eugenius, emperor in the west, 392–394

Arcadius, emperor in the east, 395–408

Honorius, emperor in the west, 395–423

Theodosius II, emperor in the east, 408–450

Alaric sack of Rome, 410

John, emperor in the west, 423–425

Valentinian III, emperor in the west, 425–455

Vandal invasion of North Africa, 429

Pelagius, ca. 350–425

Augustine of Hippo, 354–430

John Cassian, ca. 365–433

Cyril of Alexandria, ca. 375–444

Julian of Eclanum, ca. 380–455

Council of Constantinople, 381

Nestorius, ca. 381–451

Altar of Victory controversy, 382–384

Melania the Younger, ca. 383–439

Theodoret of Cyrrhus, 393–466

Jerusalem Talmud, ca. 400

Pelagian controversy, beginning 411

Disappearance of Jewish patriarchate, ca. 425

Council of Ephesus I, 431

Nestorius condemned, 431

Formula of Reunion, 433

Council of Chalcedon, 451

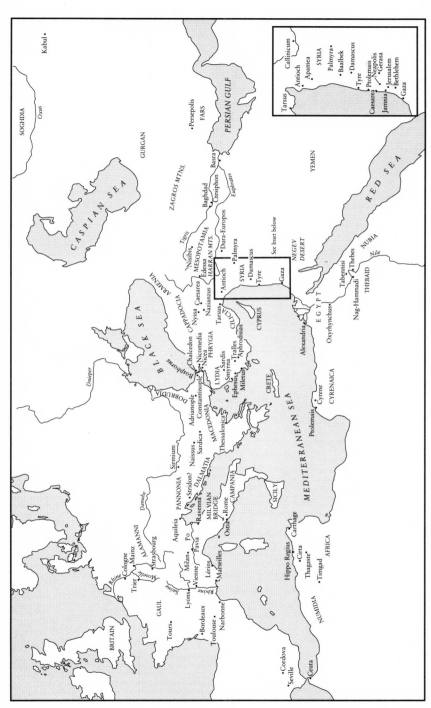

The Mediterranean World of Late Antiquity

Introduction

EVERY RELIGION MAPS ITS OWN UNIVERSE. Each in its own way locates where we humans are, where we have come from, where we are going. Each deals with the perils of the journey, the pain, suffering, and death, the disparities of rich and poor, of injustice and war. We all live and have lived in the same world, but the ways in which we see and understand this world differ markedly. For those of us who were brought up on *Star Trek* and a universe of ever-expanding horizons, the notion of a closed universe with the earth at the center and heaven above the realm of the fixed stars is endearing and quaint. Yet an application of this notion—namely, that Christ "ascended" into heaven—lies behind the creed recited by Roman Catholics at every Mass as well as by many other Christians. The theory of the evolution of species on this planet was shocking to people in the nineteenth century (as it is to some today), who believed that the earth had been created by God exactly as they saw it. To someone who believes that death is part of the natural cycle of life, clinging to life, however minimal or at whatever cost, is bizarre. Someone who believes in a personal existence after death looks at life quite differently from someone who sees life flowing on only in his or her children.

We do not receive information from outside as if we were blank photographic plates. Rather, our experiences are encoded into a system of signs and symbols that are part of our social culture and upbringing and that are often beyond awareness. This social web of symbols helps us give meaning and order to the innumerable random events of a day. Such assumptions about the world we live in can be called our worldview, the way we see and make sense of our life in this world. When we get a pain in our side, most of us, if we are modern Westerners, schedule a visit with a trained health care practitioner; we do not go, as others did and do, to a shaman or holy man or woman to be protected against the attack of an evil spirit. But all of us, wherever we are in space and time, whether devoutly religious or decidedly atheistic, endow the world with meaning and significance.

In this book I wish to explore how early Christian intellectuals expressed their understanding of the cosmos. There are many ways to approach the study of a worldview. Ninian Smart proposes one way—by looking at what he considers the six dimensions of a worldview:

1. The experiential, e.g., the feelings of awe and wonder in the presence of the numinous
2. The mythic, i.e., the sacred stories of a religious tradition
3. The doctrinal, e.g., the Roman Catholic doctrine of transubstantiation at the Eucharist
4. The ethical, e.g., the Ten Commandments
5. The ritual, e.g., baptism as an initiatory rite
6. The social, e.g., whether there is an ordained hierarchy or not[1]

On the basis of these categories, I must confess straightaway that this book belongs most easily to the doctrinal dimension. I do not discuss the various ways early Christians experienced the presence of God and Christ, either in visions and revelatory experiences, in the reading of sacred Scripture, or in a mystical ascent through the heavens. I do not discuss the growth of the rituals of the Eucharist, baptism, penance, and community prayer forms. I do not treat the growth of episcopal organization, nor do I address the fascinating web of interlocking relationships among leaders in the early Christian movement, a topic so well presented in the work of Peter Brown and Elizabeth Clark.[2] I am concerned, not with ethical codes of behavior for Christians, but rather with how their lifeways distinguished them from other religious groups. I discuss the interpretation of the sacred stories of Christians but not the development of a canon whereby some writings were excluded. I admit cheerfully that this book discusses the way early Christian intellectuals thought about God and his/her relationship with this earth and the humans on it. This book is thus intellectual history and not a blow-by-blow description of the events of the early church. There are many fine books that already undertake the latter task. And even though there are many books on the development of Christian doctrine, from the work of John Henry Cardinal Newman to that of Jaroslav Pelikan,[3] this book is different for two reasons: It eschews the mustard-seed fallacy, and it approaches early Christianity as a worldview.

THE MUSTARD-SEED FALLACY

The first way in which this book differs from other treatments of early Christian intellectual history is that it avoids what I call the mustard-seed fallacy. The fallacy has its basis in a parable in the Christian Scriptures that, in its version in the Gospel of Mark, reads, "[The kingdom of God] is like a mustard seed, which, when sown upon the ground, is the smallest of all the seeds on earth; yet when it is sown it grows up and becomes the greatest of all shrubs, and puts forth large branches, so that the birds of the air can make nests in its shade" (Mark 4:30–32).

This parable, which originally stressed the miraculous, unexpected nature of God's dealings with humans, became in the hands of the church fathers, and many present-day preachers, an allegory of the growth of the Christian church. The kingdom of God was equated with the church, the birds of the air with the Gentiles. As an allegory of the church, the parable stressed the inevitability of Christian growth and progress in the world. The church was seen as self-standing, autonomous: It may have taken time to achieve proper growth, but an inner dynamic led it on.

When we push the mustard-seed simile too hard, we wind up treating the history of the church as somehow independent, as if the church were an entity existing apart from Christians living in particular times and places. Such a treatment neglects how the history of Christianity was influenced and shaped by its cultural environment. The mustard tree must be seen as part of an ecosystem, not an independent entity.

As latecomers on the religious scene of Mediterranean antiquity, the early Christians interacted with older societies in which questions of the structure of the universe and of suffering had been answered in varying ways. The early Christians used the language of previous societies to describe their own particular vision of the universe. To be sure, every new religious movement reinterprets the language of the preceding religious tradition out of which it grows, but the early Christians faced a more complex situation. Jesus was a Jew who had lived in Galilee and Judea, but as people from the other religious traditions of the Mediterranean basin joined the Christian movement, the religious syntax of their societies also became part of the evolving articulation of the Christian worldview. The delicate task of Jews interacting with other religious traditions had already been anticipated to some extent in the way that certain Jewish authors had articulated their religious tradition in traditional Greek terms—for example, Abraham and Moses became inventors of benefits to humankind, just as the Greek gods had been. While Jesus was presenting his provocative parables, which did not explicitly state what the kingdom of God was but rather forced his listeners to rethink their assumptions about God's reign, Philo, a Jew in Alexandria, was discovering within the traditional Jewish religious literature ideas and ways of behavior similar to those advocated by Greek philosophers. Philo, who had been well educated in Greek philosophy, is one of the major representatives of the Middle Platonic school of philosophy. Yet most of his extant work is his reading of the Hebrew Scriptures as understood in Middle Platonist terms. As the maxim goes, whatever is received is received according to the mode of the receiver. As the gods appeared to humans according to each human's capacity, so the religious text was received according to each one's education. I therefore deem it important to discuss at some length the others who made up the world in which early Christian intellectuals worked.

First, we must recognize that it was a world in which the position of Christians had changed radically. From being a small minority, often persecuted, they had acquired by the fourth century a privileged position in the Roman Empire. This change is outlined in Chapter 1. Then, I discuss the intellectual worldview of Greek philosophers that formed part of the education of Christian leaders. In the mid-second century C.E., for example, Justin Martyr described his visit to various schools of Greek philosophy before he adopted the philosophy of Christianity. Chapter 2 therefore deals with the cosmos as envisaged by Stoic and Platonic philosophers.

Next, I examine the Hebrew Scriptures, the one constant ingredient in the Christian worldview. They, of course, became the Old Testament for Christians. We must not forget, however, that the world in which the early Christians lived was also a world in which Jews still continued to flourish and practice their faith. In Chapter 3, I bring together some of the evidence for the continuing vitality of Judaism in the Mediterranean basin through the fifth century C.E. In Chapter 4, I lay out the wide-ranging responses of Christian intellectuals to the Hebrew Scriptures, whether those responses were complete rejection, complete acceptance, or something in between.

I also take into account the fact that our information on early Christians and their views has come to us predominantly in texts written by urban, educated, upper-class males of the Roman Empire. It is primarily their voices that we hear, for they wrote the words down. In Chapter 7, I try to hear some of the voices of women, who were so much a part of the Christian movement, and I wonder what turns Christianity might have taken if those voices had not been so silent/silenced.

But it is not just that the mustard-seed simile tends to block out important external voices or influences. It also gives the impression that the root stock of the tree is pure and unsullied. A few dead branches may have to be trimmed, but the tree is basically whole and healthy. This notion is also extended to a "golden age" view of history: Heresies were a later infection brought into the church, usually by the alien virus of Greek philosophy. Such a golden age schema was, of course, a favorite among Greco-Roman historians of a moralizing bent. From Hesiod on, it had been used to describe the course of world empires. In the Hebrew Scriptures, Daniel had used it, as had the Roman historian Florus in the second century C.E. to describe the growth of the Roman Empire. The author of the Acts of the Apostles had also portrayed the early church idyllically: "And all who believed were together and had all things in common; they would sell their possessions and goods and distribute the proceeds to all, as any had need. Day by day, as they spent much time together in the temple, they broke bread at home and ate their food with glad and generous hearts, praising God and having the good-will of all the people" (Acts 2:44–47).

Such a utopian picture is, of course, much too serene and is contradicted even by the canonical Christian Scriptures themselves. The letters of Paul, particularly 2 Corinthians, bristle with polemic. Paul spoke sarcastically of his opponents as "superlative" apostles (2 Cor. 11:5) and set out in every way to destroy their standing in the community, as they had his. On another occasion, Paul expressed the wish that his opponents, who were advocating that Christians follow the laws of the Hebrew Scriptures and hence be circumcised, would castrate themselves (Gal. 3:10). By the middle of the first century c.e., then, about twenty years after the death of Jesus, there was clear evidence of divergent views on what it meant to be a Christian apostle: Very simply, should Christians emphasize the miracle-working, revelation-filled aspect of Jesus' ministry and see him as another divine man like Moses, or should they emphasize the suffering ignominy of Jesus' death on a cross? These views, as with all theoretical positions, had profound social implications: One stressed continuity with society; the other, a marginal, outcast relationship to the world.

Paul basically chose the second model and therefore vehemently argued against Christians having to follow all the detailed laws given to Moses by God as set out in the first five books of the Bible. The author of the Gospel of Matthew, in contrast, was concerned with setting up a stable community, a church, and proper rules of behavior. Matthew had Jesus say, "I have come not to abolish [the law and the prophets] but to fulfill. For truly I tell you, until heaven and earth pass away, not one letter, not one stroke of a letter, will pass from the law until all is accomplished" (Matt. 5:17–18). Matthew's community probably did follow the Mosaic law and commandments. It interpreted them differently from the synagogue across the street, but it followed them. Certainly the letter of James in the Christian Scriptures, while not completely antithetical to Paul's position, modified it: "A person is justified by works and not by faith alone" (James 2:24). The figure of Paul, in fact, became a flashpoint in the growing Christian tradition: For the Jewish-Christian author of the Clementine Recognitions, Paul was an arch-heretic who had to be expelled from the church, whereas for some second-century Christians with strong anti-Jewish tendencies, Paul was the apostle par excellence. Perhaps the best statement of Paul's ambiguous status was made by the author of 2 Peter 3:16: "There are some things in [Paul's letters] hard to understand, which the ignorant and unstable twist to their own destruction."

But there is divergence in the Christian Scriptures not only concerning Christian apostleship but also concerning the very person of Christ. Who is this Jesus? The four canonical Gospels of Matthew, Mark, Luke, and John presented four different kinds of Christ. Take, for example, what each writer had Jesus say as his last words.

Matthew (27:46) and Mark (15:34) are identical: "My God, my God, why have you forsaken me?" Here the language of Psalm 22:1 is used to express the despair and rejection of the lonely figure on the cross, which is the very antithesis of the astonishment and news of his resurrection.

At Luke 23:46, a passage from Psalm 31:5 is used as the last words of Jesus: "Father, into your hands I commend my spirit." With these trustful words, Jesus, the innocent victim, becomes the model for followers like Stephen, the first martyr in Acts 7:59.

John 19:28–30 says, "After this, when Jesus knew that all was now finished, he said (in order to fulfill the scripture), 'I am thirsty.' A jar full of sour wine was standing there. So they put a sponge full of the wine on the hyssop and held it to his mouth. When Jesus had received the wine, he said, 'It is finished.' Then he bowed his head and gave up his spirit." Nothing quite captures John's portrait of Jesus as this supreme instance of control over bodily functions: Jesus dying when he wills. In John's gospel, Jesus is the one who comes down from heaven and dwells in his body and has complete control over it. There is no despair in this scene, nor is Jesus a model for others: He is a unique figure.

We could pursue these variances in the fourfold presentation of the one Jesus—and scholars have done so. What I wish to underscore is that, if there was a symbiosis (whether peaceful or tense) between a gospel and the community/audience for which it was written, then there were different ways in which a person could be a Christian *from the very beginning of Christianity.* What I am concerned to present in this book are the vitality and validity of the many ways in which early Christian intellectuals envisioned the world. Frequently, the development of early Christian doctrine is imagined in almost evolutionary terms, as providentially leading to what is best in an almost inevitable, inexorable movement, with the rest imaged as nonadaptable organisms, as relics to be discarded, as wrongheaded heretics. What I wish to stress are the positive qualities of those Christian views later deemed heretical and to suggest what was lost when they were rejected—the recognition that history is not an inescapable upward thrust but a very human process of making choices. It is this fascinating process that is skipped over or undervalued by the mustard-seed simile.

THE WORLDVIEW APPROACH

The second way in which this book differs from other treatments of early Christian intellectual history lies in the questions that undergird its structure. I try to treat early Christianity as a worldview, a religion. I attempt to ask of early Christianity the questions that a student of any religion has to ask: How does the religion structure the world? And how does it explain suffering and death? In his famous essay on religion as a cultural system, Clifford Geertz underscores that every religion has to formulate conceptions of a general order of existence.[4] The world has to be comprehensible, not chaotic, have an order and structure that make sense of, and give meaning to, everyday incidents. Structure here means not only the placing of the earth, moon, sun, and stars in sequence, which can be important parts of a worldview, but also and primarily the designation of where the source of power lies in the universe. Through oracles, the gods of the Mediterranean world of the second and third centuries C.E. gave advice on when and whom to marry, how to become pregnant, when to plant crops, and how to avert plagues and famine.[5] A supplicant had to know which god or goddess was angry or which would be benevolent—that is, where the power lay. By the fifth century, many of these oracular functions had been taken over by holy men: The questions remained the same, but now the worshiper had to know how best to approach God and his Son.[6] The general order of existence also has to explain questions of suffering and injustice: Why do children die? Why do unjust, cruel humans enjoy life and go unpunished?

It is with this notion of religion that I approach the world of early Christianity. Chapter 5 deals with how Christian intellectuals structured their cosmos and where they located the source of power and protection in the universe. It examines the debates among Christians in the fourth and fifth centuries that are normally called the Arian and Nestorian heresies. I see these debates as attempts to render how the Christian cosmos is ordered. Likewise, Chapter 6 deals with the Pelagian heresy but from the perspective of how Christian thinkers incorporated the undeniable facts of suffering and injustice into a world made by a good god.

This book is intended to introduce readers to the fascinatingly dappled character of early Christian intellectual history. To achieve this goal, I purposely provide in the text itself rather lengthy quotations of primary sources. The translations, unless otherwise noted, are mine. Quotations from the Bible are from the New Revised Standard Version translation. I hope these generous quotations give the readers a taste of the literature and encourage them to delve more widely into writings by early Christian thinkers. I also provide suggestions for further reading to help readers find their way into this complicated but rewarding literature.

ᴄᴆ ONE ᵈᴏ

Christians and the Roman World:
A Sense of Belonging

ON JULY 17, 180 C.E., TWELVE CHRISTIANS from the small settlements of Scilli near Carthage stood in the chambers of the governor of North Africa in Carthage. Carrying with them the letters "of a just man named Paul," they were arraigned for being Christians. That was the only charge leveled against them. They insisted that they had never done any wrong, but being a Christian was enough in a Roman's eyes to condemn them to beheading. They went joyfully to their execution.[1]

The account of this trial is fascinating. Its very brevity and conciseness suggest that it is a trial record, without the usual embellishments so often found in the accounts of martyrs. Its starkness only highlights what was at stake. According to a letter from the Emperor Trajan in 112 C.E. to Pliny the Younger, governor of Bithynia in Asia Minor, Christians could be executed just for being Christians, for they were seen as a threat to the state. Not only were their meetings illegal, but in a society where religion and city life were so intertwined, the formal rejection of the ancestral gods for a new god was in itself an attack on society. Thus, when Polycarp, the aged bishop of Smyrna, was led before the governor in 157 C.E., he was asked to disassociate himself from the atheists, that is, the Christians (*Martyrdom of Polycarp* 9).

In the second and the early part of the third century, attacks against Christians came from ordinary people who saw the Christians as bringing the displeasure and disfavor of the gods on their cities.[2] Tertullian, writing in the late second century, caustically remarked that some considered the Christians as "the cause of every public defeat and every misfortune of the people. If the Tiber rises to the city walls, if the Nile does not rise to the fields, if the sky stays the same, if the earth moves, if there is a famine, a plague, straightaway the cry is heard, 'The Christians to the lion!'" (*Apology* 40.1–2). Even in the early fifth century, Augustine of Hippo cited as a popular proverb, "No rain? The Christians are the cause!" (*City of God* 2.3). The gruesome tortures the Christians underwent in Lyons in 177 C.E., so graphically described in Eusebius's *Ecclesiastical History* (5.1), seem to have been the result of some popular uprising against these Christian "atheists." There was no persecution from the imperial authorities, except insofar as the governor would hand down the final sentence of death, imprisonment, or slavery. One Roman governor laughed at Christians who came to him of their own accord and confessed that they were Christians; he told them that if they were so eager to die, there were plenty of ropes to hang themselves with or cliffs to jump off (Tertullian *To Scapula* 5.1). Many Christians, in fact, seem to have desired death, so that Christian leaders warned against volunteering for martyrdom (*Martyrdom of Polycarp* 3). Most officials showed no hesitation in condemning these societal malcontents.

We do not know the precise circumstances surrounding the trial of the Scillitan martyrs, but one curious fact does emerge from the trial proceedings. In stating the defense, the spokesperson for the martyrs, Speratus, argued that they had never done any wrong or stolen, "and on any purchase I pay the tax, for I acknowledge my lord who is the emperor of kings and of all nations." While belonging to this antisocietal group, Speratus engaged in normal market activity and did not try to disrupt the financial system of the city and imperial government. Such anomalies are not hard to find in the history of the Christians in the Roman Empire.

CHRISTIANITY BEFORE CONSTANTINE

A variety of attitudes to the Roman Empire was already present in the Christian Scriptures. Paul's letter to the Romans encouraged Christians to obey proper civic authorities and to pay taxes (Rom. 13:1–7). While insisting that Christians live as aliens and exiles in their society, the author of 1 Peter 2:11–17 urged his hearers to "accept the authority of every human institution, whether of the emperor as supreme, or of governors." Yet the Christians who heard the Book of Revelation saw the Roman Empire symbolized as bloodthirsty and bestial and those who were martyred as triumphing over that beast; they looked forward to a new Jerusalem that would come down out of heaven to replace Roman society.

This sense of opposition and confrontation between the Christians and the Roman Empire was perpetuated by stories about the martyrs that circulated quickly among Christians. In a commentary on Daniel, the Roman Christian Hippolytus, who lived in the early third century, applied to his own day Daniel's vision of the four beasts in Daniel 7. The last and most horrible beast was the Roman Empire, which held people in subjection with its feet of iron. Hippolytus looked forward to the empire's fall and the liberation of all peoples (*Commentary on Daniel* 2:12–13; GCS 1.68). Tertullian compared the Romans to the barbarian Phrygians (*On the Pallium* 2.6). Such an attitude was only reinforced when the Emperor Decius himself imposed persecution on the Christians in 250 by ordering them to offer animal sacrifices to the gods for the health and well-being of the empire. Decius had come to the throne at a particularly crucial time. Rome had just celebrated its one thousandth year of rule in 247, but the Goths had attacked Rome in 248. Decius had forced the Goths out of the Danube provinces and in return had been hailed emperor by his troops (he would die fighting the Goths in June 251). In the midst of this crisis, Decius appealed to the gods of the empire for help in restoring it. Forces that interfered with a harmonious relationship between the Romans and the gods were to be eliminated. That meant the Christians. Although the persecution did not last long, it was the first general persecution of the Christians by Roman authorities and was to be repeated again under the Emperor Valerian in 257–260 and under Diocletian with the great persecution, which began on February 23, 303. We must not neglect the religious motives of the persecutors: The empire was constantly under threat in the latter part of the third century. Few emperors died peacefully; most died on the battlefield. In this atmosphere of crisis, the emperors asked for help from their traditional benefactors, the gods, and sought to remove anything or anyone who might displease them.

But we should not overlook the fact that the persecutions were sporadic and provoked by some immediate crisis or that most Christians were not quite so uninvolved with worldly affairs. Some Christians were Roman soldiers, even though that would have required them to participate in the pagan rituals soldiers normally performed and leading Christians such as Tertullian, Hippolytus of Rome, and Origen opposed Christian participation in military service.[3] The Christian art remaining from the third century combines religious themes with decorative schemes common to contemporary pagan work, as, for example, in the catacomb of Domitilla in Rome, where Christ is depicted, like Orpheus, amid animals.[4] Bishop Cyprian of Carthage in the mid-third century C.E. warned against priests combining their clerical office with secular affairs, acting as bailiffs on imperial or private estates, or functioning as trustees for family pension funds (Letter 1). In Caesarea a little earlier, the great theologian Origen had been no more flattering in his portraits of Christian audiences in his sermons: men concerned about business and how to make money, women gossiping so loudly nothing could be heard (*Homilies on Exodus* 13.3).

We can sense this involvement with the world most clearly, perhaps, in the effect of the first official empirewide persecution of the Christians by the Emperor Decius. Many Christians lapsed and offered sacrifice, while others offered bribes to obtain certificates stating they had sacrificed. When Bishop Cyprian returned to his hometown after the persecution was over, he distinguished for penitential purposes between those who had actually lapsed and sacrificed and those who had only acquired a certificate (*On the Lapsed* 27–28). Presumably the ability to bribe depended on wealth and rank.

By the middle of the third century, the Christians were a recognized part of the towns in the Roman Empire. Nevertheless, the social contours of the early Christians are impossible to reconstruct with precision, and scholars still debate about how numerous and influential the Christians were in the period before the arrival of the Emperor Constantine. Robin Lane Fox holds that they "were a small minority" and that claims to an impressive advancement of Christianity before the coming of Constantine need to be treated skeptically.[5] W.H.C. Frend, in contrast, sees the advance of Christianity as "quickening," as making inroads into pagan society, and holds that Diocletian's decision to persecute the Christians in 303 c.e. was a response to the threat posed by their size and influence.[6] Without more evidence, it is impossible to give a complete picture. No doubt the answer lies somewhere in between: In some cities, wealthy Christians produced a favorable atmosphere for the acceptance of Christianity; in others, wealthy pagans ensured that the traditional religion was retained. Evidence does suggest that the Christians, no matter what their size, were a *vocal* minority.

Constantine the Great

Constantine's rise to power changed the Christians' position in society. His vision—in which he accepted Christ as his benefactor and conquered opponents with the sign of the cross—became a favorite theme of artists, and much has been written about its precise significance: Did Constantine accept Christ only as another god among the pantheon, as a more precise expression of the sun god, or was his a true conversion? We can argue all sides of the question.[7] Whatever the answer, the Christians were now the recipients of imperial benefaction. By the edict of Milan, no one could be stopped from entering the Christian religion or any other religion of his or her choice. Gifts to the Christians soon followed: the shrine of Saint John Lateran in Rome and, in the twenty-five years after his victory over Maxentius, by which he gained control of the western Roman Empire, a series of church buildings from Rome to Jerusalem, ordered by Constantine mostly at his own expense. In a letter to Eusebius of Caesarea and other bishops, Constantine gave permission to rebuild and restore churches.

> But now that freedom is restored, and that serpent driven from the administration of public affairs by the providence of the great God and by our service, I believe that the divine power is manifest to all, and that those who through fear or through unbelief have fallen into any errors will recognize the true God, and come to the true and right way of living. Therefore, remind the churches over which you preside, as well as the bishops, presbyters, and deacons presiding in other localities whom you know, to give serious attention to church buildings: either to repair the existing ones or to enlarge them, or, if necessary, to build new ones. You yourself and the others through you will ask for what is needed both from the provincial governors and from the prefects. For they have been

told to provide with all readiness what is said by your Holiness. (Eusebius *Life of Constantine* 2.46; GCS 7.60–61)[8]

Constantine also gave the very desirable gift of tax exemption to Christian clergy:

> From many instances it appears that great dangers to public affairs are brought about when divine worship, by which the greatest reverence for the most holy divinity is maintained, is set at naught, and that when it is legally restored and maintained it brings about the greatest good fortune to the Roman name and special prosperity to all human affairs, for divine beneficence bestows these blessings. Therefore, it has seemed good that those men who, with proper holiness and constant attendance upon this law, bestow their own services to the ministry of divine worship, should receive the rewards of their own toils, most honored Anulinus. Wherefore, I determine that those persons who are within the province committed to you and in the Catholic Church over which Caecilian presides, and who bestow their own services on this holy worship (those whom they are accustomed to call clerics) should once for all be kept free from all the public offices without qualification, so that they will not be drawn away by any wandering about or sacrilegious omission from the worship which is due to the Divinity, but that rather they may assist to the utmost at their own usages without any disturbance. (Eusebius *Church History* 10.7; see also CTheod 16.2.1–6, and 14)

These benefactions changed the position and standing of the Christians in Roman society. Times of persecution gave way to times of joy and benefaction. We catch a glimpse of what it meant to a Christian who had lived through these times in the oration that Eusebius of Caesarea gave on the thirtieth anniversary of Constantine's reign in 336. Within this speech Eusebius, as was proper on such an occasion, certainly lauded Constantine, but it is interesting to note the language he used. In discussing how Constantine delegated authority to his sons (without, of course, mentioning the execution of several other sons), Eusebius wrote that by the appointment of these sons as caesars, Constantine "fulfills the oracles of the holy prophets which long ago cried out, 'and the saints of the most high God shall receive the kingdom'" (*Oration* 3; GCS 7.200–201). Here Eusebius quoted from Daniel 7:15, a text that envisions the end of four bestial empires and the beginning of the time of the Son of man, that is, the beginning of the time of the saints. Daniel 7 had been used heavily by the gospel writers to predict the second coming of Jesus, as, for example, in Mark 13:26–27 and 14:62 and in the Book of Revelation 11:15–18. By the use of such loaded biblical language, Eusebius linked Constantine and his regime to the kingdom of Jesus. Eusebius reinforced this linkage by his parallel use of Constantine and the Word of God. Speaking in a mixed setting, Eusebius used the more neutral term *Word* rather than a specific reference to Christ.

The only-begotten Word of God co-reigns with his Father from ages without beginning to limitless, unending ages. So his friend [the Emperor], supplied with kingly emanations from above and empowered by the surname of the divine name, rules on earth for long periods of years. Again, the Savior of the universe arranges beautifully all of heaven, the world, and the kingdom above for his Father. His friend leads his subjects on earth to the only-begotten and saving Word and makes them fit for his kingdom. The Savior of all, by his invisible and divine power, keeps far away the rebellious powers which at times fly around in the air above the earth and attack men's souls, like a good shepherd wild beasts from his flock. His friend, adorned by him from on high with his trophies against his enemies, chastens the visible enemies of truth whom he conquered by the law of war. The Word, who has existed before the world and is the Savior of all things, imparts the seeds of reason and salvation to his followers, and makes them both reasonable and possessing knowledge of his Father's kingdom. His friend, as an interpreter of the Word of God, calls the whole human race back to the knowledge of the Mighty One, shouting out for all to hear and preaching in a mighty voice to everyone on earth the laws of true piety. (*Oration* 2; GCS 7.199)

Here, just as the Word of God guides and governs the heavens, so the emperor is placed on earth to govern it. No wonder that, for Eusebius, monarchy is the best form of government (*Oration* 3; GCS 7.201). Within that framework, the emperor is the interpreter of the Word of God—what a fascinating thing for a bishop to say. Constantine clearly did consider himself such. He himself arbitrated a dispute as to who was the legitimate bishop of Carthage, deciding on November 16, 316, in favor of Caecilian over Donatus; he deposed and exiled bishops such as Asclepas of Gaza, Marcellus of Ancyra, and the famous Athanasius of Alexandria for doctrinal as well as behavioral reasons; and he summoned bishops to councils to settle disputes that had arisen concerning the divinity of Jesus, an issue discussed in Chapter 5. After the Council of Nicea in 325, Constantine wrote a letter to the churches and described how much he had enjoyed being as one of the assembled bishops, their fellow servant (Eusebius *Life of Constantine* 3.17; GCS 7.84). According to Eusebius of Caesarea in a letter to his church (PG 20.1536–1544), Constantine undertook a forceful role in determining that the bishops accept one of the crucial terms of the Nicene Creed, *homoousion*—a term to which we return in Chapter 5.[9]

CHRISTIANITY AFTER CONSTANTINE

A year after Eusebius had pronounced in his oration to Constantine that the emperor was the interpreter of the Word of God, Constantine died. The next decades would raise with striking clarity the issue of how closely Christianity was to be related to the governing structure of society. Now that the Christian church was no longer an ostracized community but rather a recipient of imperial favor, would the church become an instrument of social control, with the emperor as God's exegete, or would it claim its own role?

Constantine's successors did attempt to achieve harmony and concord in the ecclesiastical world. Numerous councils were summoned, but the losers in these debates became disenchanted with the role of the emperor in church affairs. In *Ecclesiastical History*, written in the mid-fifth century, Theodoret of Cyrrhus detailed the persecutions that the Arians had committed against believers of the true faith (for example, 4:13–22; GCS 19.232–260). Constantius II was a particular target of disgruntled ecclesiastical leaders. Athanasius of Alexandria drew up a list of atrocities that the troops sent by Constantius had committed against those loyal to Athanasius's cause (*Apology for His Flight,* written in 357 [PL 25.643–680], and *History of the Arians,* written in 358 [PL 25.691–796]), as did Hilary of Poitiers in his *Book Against Constantius,* written in 360. "But now we fight against a traitorous persecutor, against a flattering enemy, against Constantius the antichrist" (PL 10.581).

The most violent attacks came from Lucifer of Calaris. This bishop, exiled in the late 350s, wrote to Constantius, "If to initiate false charges, to persecute God's worshipers, to introduce idolatry into the church of God, to cut the throats of those who believe in the only Son of God by means of his soldiers, if these are not evil endeavors, then these curses [from Deuteronomy] will not overtake you and your running-dogs" (*On Athanasius* 1.8; CCL 8.16). Bishop Lucifer also sent another book to Constantius entitled *On Apostate Kings* (CCL 8.135–161). Constantius could afford to be mild in the face of these attacks and comport himself as if beyond anger because his power was never really in question. These resentments, however, also sometimes led to statements, preponderantly by some bishops in the western empire, that challenged the unrestricted role of the emperor. Ossius of Cordova, who had been one of Constantine's trusted agents, wrote to Constantius, "Do not impose yourself into church affairs. Do not command us about them, but rather learn about them from us. God has put the kingdom into your hands; to us he has entrusted what pertains to His church" (quoted in Athanasius *History of the Arians* 44.7; PG 25.745). For Lucifer of Calaris, it was the duty of princes to obey bishops, and not vice versa, and Constantius should have kept within the bounds of his authority (*On Athanasius* 1.7; CCL 8.12–13). Although the words were brave, they did not stand against the emperor's forces.

A further complication in the relations of church and emperor was the rise to power of the emperor Julian, who succeeded Constantius in 361 and ruled for only eighteen months. Julian had been brought up as a Christian but had converted to paganism. His brief reign saw the taking back of all benefactions to Christians, as Julian favored pagan festivals and rituals. Christians were not exactly persecuted, but they were restricted and hemmed in. Julian's brief reign showed only too clearly how the rise to prominence of the church had been dependent on imperial favor and how fickle that favor was.

After Julian's quick exit from the scene, the Christians were once again in favor: Jovian's short reign of eight months (June 363–February 364) was succeeded by that of another Christian soldier, Valentinian I, who reigned in the western Roman Empire from 364 to 375, while his brother, Valens, ruled the east from 364 to 378. Throughout their reigns, they fought to secure the Roman borders. Valentinian was concerned with keeping the empire alive, and, as an almost contemporary historian wrote, he "remained neutral in religious differences, neither troubling anyone on that ground nor ordering him to reverence this or that. He did not bend the necks of his subjects to his own beliefs by threatening edicts, but left such matters undisturbed as he found them" (Ammianus Marcellinus 30.9.5). After Valentinian I's death, the western empire was eventually divided between his sons, Gratian and Valentinian II. On Valens's death, the eastern empire was given to a Spanish soldier, Theodosius I.

Ambrose of Milan

These next years were decisive in the articulation of the Christian church's relations with the state. One important player in this drama was Bishop Ambrose of Milan. As the residence of the imperial court, Milan was an important center: Strategically placed, Milan allowed the emperor to move quickly into Gaul, toward the Danube, down into Italy, or across into the Balkans as needed. Ambrose became bishop of Milan on December 7, 373. Born into the Roman aristocracy, he had been acclaimed bishop by the populace while governor of the province of Aemilia-Liguria, of which Milan was the administrative seat. He was a strong member of one party of Christians, the Nicenes (which are examined in Chapter 5), and was in no wise conciliatory, if not downright roughshod, toward his opponents. His chance came with the accession of Gratian, a young man of sixteen, to the emperorship of the western Roman Empire. At first Gratian had followed his father's policy of toleration, but after he met Ambrose, events changed. A council that met at Aquileia in 381 was packed with Ambrose's friends and supporters and rapidly deposed two members of the opposing Christian party. The meeting was also significant because Ambrose ran the proceedings without the interference of lay arbitrators. In his words, "Priests ought to judge lay people, not laypeople priests" (*Acts of the Council of Aquileia* 51; CSEL 82.357). When Gratian was murdered and his half-brother, Valentinian II, and mother, Justina, came to Milan, a further confrontation took place. Justina was a member of the Arians, a Christian party different from that of Ambrose. When Justina asked for a church wherein her type of Christians could worship, Ambrose refused. In a letter to his sister, Ambrose retold the surrounding incidents, which took place in 385, with evident glee. He forbade his community to communicate with soldiers who came to take over the church. With his people around him, Ambrose began to preach against Justina, whom he labeled another "Jezebel" and "Eve."

> Then the command: "Hand over the başilica." I answer: "It is not lawful for me to hand it over, nor is it proper for you to receive it, O Emperor. If you are not able by any authority to violate the house of a private individual, do you think you can appropriate the house of God?" It is alleged that the Emperor is allowed to do so, that everything is his. To this I reply: "Do not burden yourself, O Emperor, so that you think that you have imperial authority over things which are divine. Do not exalt yourself, but, if you wish to be emperor for a long time, be subject to God. It is written: "What are God's to God, what are Caesar's to Caesar." Palaces belong to the emperor, churches to the bishop. To you have been given authority over public buildings, not over sacred ones. (Letter 76.19; CSEL 82)[10]

The court of Valentinian II gave way. Ambrose, a superb politician, outmaneuvered the recent arrivals, Justina and Valentinian II, and showed who had control of the city.

Ambrose confronted another emperor, Theodosius I, in 389. When a group of monks destroyed a Jewish synagogue and a chapel belonging to the Valentinian Christians at Callinicum, a fortress town on the Euphrates, Theodosius ordered the bishop to repair both edifices and punish the offenders. Ambrose was indignant. In a letter to Theodosius (74.14; CSEL 82),[11] Ambrose argued with the emperor to let the matter drop. Ambrose described the synagogues as "a place of unbelief, a house of impiety, a shelter of madness which God himself has condemned. ... God forbids us to pray for those that you think should be vindicated." And he called the Valentinian Christians heathens. Laced throughout the letter were subtle threats of divine vengeance if Theodosius continued with his plans. Ambrose made strong use of the biblical analogy of the remonstrance of the prophet Nathan to King David, with the implied suggestion that God could withdraw his support of Theodosius. Ambrose ended his letter with another threat: "I have done what was able to be done honorably, so that you might hear me in the palace rather than, if it be necessary, hear me in the Church" (74.33; CSEL 82).

He carried out this threat. In another letter to his sister (Extra collectionem 1; CSEL 82),[12] Ambrose described the ensuing confrontation, which took place in church. During a sermon to the people on how they had to care for the church, a sermon replete with attacks on the Jews, Ambrose suddenly turned to the emperor and addressed him directly, right there in front of the congregation, and exhorted him to care for the church. Theodosius understood the hint that he should not force the Christians to rebuild the destroyed synagogue and Valentinian church. Ambrose would not continue with the eucharistic service until Theodosius indicated that he would do as Ambrose proposed. The public pressure that Ambrose brought to bear on the emperor was enormous, as both stood in Ambrose's place of power, with the Christian community around them. Theodosius relented, allowing himself to be swayed by Ambrose; he thus both showed his own clemency and publicly demonstrated the esteem in which he held the church.

Ambrose used this position of esteem in 390. That summer the citizens of Thessalonica rioted, and one of Theodosius's senior officers was killed. In retaliation, Theodosius invited all the citizens in Thessalonica to the amphitheater, and then had them massacred. Around seven thousand men, women, and children were slaughtered. Again Ambrose took up his pen and privately rebuked the emperor, urging him to do public penance, for otherwise Ambrose could not admit to communion a known public murderer (Extra collectionem 11; CSEL 82).[13] The emperor repented and accepted the public penance. The church interpreted this incident as showing that it was the link between humans and God and that in certain areas it had authority over the emperor. No one was above moral law. Ambrose was not advocating a state run by priests, however. He recognized the legitimate sphere of the emperor but also carved out a place for the interests of the church.

The Assault on Paganism

These interests were becoming more and more clear in the late fourth century. Firmicus Maternus, a converted pagan, wrote to Constantius and Constans in the middle of the fourth century, urging them to stamp out pagan religious practices:

> But necessity commands you, Most Holy Emperors, to punish and chastise this evil, and it is enjoined on you by the law of the supreme God that your severity prosecute in every way the crime of idolatry. Hear and entrust to your holy consciousness what God commands concerning this crime. In Deuteronomy this law is recorded, for it says: "But if your brother, or your son, or your wife who is in your bosom, or your friend who is equal to yourself, should ask you, saying secretly: Let us go and serve other gods, the gods of the Gentiles, you will not join with him and you will not listen to him. Your eye will not spare him, and you will not hide him. You will surely make known about him; your hand will be the first upon him to kill him, and afterwards the hands of all the people; and they will stone him and he will die, because he sought to turn you away from your Lord." He orders that neither son nor brother be spared, and directs the sword as an avenger through the beloved limbs of a wife. A friend also he persecutes with lofty severity, and all the people is roused to arms to rend the bodies of sacrilegious people. Destruction is determined even for whole cities, if they are apprehended in this crime. (*The Error of Pagan Religions* 29.1–2)[14]

Such an attitude was clearly at odds with the principles of toleration laid out by Constantine and Licinius in the Edict of Milan in 313. In 319–320,

Constantine did lay down laws that restricted access to the temples, but this was for illicit magical processes. Such magic had always been perceived by the state as threatening to public order and in particular as perhaps directed against the emperor himself. The state had always been willing to outlaw religious practices that it had judged harmful to itself: Socrates was condemned for bringing in new gods that would corrupt the city's youth; Plato had wanted to prohibit private cults.

> Upon all these cases one general law should be enacted, which will make most offend less against the gods by word and deed, and also become less foolish, through not being allowed to minister in divine things contrary to the law. Let this law be enacted for everyone without qualification: Let no one possess a shrine in private houses; when anyone decides to sacrifice, let him go to the public places to sacrifice, and hand over his offerings to the priests and priestesses to whom belongs the concern for the purity of these offerings; and let him join in the prayers with whomever he wants to pray with him. ... If anyone is known to have acted impiously, not like the sins of children, but like that of wicked adults, either by dedicating a shrine in private areas, or by sacrificing in public areas to any gods whatsoever, so as to sacrifice while impure, let him be condemned to death. (Plato *Laws* 10.909D–910D)

Cicero noted that Roman law forbade the cult of new or foreign gods unless they had been adopted officially: "No one shall have gods apart from the rest, neither new gods nor foreign gods, unless recognized by the State" (*Laws* 2.8.19). So the worshipers of Isis had been expelled from Rome in 221 B.C.E. as disturbers of Roman public order, and the last non-Christian emperor, Diocletian, had outlawed the Manichees (a group discussed in Chapter 6) in 297 C.E. as a threat to Roman security. Constantine, however, was not concerned about the use of magic for healing or for bringing about a better harvest—this was good magic (CTheod 9.16.3)—and he encouraged people to attend public cults (CTheod 9.16.1–2). The first Christian emperors, in fact, showed little inclination to enforce uniform religious belief on their subjects. Even Constantius II, who forbade the offering of sacrifices and ordered the temples closed (CTheod 16.10.5–6) after he defeated the pagan-tolerant usurper Magnentius (350–353 C.E.), did not interfere with the traditional priesthoods and kept appointing their holders. As Theodoret of Cyrrhus wrote about the Emperor Valens, "The rites of Zeus, of Dionysus, and of Demeter were performed not in a corner, as they would be in a pious reign, but bacchants were running through the middle of the forum" (*The Ecclesiastical History;* 4.24.3; GCS 19.262).[15]

Theodoret, in the mid-fifth century, was writing in a world different from that of Valens, who allowed freedom of worship for non-Christians, was an Arian Christian, and persecuted the Nicene Christians. For Theodoret, a pious Christian emperor would not allow pagan activities. But Valens's successor, Theodosius I, also allowed sacrifices at first, only prohibiting use of sacrifices for magical purposes (CTheod 16.10.7–8).

But a change was coming, as indicated in the affair of the Altar of Victory in Rome in 382. To this goddess, worshiped by the army, Augustus had erected an altar in the Senate in 29 B.C.E., and it was a symbol of the favor that the gods bestowed on the Roman Empire. Constantius II had removed it in 357 C.E., but it had been replaced after debate by the Emperor Julian, in part as an act of defiance against the Christians. Now Gratian in 382, under the influence of Ambrose of Milan, refused to accept the traditional title of *pontifex maximus,* or pontiff, and once again removed the statue and Altar of Victory from the Senate. The final blow came when Gratian cut off imperial treasury funds to pagan priests and the Vestal Virgins and refused to fill vacancies in the priests' ranks. After Gratian's murder in 383, Symmachus, a pagan Roman senator and relative of Ambrose, wrote to Valentinian II to request that the Altar of Victory be returned to the Senate.

Let your Eternity accept the other deeds of this same Emperor [Constantius] which he properly put into practice. He took away nothing from the privileges of the Vestal Virgins; he filled the priesthoods with men of noble birth. He did not refuse the expenses for Roman ceremonies; he followed a joyful senate through all the streets of the Eternal City and calmly looked at its shrines, and he read the inscribed names of the gods on the pediments; he asked about the origins of the temples; he admired their founders and, although he himself followed other rites, he safeguarded these [Roman ceremonies] for the Empire.

Everyone has his own custom, each his own religious ceremonies. The divine mind assigned to the cities various protectors so that, just as souls are apportioned to children being born, so the destined tutelar deities are apportioned to peoples. Besides this there is the usefulness which especially sets the gods near to humans. For since everyone's judgment moves in secret, from where shall his knowledge of divine commands more properly come than from the memory and the lessons of favorable events. If long space of time gives authority to religious observances, one should keep faith with so many centuries, and we should follow our parents, who followed their parents and were treated favorably.

Let us now think that Rome herself appears and addresses you with these words, "Noble emperors, fathers of your country, respect my years, which I attained by dutifully performing religious ceremonies. Let me practice my hereditary ceremonies, for I am not ashamed: I will live by my own custom, for I am free. This worship brought the world under my laws; these sacred rites repelled Hannibal from my walls and the Senones from the Capitol. Have I therefore been preserved so that in my old age I might be censured?"

I will consider what should be established, but the correction of old age comes too late and is an affront. Therefore, we ask for peace for our ancestral gods, for our patron deities. It is reasonable that whatever all worship be considered one. We look at the same stars, the sky belongs to all, the same universe surrounds us. What does it matter by what method each seeks the truth? One cannot arrive at so great a secret by only one road. (Letter 72a.7–10; CSEL 82.25–27)[16]

Symmachus's eloquent appeal fell on deaf ears. The old order was over. Victory came, not from the gods, but from the Christian God. Ambrose of Milan threatened religious sanctions against the emperor if he listened to Symmachus: "If this were a civil case, the opposing party would be guaranteed the right of reply. This is a religious case, and I, the bishop, claim that right. ... Certainly, if anything else is decided, we bishops cannot calmly allow it and pretend not to notice. You will be allowed to come to the church, but you will find there either no priest or one who will resist you" (Letter 72.13; CSEL 82).[17] Ambrose ridiculed the rites of the pagans and the ability of wooden gods to help:

> By only one road, he says, one cannot reach so great a secret. What you do not know, we know by God's voice; what you seek by guesses, we have found from the very wisdom and the truth of God. Your ways do not agree with ours. You implore peace for your gods from the emperors; we pray for peace for our emperors from Christ. You adore the works of your hands; we reckon it wrong to think that anything which can be made is God. (Letter 73.8; CSEL 82)[18]

The debate between paganism and Christianity was not confined to exchanges of correspondence. The destruction of the synagogue and the Valentinian church at Callinicum was but one in a whole series of incidents whereby Christians sought to erase the images of traditional religions and rewrite the map of the religious world of late antiquity. The pagan rhetor Libanius wrote an oration to the emperor in 386 in which he described in biting terms what was happening:

> You then have not ordered either that the temples be closed or that no one should enter them. You have not driven out from the temples and altars fire or incense or the offerings of other perfumes. But this black-garbed mob, who eat more than elephants and who, by the huge amount of cups drained, make it a hard job for those who accompany their drink with songs, who conceal these deeds by the paleness which they artificially acquire—these people, O King, although the law remains in force, run against the temples carrying cudgels and stones and bars of iron, while some, without these, use hands and feet. Then there is complete destruction as roofs are pulled down, walls demolished, statues are dragged down, altars pulled up, and the priests must either be silent or die. When the first is destroyed, there is a rush to a second and a third, and, contrary to law, trophy is heaped on trophy. Most take place in the countryside, but some even in the cities. The attacking forces in each case are numerous, but after countless abuses these separate groups come together and demand an account from each other of what they have done, and it is shameful not to have done the greatest damage. So they spread through the fields like flooding rivers, and plunder the fields by means of the temples. For wherever they pluck out a

temple from a field, that field is blinded and lies inactive and dies. (*Oration* 33.8–9)

Imperial legislation was indeed slower than the attacks of the monks. Just as the Christians had at first been seen as angering the gods, so now non-Christians brought disaster and by the worship of their gods hindered the kindness of the Christian God. On February 24, 391, Theodosius issued an edict that prohibited all sacrifices, and on June 16 he basically closed down the temples: "Let no one pollute himself with sacrificial animals; let no one slaughter an innocent victim; let no one approach the shrines, go through the temples, or honor the images formed by mortal action, lest he become liable to divine and human penalties. Let the authority to sacrifice be granted to no one, let no one go around the temples; let no one honor the shrines" (CThead 16.10.10–11).

The Christians of Alexandria immediately took advantage of the edict to destroy the wondrous temple of Sarapis in Alexandria.[19] The final legal blow came during the usurpation of imperial power in the west by Eugenius in 392–394. Theodosius issued a decree on November 8, 392, that completely suppressed the freedom of the pagan cults.

> Let no one at all, of whatever origin or order of men or of dignities, whether placed in authority or enjoying the dignity, whether he is powerful by the lot of birth or is humble in origin, rank or fortune, slaughter an innocent victim to images which lack sensation in any place at all or in any city. Let him not, by a more secret rite, venerate his lar with fire, his genius with wine, his penates with fragrant odors; let him not burn lights to them, lay incense before them, or hang up garlands for them. (CTheod 16.10.12)

The Christian God once more triumphed over the pagan gods in battle, and Eugenius was defeated in September 394. Two years later, the sons of Theodosius revoked the privileges accorded to pagan priests: "If any privileges have been granted by ancient law to priests, ministers, prefects, hierophants of the sacred mysteries, or by whatever name they are called, let such privileges be completely abolished. Let such people, whose profession is known to be condemned by law, not rejoice in the fact that they are protected by any privilege" (CTheod 16.10.14).

No pagan was forced to convert, and processions and spectacles were too popular to destroy overnight. But public prayers and sacrifices to the gods were forbidden. The empire was publicly Christian. As Prudentius wrote in his poem *Against Symmachus*:

> Instructed by such edicts, the city [Rome] fled her ancient errors and dispelled the thick clouds from her wrinkled brow, as her leaders were ready to attempt the eternal ways, to follow Christ at the call of their high-minded guide and place their hope in eternity. Then Rome, docile in old age, first blushed for her

past centuries, was ashamed of the time gone by, and hated the past years with their detestable religious rites. (1.506–513; CSEL 61.238)

Pour in then Almighty, to these harmonious lands! The world, which Peace and Rome hold by a united bond, now holds you, O Christ! You command these to be the source and culmination of events, and Rome without Peace is not acceptable to you. (2.634–637; CSEL 61.270)

Here the new creation, Christianity, encompassed a renewed world empire, the Roman.

Augustine of Hippo

But it was a Christianity of a particular kind. Throughout the fourth century, emperors had exiled bishops who had disagreed with them, but the end of that century saw the use of imperial troops to enforce orthodoxy against recalcitrant heretics and schismatics. The most fascinating case study for the development of this policy on the use of force remains Africa and the Donatist schism[20] and within this the development of the ideas of Augustine, bishop of Hippo, whose career is examined in more detail in Chapter 6. When Augustine was first priested in 391, he was eager to persuade both his congregation about right observances and his Donatist opponents about correct faith. Stubborn, and sometimes violent, resistance to his efforts at persuasion slowly changed his mind. When imperial agents arrived in Africa in 399 to close pagan shrines, Augustine supported them. "Do we say, 'Wish not what you wish?' Rather, let us even give thanks that you wish what God wishes. For God wishes that all superstition of the pagans and Gentiles be destroyed. God commanded, God foretold, God now begins to fulfill, and in many parts of the earth he has already in great part fulfilled" (Sermon 24.6; CCL 41.331).

In 401, the Catholic bishops of Africa asked the government for repressive measures against the Donatist schismatics. It is not known whether Augustine endorsed these policies expressly, but there is no reason to suppose that he would have opposed them. He was, however, not fully supportive. In Letter 93, written in 408, however, he explained his changing position on the use of force:

93.2   If anyone were to see his enemy, delirious with dangerous fever, running headlong, would he not be returning evil for evil if he were to let him go on so, rather than if he had him caught and bound? Yet he might then seem to the man himself most hateful and most hostile when he would have shown himself most helpful and merciful. But, when he recovered his health, he would be as exceedingly grateful as he had previously thought that he should leave him alone. Oh, if I could show you how many active Catholics we now have from the very ranks of the Circumcellions who condemn their former life and the wretched error by which they thought that whatever they used to do in restless recklessness they were doing on behalf of the church of God. Yet they would not have been

brought to this state of health unless they had been restrained, like those with fever, by the bonds of those laws which displease you. What of that other kind of
deadly illness of those who had no troublesome insolence, but who were long
weighed down with inertia and would say to us: "What you say is true; we have
no response. But it is hard for us to relinquish the way of our parents"? Should
they not, for their own good, be shaken up with the stick of temporal troubles,
so that they might come out as if from a lethargic sleep and awaken to the health
of unity? Also, how many of those who now rejoice with us find fault with the
former weight of their deadly custom, and confess that we were right to trouble
them so that they might not perish as in a deadly sleep from a disease of long-
standing habit?

93.3   But on the other hand, with some those measures do not succeed. Is a
medicine, then, to be disregarded because some have an incurable plague? You
pay attention only to those who are so hardened that they do not accept this discipline. For about them it is written: "In vain have I smitten your children; they
did not accept discipline" (Jer. 2:30). I think, however, that they have been
struck in love, not in hatred. ...

93.9   No instance is found in the Gospels or the letters of the Apostles where
any help was sought from the kings of the earth for the Church against the enemies of the Church. Who denies that one is not to be found? That prophecy was
not yet fulfilled: "Now, O kings, understand; receive instruction, you that judge
the earth. Serve the Lord in fear" (Ps. 2:10–11). But up to the present, that other
passage earlier in the same psalm was fulfilled, in which it is said: "Why have
the nations raged and the people plotted vain things? The kings of the earth
stood up and the princes met together against the Lord and against his Christ"
(Ps. 2:1–2). Truly, if past events in the prophetic books were figures of future
ones, both periods were foreshadowed in the king named Nabuchodonosor:
what the Church experienced under the Apostles, and what she now experiences. So, in the time of the Apostles and martyrs, that part was fulfilled which
was prefigured when the renowned king tried to force devout and upright men
to adore an idol, and threw them into the fire when they refused. But now that is
fulfilled which was prefigured a little later in the same king when he was converted to the true God and decreed for his kingdom that whoever blasphemed
the God of Sidrach, Misach, and Abdenago should suffer due penalties. Therefore, the first part of that king's reign signified the earlier periods of unbelieving
kings, whom the Christians instead of the impious endured, but the latter part
of that king's reign signified the periods of later faithful kings whom the impious endured instead of the Christians. ...

93.17   I have, then, yielded to these examples furnished to me by my colleagues. For my opinion at first was that no one should be forced into the unity
of Christ, but that we should act by speaking, fight by disputing, and conquer
by reasoning, lest we make pretended Catholics out of those whom we knew as
open heretics. But this opinion of mine has been overcome, not by the words of
those opposing me, but by the examples of those proving their point. For first of
all was set before me the case of my own city, which had been wholly Donatist,
but was converted to Catholic unity by the fear of imperial laws, and which we

now see so detests the mischief of your animosity that one might believe it had
never existed there at all. ...

   93.19   With these gains of the Lord round about to contradict me, should I
stand in the way of my colleagues so that the sheep of Christ, wandering on your
mountains and hills—that is, on the swellings of your pride—should not be
gathered into the sheepfold of peace, where there is "one fold and one shepherd"? (John 10:16; CSEL 34.446–463)

Here Augustine outlined how his change of opinion was based on the ef-
fectiveness of the strong-arm methods used by his episcopal colleagues.
Against those who objected to the use of the imperial military to settle
intrachurch disputes, Augustine skillfully retorted that different times required different methods. His main purpose was to characterize his Donatist
opponents as sick and unsound, therefore not amenable to argument and requiring extreme treatment. To characterize an opponent as mentally unstable and in need of restraint was to take a step down a slippery path, but
Augustine would not change his mind. The most famous bolstering of this
attitude was Augustine's interpretation of part of the parable of the wedding
feast in Luke 14:15–24. In Luke's version of the parable, when all the invited
guests refuse to come to the feast, the host sends out his servants to bring in
people to dine; but there is still room, and the host then says to his servants,
"Go out into the highways and byways and compel them to come in."
Augustine seized on this marvelous hyperbole and announced, "Do you
think no one should be compelled to do right, when you read that the master
of the house said to his servants: 'Whomsoever you find, compel them to
come in'?" (Letter 93.5; CSEL 34.449).

This attitude toward religious coercion would seem to categorize
Augustine as a firm adherent of imperial Christianity, as Eusebius of Caesarea was. Yet Robert A. Markus demonstrates with great clarity how this
view was in tension with deeper currents in Augustine's thought.[21] It is true
that Augustine, in works dated to 399–400, was first caught up in
triumphalist Christianity, which held that the spread of Christianity was the
fulfillment of biblical prophecies:

> For all those things, which you now see taking place throughout the whole
> world in the Church of God, and under the name of Christ were already pre-
> dicted long ago: what we see corresponds to what we read. By means of these
> things we are built up in faith. ... It was foretold not only by the prophets, but
> also by the Lord Jesus Christ Himself, that His Church would exist throughout
> the whole world, spread abroad by the martyrdoms and sufferings of the saints.
> This was foretold at a time when even His name was hidden from the nations
> and, where it was known, was laughed at. By the power of his miracles, how-
> ever, whether he performed them himself or through his servants, we already
> see that what was predicted is fulfilled as these things are being reported and be-
> lieved; the very kings of the earth, who formerly persecuted Christians, are now

subject to the name of Christ. (*On the Catechising of the Uninstructed* 27.53.1.7; CCL 46.175–176)

When the imperial troops arrived to destroy the pagan temples, Augustine emphatically identified these events with the ushering in of a new era:

> For what is fulfilled by Christians was not predicted in Christian times, but long ago. Those very Jews who have remained enemies to the name of Christ, about whose future faithlessness these prophetic writings have not been silent, themselves possess and read the prophet who says: "O Lord my God, and my refuge in the day of evil, to you the nations shall come from the ends of the earth, and say, 'Surely our fathers have worshiped lying idols, and there is no profit in them'" (Jer. 16:19). Behold, that is now being done. Behold, now the Gentiles are coming from the ends of the earth to Christ, saying these things, and breaking their idols! (*The Harmony of the Gospels* 1.26; CSEL 43.39)

As late as 417, Augustine appealed to the notion of a changing world to justify the use of coercive power against the Donatists: "Those who do not wish to enact just laws against their own wicked deeds say that the Apostles did not seek such things from the kings of the earth. But they do not consider that it was a different time then, and that all things have to be done at their proper times. For which emperor then believed in Christ, or who would have served Him by enacting laws on behalf of religion and against irreligion?" (Letter 185.19; CSEL 57.17).

Gradually eclipsing this triumphalist strain, however, was another motif that would dominate Augustine's great *City of God:* "All history [outside the scriptural canon] is starkly secular, that is to say, it is incapable of being treated in terms of its place in the history of salvation."[22] There was to be no Christian empire. In discussing the prophecy concerning Gog and Magog in the Book of Revelation 20:7–15, Augustine refused to interpret it as applying to some contemporary races outside Roman dominion but understood that prophecy as applying to some events at the end of the world, whenever that might be (*City of God* 20.11). The sack of Rome by the Visigoths under Alaric in 410 had led to questions about the new "Christian times." Had the abandonment of the traditional Roman gods brought about this destruction? Why could not the Christian God have saved Rome?

Such questions led Augustine to write the *City of God,* which quickly outran the bounds of its immediate causes to become a profound meditation on the relation of Christianity to paganism, of the Christians to the world in which they lived. Augustine's thought is dominated by the image of the church on a pilgrimage. Here the city of God is intermingled with the city of this world, and it can never attain true peace until God decrees the end of time (19.26–27), just as there can never be true justice, the proper requirement for a city, until all things and people are fully subject to God (19.21). In a letter from 418, Augustine argued that no one should try to calculate the times and seasons of the coming kingdom of Christ:

> However, I do not know whether we can discover anything more definite on this question—if we are able by any reasoning or ability—than what I wrote in my previous letter about the time when the whole world will be filled with the Gospel. For what your Reverence thinks, namely, that this has already been brought about by the Apostles themselves, I have not proved by sure authorities. For that there are among us, that is, in Africa, innumerable barbarian tribes among whom the Gospel has not yet been preached is daily taught to us clearly from those who are brought from thence as captives by the Romans and are mixed in with Roman slaves. ... The Lord did not promise by means of an oath the Romans but all nations to the seed of Abraham. ... In whatever nations the Church is not yet, it must be that it will be. (Letter 199.46–48; CSEL 57.784–787)

There were still plenty of barbarian peoples to be preached to and, even in the Roman Empire, much to be done. Commenting on Psalm 61:5, Augustine said, "Those people who fill the churches on the festivals of Jerusalem fill the theaters for the festivals of Babylon" (PL 36.73). Such a view led to a radical secularization of political life. As Markus so eloquently states:

> The true Church was both holy and worldly; in some sense it had also to suffer persecution from the world. In no way, at any rate, could it be identified with any worldly institution, and conversely, no worldly institutions could ever validly claim to be "Christian" or "sacred." In Augustine's eschatological perspective the distance between the only true Christian society and any historical society, past, present, or future, was infinite. His recasting of the vocabulary of ecclesiology implied that in so far as one could speak of any society possessing any quality of sacredness, one could do so only in virtue of its eschatological orientation. ... Augustine sharply rejected the notion that any society might be modelled on the heavenly city, or reflect it as an image reflects its archetype.[23]

The use of a metaphor of pilgrimage and alienation, however, is also radically different from that in the writings of the first Christians: Augustine was not advocating an escape from the world. The world is the arena in which Christians live, and they, too, must seek to live harmoniously in it. We must remind ourselves that Augustine was no fringe person: He was a bishop of a small town, whose daily activities involved arbitration in lawsuits and whose correspondence was with important imperial officials.[24] Augustine was very much an establishment figure, as evidenced by his insistence on the notion of order in society. Even though Augustine broke with the late Platonic notion of human perfectibility through human society, he nevertheless asserted that Christians have a duty to serve in society. He was deeply aware of the problems of social living: "Who would have the strength to number or who would be adequate to estimate with how many and with what enormous woes human society abounds amidst the tribulation of this mortality?" (*City of God* 19.5). He discussed in minute detail the difficulties of a judge in lawsuits, the ignorance that forced him to sometimes condemn the innocent or torture witnesses to obtain knowledge: "In these dark areas of life in society, will that wise man sit as a judge, or will he not dare to do so? Clearly, he will sit; for the claims of human society constrain him and draw him to this duty; to desert society brings offense" (*City of God* 19.6).

The Christian *will* take a place within society to make sure that it functions properly. "The sphere of politics is relative and restricted; within its restricted area, it is autonomous; but in its very autonomy it is a matter of deep concern to the citizen of the heavenly city."[25]

> Therefore the use of those things necessary for this mortal life is common to both types of humans and households, but each has its own very different goal in using them. So the earthly city, which does not live by faith, seeks an earthly peace, and sets up an agreement as regards commanding and obeying so that there may be a certain accommodation of human wills concerning the things that pertain to this mortal life. But the heavenly city, or rather the part of it that sojourns in this mortal life and lives by faith, uses of necessity this peace too, until this mortality for which such a peace is necessary passes away. ... It does not hesitate to obey the laws of the earthly city by which those things that are fit to sustain mortal life are administered so that, since this mortality is common, harmony may be preserved between both cities in the things that pertain to this mortal life. ...
>
> Therefore, this Heavenly City, while it sojourns on earth, summons citizens from all peoples, and gathers an alien society of all languages. It does not care whatever difference there may be in manners, laws and institutions by which earthly peace is procured or maintained, and does not abolish or destroy anything of these, but rather preserves and follows them. For, however different they may be among different nations, they aim at one and the same goal of earthly peace, as long as they do not hinder the religion by which the one most high and true God is taught to be worshiped. Therefore, even the heavenly city in this sojourn uses the earthly peace, and guards and seeks the harmony of human wills concerning the things that pertain to the mortal nature of humans, as far as it agrees with sound piety and religion, and refers the earthly peace back to the heavenly peace. (*City of God* 19.17)

Augustine here provided a rationale for young men to enter public life, to be part of the imperial governmental bureaucracy. As Peter Brown so gracefully says, "The *City of God,* far from being a book about flight from the world, is a book whose recurrent theme is 'our business within this common mortal life'; it is a book about being otherworldly in the world."[26] The Christian, in Augustine's view, was still an alien in the world but was now a resident alien.

CONCLUSION

In cities large and small Christians were born, lived, worked, married, reared children, paid taxes, and died. But from the fourth century on, Christians were redoing the cultural map of Roman society. Now the Christian liturgies were openly celebrated, and the ebullient processions and feasts in honor of the gods and goddesses were discontinued. The birth of Christ at Christmas was celebrated instead of the feast of the unconquered sun, and the Christians took over the liturgical calendar. The oracular site of Sarpedon in Asia Minor became the shrine of Saint Thecla. Pilgrims flocked to Simeon Stylites on his pillar outside of Antioch in Syria in the first half of the fifth century, rather than to the oracle of Apollo, to ask questions, and medallions of Simeon hung on the doorways of shops in Rome, rather than statues of the gods and goddesses, warded off evil. Orthodox Christians, wherever they fell on the issues concerning the relationship of church and state, were no longer a persecuted minority but a potent cultural force in society. But how were these Christians going to structure their world? What was to be their worldview? How would they explain the existence of the world or see its structure and organization? How would they account for the physical suffering and moral injustice that they still witnessed in it? It is to these questions that we now turn.

Suggestions for Further Reading

Barnes, Timothy D. *Constantine and Eusebius.* Cambridge, Mass.: Harvard University Press, 1981.

_____. *Early Christianity and the Roman Empire.* London: Variorum, 1984.

Brown, Peter. *Augustine of Hippo.* Berkeley and Los Angeles: University of California Press, 1967.

_____. *Religion and Society in the Age of Saint Augustine.* New York: Harper, 1972.

_____. *Power and Persuasion in Late Antiquity: Towards a Christian Empire.* Madison: University of Wisconsin, 1992.

Cadoux, Cecil John. *The Early Church and the World.* Edinburgh: Clark, 1925.

Fowden, Garth. "Bishops and Temples in the Eastern Roman Empire, A.D. 320–435." *Journal of Theological Studies* 29 (1978):53–78.

Frend, W.H.C. *Martyrdom and Persecution in the Early Church.* Oxford: Blackwell, 1965.

Markus, Robert A. *Saeculum: History and Society in the Theology of St. Augustine.* Cambridge: Cambridge University Press, 1988.

Sainte-Croix, G.E.M. de. "Why Were the Early Christians Persecuted?" *Past and Present* 26 (1963):6–38.

❧ TWO ❧

Cosmos: The Quest for Order

ABOUT HALF A CENTURY BEFORE Jesus was born, the philosopher Posidonius of Apamea died (ca. 135 B.C.E.–ca. 51 B.C.E.). Wide-ranging in his interests and a keen observer, Posidonius was visited at his school on Rhodes by such eminent people as Cicero and Pompey the Great. What Posidonius wrote has survived only as excerpted by later writers, but as we begin our exploration of how the early Christians viewed their universe, we might pause to see how Posidonius saw his.

He first observed that the cosmos is a body. From that starting point, he inquired what kind of a body it is: Is it simply a mass of independently existing bodies, like a herd of goats? Is it a unity of different things combined together, like a ship or a house? Or is it a unity the way plants and animals are unities? Aware of the effect of the moon on tides, Posidonius first argued that the cosmos is a unified body and then went on to argue that it is like an animal; the cosmos is an ensouled body.

> Therefore, since the cosmos also is a body, it is either a unified body or one of combined or separate parts. But it is neither of combined nor of separate parts, as we prove from the sympathies in it. For according to the waxings and wanings of the moon, many sea and land animals wane and wax, and ebb tides and flood tides occur in some parts of the sea. So, too, changes in the atmosphere and all kinds of change in the air take place after certain risings and settings of the stars, sometimes for the better, but sometimes pestilential. From these facts it is clear that the cosmos is some kind of a unified body. For in the case of bodies formed from combined or separate parts, the parts do not sympathize with one another, since if it happened that all the soldiers in an army were to perish [save one], the survivor is not seen to suffer through contagion; but in unified bodies there is a certain sympathy, since when a finger is cut, the whole body is affected. Therefore, the cosmos also is a unified body.
>
> But since some unified bodies are held together by simple constitution (like stones and sticks), others by nature (like plants), others by soul (like animals), the cosmos also is controlled by one of these. Now, it would not be held together by simple constitution. For the things held together by simple constitution like sticks and stones do not admit of any important change or variation, but suffer only the conditions produced by loosening or contraction. But the

cosmos admits of important changes, as the atmosphere becomes sometimes icy, sometimes hot, and sometimes dry, sometimes moist, and at other times changing according to the motions of the heavenly bodies. Therefore, the cosmos is not held together by simple constitution. But if not by this, then assuredly by nature; for even the bodies controlled by soul were first held together by nature. Necessarily, then, it must be held together by the best nature, since it contains the natures of all things. (Sextus Empiricus *Against the Physicians* 1.79–84)

This idea of the cosmos as a living unity was not original to Posidonius. It was part of an intellectual discussion of considerable antiquity, and Posidonius was in some sense simply handing on that tradition. Thus, the world the Christians entered was already an old world, rich in intellectual tradition. Socrates, who lived in the fifth century B.C.E., was already part of a philosophic tradition, and he and his successor Plato, who died in 347 B.C.E., left behind them a legacy that would dominate the intellectual outlook of the Greco-Roman world and that would still be an influence in oracular responses of the god Apollo in the second century C.E.

By the time the earliest Christian Scriptures were written down, a tradition of philosophic debate, of master questioning and debating with pupils, had already been in place for four hundred years—that is, a time span longer than the one from the landing of the Mayflower at Plymouth Rock to the present. So when Christian intellectuals sought to explain their new lifestyle, how they saw their place in the world, how they envisioned the world, they came face to face with explanations already molded and formed in the Greek philosophic heritage. Questions of physics and cosmology (How was the earth formed? By whom? When?) and questions of ethics (What is the right way to live? Do humans have free will?) had already been raised and grappled with. This chapter explores some of that philosophic heritage to provide certain broad outlines that we need for subsequent readings in early Christian authors.

But these philosophic writings did not exist in a vacuum. They were read and understood and commented on, a fact often forgotten by students of early Christianity as well as by historians of classical philosophy, who frequently concentrate on the major figures of Greek philosophy—Plato and Aristotle, the Stoics, the Epicureans and Skeptics, and then no one until Plotinus. The philosophic tradition exerted a constant pressure on the intellectuals of the second and subsequent centuries as teacher after teacher commented on the writings of the great masters, especially Plato. In *Life of Plotinus* by Porphyry, Plotinus is ranked by another intellectual, Longinus, among a host of other philosophers:

Of the first kind [i.e., those who set down their views in writing] were the Platonists Eucleides and Democritus, and Proclinus, who lived in the Troad, and

Plotinus and his friend Gentilianus Amelius, who are still publishing in Rome, and the Stoics Themistocles and Phoebion and the two who were flourishing till recently, Annius and Medius, and the Peripatetic Heliodorus, the Alexandrian. Of the second [i.e., those who did not write] were the Platonists Ammonius and Origen, with both of whom I visited for a very long time, men who much surpassed their contemporaries in insight, and the Successors at Athens, Theodotus and Eubulus. (*Life of Plotinus* 20)

We know next to nothing about all the scholars mentioned, yet we can sense the vitality and continuity of the cosmological debate. Perhaps the best analogy is the legal tradition in the United States. We can look at the Constitution as a historical document limited and defined by the language, culture, and political maneuvering of the late eighteenth century. But it is also part of the two-hundred-year-old living tradition formed by each of the justices who have read that document in the light of their times. This tradition framed the way questions were posed and problems discussed.

THE COSMOS AS A LIVING BODY

Posidonius's first observation was that the cosmos is in some sense a unity, yet a unity with many parts. This observation forces us to reflect a little on the differences between the presuppositions of the Greeks and our own concept of the universe. What do we envision when we hear the words the *universe* and the *world*? We probably imagine something that started with a big bang, is rapidly expanding with black holes, and contains distances so vast that they can be measured only in light years. When coming to the philosophic tradition of the Greeks, we have to change our viewpoint. They had much less to work with than modern scientists do: The Greeks had their eyes and ears and the observations of others, such as the reports of sailors on sea voyages and the records of Babylonian astronomers. What impressed most Greeks was the unity of the world even in its great diversity. The very word *kosmos*, from which our word *cosmology* is derived (as well as *cosmetics*), has a sense of order and arrangement, which, for the Greeks, leads to beauty. Amid all the plurality of phenomena, the Greeks passionately believed there is order. The world humans live in must be a cosmos, must have order.

The early cosmologists sought to find it by claiming that everything in the world was formed out of (perhaps consisted of) some single material: Thales suggested water. The problem presented itself most forcibly in the sayings of two philosophers before Plato: Heraclitus of Ephesus and Parmenides of Elea. What Heraclitus actually believed is debated: He was charged with holding that everything in the world is constantly changing, whereas he may in fact have emphasized the stability within constant change.[1] But Plato, followed by Aristotle, laid down that he was a proponent of constant change, and the charge stuck. "Heraclitus says somewhere, 'All things give way and nothing remains,' and likening the things that exist to the current of a river, he says, 'You cannot step twice into the same stream'" (Plato *Cratylus* 402a).[2]

Parmenides took a different tack. In a dense poem (of which only fragments survive) in the form of a discussion between himself and a goddess,[3] he distinguished clearly between what is and what is not: "On the one hand, that (a thing) is and it cannot be. ... On the other hand, that (a thing) is not and that it of necessity must not be" (Frag. 2.35). Something either exists, or it does not exist. If it does not exist in the present, it will not exist in the future. Therefore, only what exists here and now will exist in the future. Nothing can come out of what does not exist. From this logical assumption, Parmenides concluded that there is in reality no motion or change: "Generation is extinguished and destruction not to be heard of" (Frag. 8.21). In spite of appearances, the universe is solid throughout and immobile, continuous throughout and indivisible. Logically, for Parmenides, there can be no change. Here we confront a persistent problem in Greek cosmological theory: the problem of change, the reconciliation of unity within plurality. All subsequent Greek thinkers had to come to terms with Parmenides. The cosmos is one, but the question is, How? Few followed Parmenides in his radical assertion that reason alone can be trusted and that the evidence of the senses that things do in fact change be discounted.

Posidonius emphasized that the cosmos is one through a sympathy that links the different parts together, thus combining unity with diversity. But this is an older notion that can be found in the two main philosophic traditions that influenced early Christianity: Stoicism and Platonism. Both these schools of philosophy held that the world exhibits design and order; thus natural science reveals the operations of mind in the cosmos. Both also held that the cosmos is a perfect unity and is therefore ensouled, a living animal. For many, this sense that the world itself pulsates with life, is a living animal, is a hard notion to penetrate and is often dismissed with labels such as "animism" or "prescientific." Rather, we must empathize with the Greeks' wonder at the traces of something larger than humans in the sky and planets, at the power manifested in thunder and lightning, at the divine hush surrounding a shrine such as Delphi. This idea of the cosmos as a living unity was shared by both the Stoics and the Platonists, but the two groups used different images and metaphors to describe the cosmos.

The Stoics

The metaphor the Stoics used to explain the origin of the cosmos was that of human generation. According to the Stoics, within an original unity there are two "principles," or originating causes: a passive one and an active one. At first glance this conception may seem abstractly innocuous enough. The passive principle, which is without shape or form and immobile, is capable of receiving any quality. The active principle gives shape, form, and movement to matter. The active principle can be said to be the maker (demiurge) of the cosmos and all things in the cosmos. It can be called god, but in the Stoic view nothing exists that is not a body. For the Stoics, everything real is corporeal: what is spatially extended in three dimensions with resistance or what is capable of acting or being acted on. Cleanthes, head of the Stoic school after its founder Zeno from 263 to 232 B.C.E., listed examples in which wounds to the human body cause pain to the soul and in which passions of the soul, such as anger, affect the body. He concluded from such mutual interaction that the soul and mind are corporeal. So when the Stoics said that god/mind (*Logos*) penetrates the whole cosmos, they were referring to some kind of bodily interpenetration. Thus, the cosmos is one, but there are in it two eternally coexistent bodily principles that produce the cosmos we have today. This insistence on two principles, an active and a passive, reflects a view of human generation where the male semen gives movement and form to the matter supplied by the female.

The cosmos, for the Stoics, is a living being, ensouled, intelligent, and endowed with both the power of sensation and the power of reason, which are corporeal entities. Just as breath is a clear marker of life in animals, so the cosmos is unified by *pneuma*, "breath" or "spirit," which is a form of the active principle. This pneuma wholly pervades the universe, just as breath pervades a living body. So for the Stoics there is no mind/body dichotomy, for all that exists is body, is corporeal. They did bequeath, however, important words for Christian thought: pneuma and Logos. The author of the pre-Christian work *The Wisdom of Solomon,* which later became part of the early Christian Bible, described wisdom in this way: "There is in [Wisdom] a spirit [*pneuma*] that is intelligent, holy ... and penetrating through all spirits [*pneumata*] that are intelligent, pure and altogether subtle. For Wisdom is more mobile than any motion; because of her pureness she pervades and penetrates all things. She is a breath of the power of God, and a pure emanation of the glory of the Almighty" (*Wisd. of Sol.* 7:22–25).

The Logos pervades the cosmos and orders it all. The word *Logos* is interesting—it referred primarily to discourse, to rational speech rather than just to sounds (*phonai*), and then was transferred to the mind ordering the speech. Consider the opening words of the Gospel of John: "In the beginning was the Word [*Logos*] and the Logos was with God, and the Logos was God. He was in the beginning with God. All things came into being through him, and without him not one thing came into being" (John 1:1–3). How would someone trained in Stoic thought interpret these words? In the third century C.E., Origen had to argue forcibly that God is indeed incorporeal; in the late fourth century, Augustine of Hippo complained how he, as a reasonably well-educated person, still could not conceive of anything that was not corporeal; and some monks in Egypt threatened to depose the bishop of Alexandria for daring to hold that God is incorporeal. Not that all Christians were Stoics or had even heard of the Stoics, but there are many possible interpretations of religious texts such as the Gospel of John.

The Logos of the Stoics therefore contains within itself the active forms of all the things that are to be. These forms are the *logoi spermatikoi,* the "seminal logoi," with their association with generation, and these seminal logoi unfold themselves into the forms of individual things. These forming principles of individual things are parts of the universal principle in the most literal sense, pieces of God, but they are not separated or cut off from the whole. The rational soul of humans is a fiery breath, a pneuma, that is part of the universal fiery breath, the divine reason or God, which pervades, controls, and determines everything in the universe. Given this view of the world as a living being that is perfect and divine, a person's whole object in life must be to live in accordance with this reason—humans must live *homologoumenos,* "conformably," or, as later developed, *homologoumenos te physei,* "conformably with nature." Humans will ultimately be forced to obey the decrees of the divine Logos, which is fate, determining everything in the universe, but a human is free to *choose* how he or she will obey—either joyfully and willingly or miserably and defiantly.

This striving to live according to nature/reason/divine principle gave rise to the characteristic notion of the Stoics, for which English has preserved the word *stoical:* that the emotions, desires, and passions are not part of reason. They are not simply to be controlled or governed by reason; they are to be eradicated. The ideal is *apathy,* freedom from all passion, emotion, affections, from all the ways in which things can affect the soul, whose reason they pervert. This paints a rather grim picture of someone indifferent to all external things—to riches, health, power. But the later philosopher Epictetus, at first a slave in Rome under the Emperor Nero, talked about this ideal joyously:

> For if we had understanding, what else ought we do both publicly and privately except hymn and praise the Deity, and discuss fully his benefits? Should not that hymn to God please us as we dig and plough and eat? "Great is God, because he has given us hands, a throat, and a belly, to grow unconsciously and to breathe while asleep." This is what we ought to sing at every opportunity, and above all to sing the greatest and divinest hymn, because God has given us the power to understand these things and to use them on the way. (*Discourses* 1.16.15–18)

> Come, now, let us go over what we agree on. The unhindered man, who finds things ready to hand as he wants them, is free. But the man who can be hindered or compelled or thwarted or thrown into something unwillingly is a slave. And who is unhindered? The man who longs for nothing foreign. And what things are foreign? Those things that are not under our control, either to have, or not to have, or to have of a certain quality, or in a certain way. Therefore the body is foreign, its members are foreign, property is foreign. If, then, you strongly desire

one of these things, as though it were your own, you will suffer punishment appropriate to one who longs for what belongs to another. This is the road which leads to freedom, this is the only release from slavery, to be able to say at any time with your whole heart,

> Lead thou me on, O Zeus, and you, O Destiny,
> To where long ago I was appointed by you. ...

Are *you,* then, free, says someone?—By the gods I wish and pray to be, but I am not yet able to look my masters in the face, I still honor my little body, I take great pains to keep it perfect, even though it is not perfect in any case. (*Discourses* 4.1.128–131, 151)

Here there is no despair, no sense of being crushed by inexorable fate. Rather, the Stoic is portrayed as liberated into gladness, and his call to freedom from slavery to the passions and his sense of inner struggle resonate with the call of the apostle Paul to Christians to live by the Holy Spirit and not to gratify the desires of the flesh, to live in freedom and not to submit to the yoke of slavery (Gal. 5:16–21). The Stoics' view of a world governed and infused by a divine Logos/reason, of which each human's mind is a part, will recur in various ways in Christian thought.

The Platonists

Plato. Whereas the Stoics used the metaphor of biological generation to discuss the origin and cosmology of the universe, the Platonists used that of the craftsman fashioning an object. In contrast to the Stoics, who insisted that only bodies exist, Plato clearly distinguished the mind from the body. In the *Timaeus,* he stated, "We must say that soul is the only existing thing which is appropriate to possess intelligence; this is invisible, whereas fire and water and earth and air are all visible bodies" (46D). In describing the formation of humans, Plato wrote:

First [God] ordered all these; then out of them he organized this universe, one living being containing all living beings in itself, both mortal and immortal. He was himself the fashioner [demiurge] of the divine, but he enjoined his own children to make the generation of mortals. In imitation of him, they took the immortal principle of soul, and framed a mortal body round about it and gave the whole body as a vehicle. They added another kind of soul—a mortal one—which had in itself fearsome and necessary feelings: first pleasure, the greatest incitement to evil, then pains, which frighten us from good; moreover confidence and fear, a pair of foolish counselors, anger hard to appease and credulous hope. They mixed these of necessity with irrational sensation and desire, which will attempt anything, and so organized the mortal soul.

Since they feared to pollute the divine element no more than was absolutely necessary, they made the mortal element dwell in another chamber of the body, and built the neck as a kind of isthmus and boundary between the head and the breast to keep them apart. ... The part of the soul which is fond of competition

and which shares courage and anger they located nearer the head between the
midriff and the neck so that within hearing of reason it combines with it to forcibly restrain the group of appetites when they wanted not at all to obey the word
of command from the citadel. ... The desire of the soul for food and drink and
other natural needs of the body they located between the midriff and the navel
as its boundary. (*Timaeus* 69B–70E)

A human is thus divided into three parts: a rational part, a courageous or
spirited part, and an appetitive part. (Plato and the Platonic tradition seem
to have liked threes.) Plato's own description of the soul—whether it is indivisible or not—is not completely consistent, but it will be a standard feature
of later interpreters. Plato's insistence on the incorporeal nature of mind,
that something other than bodies can exist, though it had forerunners in
Greek philosophical tradition (Anaxagoras, for example, said that mind is
the cause of all things), was to have a profound influence on the intellectual
history of the Greco-Roman world and its successors in the Western tradition.

The incorporeal nature of mind was coupled with Plato's theory of ideas.
Scholars dispute whether Plato ever had the theory of ideas or forms that
some later interpreters posited he did. Whatever the case, in an attempt to
answer the question of unity within plurality, Plato searched for definitions
of things. When, in Plato's dialogues, Socrates asked what justice is, if it is
good or beautiful, he was not satisfied with answers that simply gave examples of just deeds or good acts or beautiful objects. He sought the definition
of justice, goodness, beauty, the universal by which these particular examples can be said to be just or good or beautiful. Plato's ideas, in their simplest
statement, are logical definitions: They are universals that all discourse in-
volves. Those definitions may sometimes be hard to arrive at, but without
them discourse is impossible. But often in Plato these universals are not just
logical definitions; they are also really existing, eternal forms. This world of
ideas or forms is the true world of authentic being, of which the world we
live in is but a shadow. That world of ideas is eternal and imperishable; this
world of ours is mortal and subject to decay. How the two worlds are related
is described in metaphor; this world participates somehow in that eternal
idea of which it is a reflection.

An example of how this notion of two worlds was later used is the discussion by Philo of Alexandria, a contemporary of Jesus, of the creation accounts in Genesis 1 and 2. Philo noted that there are two differing accounts
of how humans were created, one in Genesis 1:26–28, the other in Genesis
2:7. He saw in these two accounts the creation of two different levels of existence—the human who exists in the world of ideas and the earthly, physical
human.

After this he [Moses] says, "God formed man by taking clay from the earth, and
breathed into his face the breath of life" (Gen. 2:7). By this he shows most

clearly that there is a great difference between the one [man] just now formed and the other [man] who earlier came into being according to the image of God (Gen. 1:26–27), for the one who is formed already partakes of a perceptible quality, consists of body and soul, is a man or a woman, by nature mortal; but the one according to the image is an idea or genus or seal, intelligible, incorporeal, neither male nor female, by nature incorruptible. (*On the Creation* 134)

So when Plato began to outline his cosmology in the *Timaeus*, he first distinguished

between that which always is and has no coming-into-being and that which is always coming-into-being but never is. The one is comprehensible by thought by the aid of reason, being eternally the same, the other is conjectured by opinion with the aid of irrational sensation, coming to be and perishing, but never truly existent. (27D–28A)

If this cosmos is beautiful and its fashioner good, it is clear that he was looking at the eternal; but if [this cosmos is not beautiful and its fashioner not good,] something which cannot be uttered without blasphemy, [he was looking] at that which came into being. Obviously, of course, he looked at the eternal; for the cosmos is the fairest of all things which have come into being and he is the best of causes. (29A)

So the artificer (demiurge, whom we met in the Stoics) is outside and distinct from the world. When he decides to create an orderly world, a cosmos, he looks at an ideal model, called by Plato live or animated being, containing in itself ideas, and then proceeds to make an image of it out of a preexisting chaos, called space, nurse, or receptacle. As this image is also to be animated and intelligent, the artificer fashions a cosmic soul out of a stuff, the ingredients of which are called the indivisible and that which is divisible about bodies, the same and the different. He then creates the elements (fire, air, water, earth) by imposing geometrical forms on rudiments already present in the chaos, builds out of them the body of the world, and wraps a cosmic or world soul around it, creating an orderly world that is an animated being. The cosmos is therefore alive, is in fact perfect and divine, and consists of a world soul imposing order on the irregular and disorderly motion inherent in the receptacle.

After the cosmos is formed, the artificer then proceeds to form all kinds of beings to inhabit this cosmos, particularly individual souls. He fashions them out of the same kind of stuff as the world soul, though the mixture is less perfect. The sun, moon, planets, and stars are all ensouled and are divine (the Greeks could only believe they were self-moving), and these subgods, the visible, created gods, are given the task of framing the mortal parts of humans. There is thus a close correspondence between macrocosm and microcosm, but Plato also worked with a gradation of beings, of levels of existence, between the demiurge and existence on the earth: the world soul; the visible, created gods of the sun, planets, and stars; the human soul; other living beings, such as animals and plants; and then the nonliving.

One of Plato's successors, Xenocrates formalized the hierarchy even further and talked of a triadic division of the universe where the moon occupies a median position. He seems to have connected the gods with the solar realm and immortality, the demons or minor spirits with the lunar realm since they share immortality with the gods but are subject to human emotions, and humans with the earth.[4] In all of this is seen the desire to stagger the universe, but we also glimpse how the cosmos is alive and populated. This sense of a hierarchy of being also surfaces in the doctrine of transmigration, whereby the souls of men can move into the bodies of other men or descend into female bodies or beasts (*Timaeus* 90E–92B). Plato's worldview is therefore an ordered hierarchy, a gradation of intelligence and of levels of existence. There are many intermediaries between the demiurge and humans.

Plato's worldview also evokes many questions. Who is this artificer? Where do the forms or models at which the artificer looks to fashion the cosmos reside? Will there always be opposition between the order imposed and the irregularity of the receptacle? The *Timaeus* is cast in the form of a dialogue, and such a form by its nature does not pretend to give a complete and definitive treatment of a subject.

In the Platonic conception of the cosmos, another analogy is also at play. Plato seems to have been fascinated by mathematics—in some way the abstraction needed to discuss geometric forms, which are divorced from matter, was what Plato saw as a prerequisite for philosophic studies. One of Plato's great achievements in the history of science was his insistence on the understanding of natural phenomena in terms of mathematics, and one notable result was the astronomical model developed by Plato's pupil Eudoxus. Numbers were also involved in the questions raised by Parmenides and Heraclitus—the problem of change, of the one and the many, of unity among the multiplicity of phenomena.

In Plato's later years, he formulated a fundamentally mathematical model for the origin of the cosmos. First came the problem of the generation of numbers. If there were to be numbers, a number beyond one had to be posited, for out of these two numbers all other numbers could be formed—three by adding one to two, four by adding one to three, and so forth. Plato saw one to four as the primal numbers, for added together they produce the perfect number (for Plato), ten. Plato therefore suggested that two first principles were required to create the cosmos—the One and what he called the indefinite dyad or two. Out of these two principles came all other beings. Without the assumption of an indefinite dyad, all being would be frozen in the Parmenidean One. The One would impose limits on the opposite principle, for the dyad would be infinitely extensible or divisible, simultaneously infinitely large and infinitely small.

Another problem arose from the relation of numbers to solids. Plato was trying to find a unified theory to explain the universe. Plato saw geometrical shapes underlying the physical entities of this world, and behind geometry lie numbers. The four primal numbers, one to four, correspond to geometrical shapes in this way: The point corresponds to one, the line to two (as Plato did not think that a line could be analyzed into points), the plane to three (the triangle), and the solid to four (the tetrahedron). The movement progresses from numbers through geometrical figures to physical reality. Plato therefore envisioned a process whereby a being, which corresponds to the world of numbers, is somehow participated in by another being, called the world soul, which transforms these numbers into geometric shapes and then projects these shapes onto the physical world. The world soul mediates between the intelligible realm and the sensible realm. The world soul partakes of both the intelligible realm and, somehow, the subrational realm.

The Followers of Plato. Plato's followers would develop this framework in different ways, but the basic view of the cosmos in human terms was already clear: As the intellect in humans is distinct from the senses, some of which are more rational than the others, so the intelligible world is distinct from the world soul and the sensible world. As there is a hierarchy of intelligence in humans, so is there a similar hierarchy in the cosmos. The main discussions of the Platonists contemporaneous with the rise of the early church concerned, first, the stuff out of which the cosmos is made. A Platonist such as Albinus stressed the dominance of the One/God and the complete passivity of matter, whereas Plutarch seems to have granted much more autonomy to matter as a source of disorder and confusion, a positive disorderly element.

> Therefore this very old opinion comes down from writers about the gods and from lawgivers to poets and philosophers. Anonymous in origin but strongly persuasive and hard to erase, it survives in many places both among barbarians and Greeks, not only in stories and traditions but also in rites and sacrifices. It holds that the Universe is not suspended aloft by accident, unintelligent, irrational, and without guidance, nor is there one Reason [*Logos*] controlling, guiding it as if by rudders or by controlling reins, but nature brings forth in this world many things mixed with evil and good, or rather, to put it simply, nothing is unalloyed. However, there is not one steward of two large wine jars who mixes up and distributes to us affairs as a barman (distributes) liquids, but our life and the cosmos is mixed from two opposed principles and two rival powers, one of which leads straight ahead, while the other turns and bends back. If this is not true of the whole cosmos, what is around this earth along with the moon is irregular and variable and entertains all kinds of changes. For if by nature nothing happens without a cause, and if the good cannot furnish a cause for evil, it is necessary that nature have a distinct source and principle of evil, just as of good. Most people, including the wisest, hold this opinion, for they think that there

are two gods, like rivals, one the fashioner of good and the other of evil. (*Isis and Osiris* 369B–D)

This radical dualism remained within some exponents of Platonism after Plutarch. Numenius, who lived around 176 C.E. and was a major influence on Ammonius Saccas, the teacher of Plotinus, and possibly on Origen, stressed that matter is a positively evil force and that this dualism exists in each of us as much as in the cosmos: "There cannot be found in the realm of generation any condition free of vice, neither in human creations, nor in nature, nor in the bodies of animals, nor yet in trees or plants nor in fruits, nor in the flow of air, nor in the pull of water, nor even in the heaven itself, since everywhere it entwines itself with Providence like the pollution of an inferior nature."[5] Plotinus seems to have reacted against this approach, possibly in opposition to the Christian Gnostics (see Chapters 4 and 5), and stressed more the goodness of the cosmos.

The second contemporaneous Platonist discussion concerned the demiurge. Under the twofold influence of the Stoic Logos and number theory, a distinction was made between a completely transcendent, self-contemplating figure, a pure monad or One, and an active demiurgic figure (this distinction is almost reminiscent of that between pure and applied mathematics). This active demiurgic figure is a Platonic adaptation of the Stoic Logos. Later Platonists thus arrived at two entities, one basically the demiurge of the *Timaeus* and the other a completely transcendent good/One. Platonists such as Albinus, Apuleius, or Numenius would argue that there are two distinct gods. Both are minds, but one is at rest in self-contemplation, while the other is actively outgoing.[6]

Plotinus. Other Platonists based themselves on a passage in the possibly spurious second letter of Plato, where three principles are mentioned: "For [the nature of the first] is like this: all things are in respect of the king of all and all things are on its account, and that is the cause of all beautiful things. The second is in respect of the second things, and the third is in respect of the third things" (Letter 2 312E). This cryptic statement was understood to mean that three principles underlie all of existence and that these three principles are arranged hierarchically whereby the third principle is subordinate to the second, which is subordinate to the first. The world soul, or world of geometrical shapes, is subordinate to the world of numbers, which itself emanates from a primal One.

One person who did develop this trio of principles was the philosopher Plotinus. Plotinus clearly spoke of three hypostases, or principles: the One/good, the nous/mind, and the soul.

> Since, then, the simple nature of the Good appeared to us as also primal (for all that is not primal is not simple), and as something which has nothing in itself,

but is some one thing; and since the nature of what is called the One is the same (for this is not some other thing first and then one, nor is the Good something else first, and then good), whenever we say "the One" and whenever we say "the Good," we must think that the nature we are speaking of is the same nature, and call it "one" not as predicating anything of it but as making it clear to ourselves as we can. And we call it the First in the sense that it is simplest, and the Self-Sufficient, because it is not composed of a number of parts; for if it were, it would be dependent on the things of which it was composed; and we say that it is not in something else, because everything which is in something else also comes from something else. If, then, it is not from something else or in something else or any kind of compound, it is necessary that there should be nothing above it. So we must not go after other first principles but put this first, and then after it Intellect, that which primally thinks, and then Soul after Intellect (for this is the order which corresponds to the nature of things): and we must not posit more principles than these in the intelligible world, or fewer. (*Against the Gnostics* 2.9.1; LCL)

The One is all things and not a single one of them: it is the principle of all things, not all things, but all things have that other kind of transcendent existence; for in a way they do occur in the One; or rather they are not yet there, but they will be. How then do all things come from the One, which is simple and has in it no diverse variety, or any sort of doubleness? It is because there is nothing in it that all things come from it: in order that being may exist, the One is not being, but the generator of being. This, we may say, is the first act of generation: the One, perfect because it seeks nothing, has nothing, and needs nothing, overflows, as it were, and its superabundance makes something other than itself. This, when it has come into being, turns back upon the One and is filled, and becomes Intellect by looking towards it. Its halt and turning towards the One constitutes being, its gaze upon the One, Intellect. Since it halts and turns towards the One that it may see, it becomes at once Intellect and being. Resembling the One thus, Intellect produces in the same way, pouring forth a multiple power—this is a likeness of it—just as that which was before it poured it forth. This activity springing from the substance of Intellect is Soul, which comes to be this while Intellect abides unchanged: for Intellect too comes into being while that which is before it abides unchanged. (*On the Origin and Order of the Beings Which Come After the First* 5.2.1; LCL)

Here Plotinus described the unfolding of the universe, the emanation of the cosmos out of an utterly simple first principle, about which we can really speak only in negative terms. This universe is an ordered one, with each move away from the One a move down in the hierarchy of being. Plotinus's description of the One reflects his complete absorption in intellectual pursuits. His source is not intellect but is beyond intellect: "Its thinking of Itself is Itself, and exists by a kind of immediate self-consciousness, in everlasting rest and in a manner different from that of Nous/Mind" (5.4.2). Here we can get a hold on the distinction between the One and the Nous: The nous/mind for Plotinus is thinking about some object. There is an inherent duality in the notion of understanding, even of an intuitive self-thinking mind/intellect whose object is itself immediately apprehended without any seeking or movement outside itself. What intellect contemplates when it has emerged from the One is the One itself in a turning back.

Plotinus spoke of intellect emanating from the One, but this is not an automatic and necessary event that excludes freedom and spontaneity. In fact, Plotinus sometimes spoke of this emanation as an act of illegitimate self-assertion (*tolma*). It is difficult to know precisely what he meant by this, but perhaps it is connected with a desire for separate existence, the desire to *be* at all. If the universe is to exist, if multiplicity is to exist, there must be some movement away from the utterly One. But Plotinus, "in some moods, when he is concentrating on the transcendent excellence of the One, regards as regrettable [this desire for separate existence] because it must be a desire for something less than the Good."[7] Soul, in Plotinus's scheme, is akin to the previously discussed world soul: It can look back to contemplate the intellect and the One, and it is responsible for the formation of bodies in the visible world. It thus remains the intermediary between the worlds of intellect and sense perception.

We thus come back to the notion articulated at the beginning of this chapter: that the world for the Greeks is a cosmos, an ordered, closed whole. Everything in it has its proper place and proper movement: The sun and the stars move unchangingly in their same orbits. In one sense this view of the world can be said to be static, for only the lower parts of this cosmos on earth are subject to generation and decay; the sun, moon, and stars are eternal, divine. To a Platonist, calling the universe static is to pay it a compliment. For us, static often means "lifeless," but not to the Greco-Roman world. Socrates was admiringly depicted walking along and suddenly standing stark still and remaining that way all day. He was not moving, but to the Platonists he was fully alive. He was rapt in contemplation, immersed in the life of the mind.

> Reflecting on something at dawn, [Socrates] stood on the spot examining it; and when it would not go well for him, he would not let go but stood there searching it out. Already it was midday, and the men were noticing him, and said to one another in wonder: "Socrates has been standing pondering something since dawn!" At last some of the Ionians, since it was evening and they had supped— for it was then summertime—brought out their mats and were both lying down in the cool and watching to see if he would go stand through the night. He stood until dawn came and the sun rose; then he went away, praying to the Sun as he departed. (Plato *Symposium* 220C–D)

The intelligible world, in the image of Plotinus, is "boiling with life" (*Enneads* 6.7.12). "The highest life is a life of intense, inturned, self-contained contemplative activity, of which the life of movement, change, production

and action on the physical level is only a very faint and far-off image, changing (though without ever producing anything really new) because of its very
imperfection."[8]

> Here the greatest, the ultimate contest is set before our souls; all our toil and
> trouble is for this, not to be left without a share in the best of visions. The man
> who attains this is blessed in seeing that "blessed sight," and he who fails to at-
> tain it has failed utterly. A man has not failed if he fails to win beauty of colors
> or bodies, or power or office or kingship even, but if he fails to win this and only
> this. For this he should give up the attainment of kingship and of rule over all
> earth and sea and sky, if only by leaving and overlooking them he can turn to
> That and see.
>   But how shall we find the way? What method can we devise? How can one
> see the "inconceivable beauty" which stays within in the holy sanctuary and
> does not come out where the profane may see it? Let him who can, follow and
> come within, and leave outside the sight of his eyes and not turn back to the
> bodily splendors which he saw before. When he sees the beauty in bodies he
> must not run after them; he must know that they are images, traces, shadows,
> and hurry away to that which they image. For if a man runs to the image and
> wants to seize it as if it were the reality (like a beautiful reflection playing on the
> water, which some story somewhere, I think, said riddlingly a man wanted to
> catch and sank down into the stream and disappeared), then this man who
> clings to beautiful bodies and will not let them go, will, like the man in the story,
> but in soul, not in body, sink down into the dark depths where intellect has no
> delight, and stay blind in Hades, consorting with shadows there and here. This
> would be truer advice, "Let us fly to our dear country." What then is our way of
> escape, and how are we to find it? We shall put out to sea, as Odysseus did, from
> the witch Circe or Calypso—as the poet says (I think with a hidden meaning)—
> and was not content to stay, though he had delights of the eyes and lived among
> much beauty of sense. Our country from which we came is there; our Father is
> there. How shall we travel to it? Where is our way of escape? We cannot get
> there on foot; for our feet only carry us everywhere in this world, from one
> country to another. You must not get ready a carriage, either, or a boat. Let all
> these things go, and do not look. Shut your eyes, and change to and wake an-
> other way of seeing, which everyone has but few use. (*On Beauty* 1.6.7–8)

In this passage, Plotinus contrasted two figures from Greek tradition. On
the one hand, Narcissus, the youth so self-absorbed in his own beauty that
he sits entranced by his reflection in a pool, not harkening to the call of the
nymph Echo but wasting away. The other is the Homeric hero Odysseus,
who, amid myriad trials, always strives to return from the battle against the
Trojans back to his native island of Ithaca. Odysseus is not distracted by the
seductive charm of the goddess Circe, who bewitches humans and turns
them into animals. Plotinus wanted his followers to be heroic like Odysseus,
not a failure like Narcissus, and interpreted their stories allegorically: A person must leave physical beauty to seek a true homeland amid intelligible

beauty. The physical world is the last of a series of descending emanations, the mortal as opposed to the immortal. These levels of existence within the universe, down to and including a person's true self, can be called gods or divinity, but in a way that is at odds with our use of those terms. Plotinus's search was a quest for an intuitive grasp of the order in the cosmos. Plotinus, so his biographer Porphyry claimed, several times came to a mystical union with the One (*Life of Plotinus* 23).

This desire to grasp the divine in a mystical union was not peculiar to Plotinus. Another pagan philosophic group also sought divine knowledge. A prayer thanking the god Hermes-Thoth for revealing secret knowledge to the group concludes a revelatory discourse called the Perfect Discourse. Hermes-Thoth was an amalgam of the Greek god Hermes and the Egyptian god Thoth, the god of letters who was understood in late antiquity to be a revealer of secret knowledge.

> This is the prayer that they spoke: "We give thanks to Thee! Every soul and heart is lifted up to Thee, O undisturbed name, honored with the name God and praised with the name Father, for to everyone and everything (comes) the fatherly kindness and affection and love and any teaching there may be that is sweet and plain, giving us mind, speech, (and) knowledge: mind, so that we may understand Thee, speech, so that we may expound Thee, knowledge, so that we may know Thee. We rejoice, having been illumined by Thy knowledge. We rejoice because Thou hast shown us Thyself. We rejoice because while we were in (the) body, Thou hast made us divine through Thy knowledge.
>
> The delight of the man who attains to Thee is one thing: that we know Thee. We have known Thee, O intellectual light. O life of life, we have known Thee. O womb of every creature, we have known Thee. O womb pregnant with the nature of the Father, we have known Thee. O eternal permanence of the begetting Father, thus have we worshipped Thy goodness. There is one petition that we ask: we would be preserved in knowledge. And there is one protection that we desire; that we not stumble in this kind of life."
>
> When they had said these things in prayer, they embraced each other and they went to eat their holy food, which has no blood in it.[9]

This prayer, with its use of the second person plural and the comment about what "they" did, presupposes a community gathering of some kind, with its own rituals for eating together and for embracing. The larger collection from which this prayer comes charts a pagan intellectual milieu interested in questions of cosmology.[10] What is fascinating about this text is that the earliest manuscript evidence we have for it is in a collection of Christian documents hidden sometime during the fourth century C.E. and rediscovered only in 1945. The appropriation of such texts by some later Christians evidences an interaction, but for the first stirrings of awareness by pagan thinkers about Christians, we have to turn to the second century.

PAGANS ON CHRISTIANS

For reasons unknown to us, there was a surge of interest among second-century Greek intellectuals about Judaism and Christianity. Regardless of whether this interest arose because of the migration of men such as Numenius—who came from Syria, said that "Plato is nothing else than Moses speaking Greek," and may have been the impulse behind Plotinus's desire to investigate Persian and Indian philosophy—or because some Christians were beginning to philosophize, statements about Jews and Christians began appearing among pagan writers.[11]

One of the most interesting pagan writers on Christians is Galen, whose work *On the Parts of the Human Body* appeared between 170 and 180 and became a classic in the history of medical thought. While talking about human eyebrows, he distinguished in an aside clearly between his approach and that of the Jews (and Christians). For Galen, the Jews were better than the Epicureans because for Epicurus the cosmos developed out of a collection of atoms in space. Natural movements first separated from each other the sky, air, sea, and earth, and then later plants and animals developed, again naturally, without any intervention from the gods. For holding such views the Epicureans were branded as the atheists of the ancient world—not because they did not believe in the gods (they did), but because they held the gods gave no thought to human existence. (Christians are often ranked with Epicureans in martyrdom accounts.) This sense of randomness/chance was abhorrent to the Greco-Roman philosophic tradition, where the cosmos is beautifully ordered by the plan of a demiurge. Galen shared with Jews and Christians a belief that the origin of generation comes from the fashioner, but Galen rejected a simple act of divine will as the explanation of the cosmos. "We say that certain things are impossible by nature, and that God does not attempt these things at all but that he chooses the best out of what can come into being" (*De usu partium* 11.14; Helmreich 2.159).[12]

Here the Platonic metaphor of the architect creating a building comes into play—as the architect has to place his model into concrete, to contend with the material, so the demiurge has to work with the stuff of the universe. The question here is not that Jews and Christians believed that God created the cosmos out of nothing, whereas Galen held that there was some coexisting material. (That question would occur only later.) Rather, it is that Jews and Christians had not attempted a fully reasoned—that is, functional—account of the cosmos. For both the Jews and the Christians, Galen held, everything depends on God's will. According to them, God can even make a man out of a stone, Galen exclaimed in astonishment. For him, such a view allows for capriciousness, not order. The cosmos is a beautiful work of art (*De usu partium* 3.10; Helmreich 1.174–177), suffused with intelligence (*De usu partium* 17.1; Helmreich 2.446–449). So admiration is mixed with criticism.

Celsus, writing his *True Doctrine* about the same time as Galen, clearly despised Christians. The work of Celsus is known to us only through the quotations Origen made in refuting Celsus. (The references are thus to Origen's *Against Celsus.*) The importance of Celsus's attack in the eyes of Christian intellectuals can be seen in the fact that Origen found it necessary to write a refutation over fifty years after Celsus had written. Celsus, for all his distemper, raised questions that go to the heart of Christian self-definition.

First, like Galen, Celsus questioned the view that God's will is a sufficient explanation of the world. He insisted that the Christians were wrong to hold that anything is possible to God, there are limits on the power of God, and there are things that God simply does not do (7.14), that are beneath his dignity. But Celsus was particularly insistent that God does not come down to earth (4.2–7). The staccato questions found at 4.3—"What would God intend by such a descent? To learn what transpires among humans? Does he not know everything? If, then, he knows but does not correct, is he not able to correct by divine power? Is he not able to correct humans by divine power unless he sends someone by nature for this purpose?"—evidence the incomprehension on the part of a Platonist, because of his exalted view of the divine, at the need for a supreme god to visit humanity.

> God is good and beautiful and blessed and among the fairest and noblest. If then he comes down to humans, he must undergo a change, but a change from the good to the bad, from the beautiful to the ugly, and from blessedness to unhappiness, from the noblest to the worthless. Who would choose such a change? Indeed, it is the nature of mortals to alter and to be reformed, but for immortals to remain the same. Therefore, God would certainly not entertain such a change. (4.14)

But Celsus also reacted against the Christians because the cosmos as a whole is eternal; there is no need for God to visit the earth (4.62).

Celsus compared Jesus to other figures in order to show his unimportance. The stories told about Jesus' birth are like stories of other heroes (1.67), his wandering habits like those of other crazy Syrian prophets (7.9), his miracles like those of others (2.55). In fact, Celsus claimed that Jesus' miracles are no better than magician's tricks (1.9, 68), not worthy deeds like those of Heracles, which would have merited hero status (1.67). The doctrines of Christians are similar to those of others: the end of the world by fire (4.11–13), the figure of Satan (6.42). Celsus's reasoning here led to the major argument against the Christians: Their doctrines are simply a misunderstanding of ancient doctrines, the Christians are a nontraditional religion (2.1), yet nothing in their beliefs is new. This question of the novelty of Christianity tied in with the question, Why did Christianity appear only now? (4.7), and was taken up by Porphyry, the disciple of Plotinus, at the end of the third century and driven home:

> If Christ says that he is the way of salvation, the grace and the truth, and posits that in himself alone is the return to God for those who believe in him, what did the men who lived so many centuries before Christ do? Leaving aside the time before the kingdom of Latium, let us take the time of Latium as if it were the beginning of the human race. In Latium itself gods were worshipped before Alba was built; in Alba, divine worship and temple rites flourished equally. For a not shorter period, even for a long expanse of centuries, Rome itself was without the Christian law. What, then, is to be done with so many innumerable souls, who were in no wise at fault, if indeed the one in whom it is efficacious to believe would not accommodate his coming to humans? The whole world, moreover, was as zealous as Rome itself in temple rites. Why, then, did he who is called the Savior withdraw himself for so many centuries? Let it not be said that the human race was taken care of by the ancient Jewish law. The Jewish law appeared and flourished after a long time within the narrow area of Syria; afterward indeed, it crept forth to the coasts of Italy but after Gaius Caesar, or, at the earliest, while he was emperor. What, then, is to be done with the souls of those who lived in Rome and Latium who were deprived up to the time of the Caesars of the kindness of Christ, because he had not then come?[13]

These are major criticisms against Christianity—stories about Jesus are no different from other stories, and Christian doctrines are no different, so why should Christians consider themselves importantly different from the rest of society? Porphyry, in fact, allowed for a view of Jesus that integrates him into the cosmology of Platonists—he is a divine hero, not quite of the level of Plotinus but better than most other humans (cited in Augustine *City of God* 19.23).

CONCLUSION

The view that the universe is a perfect creature in which everything is well ordered and that the world of change stands in contrast to the static world of intellectual beings would present a challenge to early Christian intellectuals. The changeless fashioner of the universe cannot undergo change by coming to visit this world. The One of Plotinus does not act in this world, and certainly not capriciously. Yet if Jesus is not this changeless fashioner, in what way does he differ from other humans, like Socrates and Alexander the Great, who had been seen as acting in a more-than-human fashion and so given divine honors? Before we look at how Christians responded to this challenge, we should consider another problem for the early Christians. Galen had lumped together both Jews and Christians in criticizing their view of the universe. This alerts us to the continuing presence of Jews in the Mediterranean world, and it is to explore that presence that we now turn.

Suggestions for Further Reading

Armstrong, Arthur H., ed. *The Cambridge History of Later Greek and Early Medieval Philosophy.* London: Cambridge University Press, 1967.

_____. *Classical Mediterranean Spirituality: Egyptian, Greek, Roman.* New York: Crossroad, 1986.

Blumenthal, H. J., and R. A. Markus. *Neoplatonism and Early Christian Thought: Essays in Honour of A. H. Armstrong.* London: Variorum, 1981.

Dillon, John. *The Middle Platonists: 80 B.C. to A.D. 220.* Ithaca: Cornell University Press, 1977.

Fowden, Garth. *The Egyptian Hermes: A Historical Approach to the Late Pagan Mind.* Cambridge: Cambridge University Press, 1986.

Long, A. A., and D. N. Sedley. *The Hellenistic Philosophers.* Cambridge: Cambridge University Press, 1987.

Walzer, Richard. *Galen on Jews and Christians.* London: Oxford University Press, 1949.

Wilken, Robert. *The Christians as the Romans Saw Them.* New Haven: Yale University Press, 1984.

❧ THREE ❧

Jews in the Roman Empire

HISTORY RECORDS THE MAJOR FIGURES and upheavals of a period; ordinary, day-to-day activities are presupposed and not written about, a subtext to the historical record. This is particularly true for the position of the Jews in the Roman Empire.

There are no words to describe adequately the significance of the destruction of the Temple in Jerusalem in 70 C.E. for the Jews in Judea. The Temple had been the center of Jewish religious and national life, the place where the God of Israel was worshiped and appeased.[1] Huge crowds would converge on Jerusalem to celebrate the major festivals. With the Temple, the house where God dwelt, burned, how could sacrifices be offered to God? Without sacrifices, how was the nation to follow the commandments of God? The trauma of the Temple's destruction is captured in works such as 4 Ezra and 2 Baruch. For example, in 4 Ezra, a work written at the end of the first century, the prophet Ezra is shown reproaching God for what has happened to Israel:

> I want to ask ... about those things which happen to us every day: why Israel has been given to the Gentiles and why the people whom you loved has been given to impious tribes, and the Law of our fathers has been made worthless, and the written orders are for nothing; why we pass from the world like locusts, and our life is like a vapor, and we are not worthy to obtain mercy. (4 Ezra 4:23–24)

It is difficult to trace precisely what happened among Jewish leaders in Israel after the destruction of the Temple. Stories about personalities and events from this time are embedded in much later writings, such as the Palestinian Talmud, written around 400, and the Babylonian Talmud, written around 600, but it is extremely problematic to tease reliable historical data out of these works, which were not written to record history. We know that a meeting of various Jewish leaders took place at Jamnia around 95, but not what was decided there. One attempt to restore Jewish independence, recapture Jerusalem, and renew the former Jewish way of life was undertaken by Simon bar Kosiba in 132, but it failed. As a consequence, the Romans decided to build a temple to Zeus where the Temple to Yahweh had stood, and no Jews were to be allowed to dwell in Jerusalem. A response by one group of Jews to the destruction of the Temple and the revolt of bar Kosiba resulted in a document at the end of the second century—the Mishnah. But it does not mention these traumatic events at all. In fact, the Mishnah makes no reference to historical events. It is an inward-looking document that constructs a world complete in itself, a way of holiness and sanctification almost insulated from the outside world. The Mishnah concentrates on rules for ritual purity and the fulfillment of Torah commandments in a world without a temple and sacrifices.

JEWS IN DIASPORA

The Mishnah was the response of one group of Jews, most of them male, living in Galilee. What I want to explore in this chapter is the story of the Jews living outside the homeland in the cities of the Mediterranean world. What we can learn of Jews in the early centuries of the common era suggests how widespread this Diaspora was. From Philo of Alexandria's report of a letter of King Agrippa I to Caligula, we can sense the extent of Jewish settlement in the Mediterranean basin:

> As for the holy city, I must say what is appropriate. As I said, it is my native city, but it is also the mother city not of one country, Judea, but of a great number because of the colonies which it sent out at various times both to the neighboring lands—Egypt, Phoenicia, Coele-Syria as well as the other part of Syria—and to the lands lying far away—Pamphylia, Cilica, most of Asia up to Bithynia and the farthest reaches of Pontus, and likewise also into Europe, Thessaly, Boeotia, Macedonia, Aetolia, Attica, Argos, Corinth, the greatest and best parts of the Peloponnese. Not only are the mainlands full of Jewish colonies but also the most excellent of the islands, Euboea, Cyprus, Crete. I keep silent about the countries beyond the Euphrates, for all, except for a small part, have Jewish colonists—Babylon and those of the other satrapies with fertile land round about.
> (*The Embassy to Gaius* 281–282)

Archaeological and inscriptional evidence supports this wide-ranging list of Jewish communities, although for most of the western provinces of the Roman Empire, such evidence does not appear until the later imperial period.[2] But it is not only the geographical sweep of Jews in the early centuries of the common era that the archaeological and inscriptional evidence has revealed, but also something much more: the self-confidence and vitality of this Judaism.

Dura-Europos

The robust Judaism of the second and third centuries is evidenced in the synagogue found at Dura-Europos on the Euphrates, in the inscriptional and archaeological discoveries in Asia Minor, and in the Jewish catacombs in Rome. The synagogue at Dura-Europos is remarkably well preserved.[3] When the Sassanian army was advancing against this Roman outpost in 256, the inhabitants, in a desperate attempt to strengthen the city fortifications, tore off the roofs of the buildings just inside the city wall and filled them with sand. The wall paintings of the synagogue, completed only about five years previously, were thus kept safe both from the ravages of war and of time. The Jewish community at Dura-Europos was a minority in a pagan city, but still much larger than the Christian group. In the late second or early third century, a private house was remodeled to form a synagogue, and this was enlarged in 244–245 to create the one discovered.

The wall paintings are remarkable and show that the artists drew on the artistic resources of their environment: Major biblical figures such as Moses and Joseph are dressed as Roman citizens and the Israelite army as Roman soldiers; elsewhere Mordecai and Ezekiel are portrayed in Parthian dress. On the ceiling of the prayer room are fertility symbols of branches of fruit and grain and female heads, and the wall paintings themselves are separated by borders of running grapevines. Yet the paintings also evidence a distinct Jewish self-consciousness. Major biblical symbols are portrayed—the Exodus, the Temple, the priesthood of Aaron, the binding of Isaac, the anointing of David—and there is a niche in the west wall facing toward Jerusalem, presumably for the Torah scrolls. More boldly, the paintings portray the events of the Book of Esther, with the Jews triumphing over the Persians; the biblical narrative of 1 Samuel 5:1–8, where the Philistine god Dagon in Ashdod is destroyed, with the defeated god's ritual objects those of pagan religions at Dura; the story of Elijah triumphing over the priests of Baal (1 Kings 18); and Ezekiel's vision of national restoration through the quickening of the dry bones (Ezek. 37). These are scenes of Jewish triumph and restoration over surrounding enemies and defeat. Such depictions would bolster the self-esteem of a minority community, but the boldness and beauty of these paintings suggest a self-confident Judaism, secure in its heritage and traditional values.

Asia Minor

Among much evidence for Jews in Asia Minor we might first note an important inscription from Aphrodisias. There, inscribed on two faces of a marble block, which may have functioned as a doorjamb, is a fascinating witness to the importance of Jews in this small city. Both faces list names that are clearly Jewish and that describe people who contributed to the foundation of something (scholars are not quite sure what). Whether the list of names on the second face is connected to the previous list of contributors is uncertain. First listed are the male members of a Jewish community—Joseph, son of Zenon; Manases; Judas; Joseph; Jacob; Reuben; Samuel; Simeon; Zacharias—and then follows a list of city councillors who are called *theosebeis* ("god-fearers") and are to be distinguished from others in the inscription called "proselytes."[4] Here then is evidence of quite close connections between the Jewish community and the ruling members of the city.

Another close link between a Jewish community and its neighbors is dramatically shown in the town of Sardis, also in Asia Minor. There the synagogue is not a separate building but one segment of a much larger structure, the Sardis gymnasium. At some time during the third century, the large south hall was obtained by the Jewish community. Within this synagogue/basilica is a lectern whose supports are lions topped by Roman eagles clutching thunderbolts: The eagle is clearly a symbol of Rome, and the lion is connected with Sardis from long in the past (Herodotus *The Histories* 1.86). The iconography of the lectern therefore ties in with city traditions and suggests a prosperous Jewish community at home in its environment and yet maintaining its Jewish identity.

Rome

Rome was the center of a Jewish community of thousands. As the second-century Roman historian Dio Cassius commented, "I do not know from whence this title [i.e., Jews] began to be used of them, but it is used also of those other people, although of alien race, who are zealous for their customs. This race exists even among the Romans, and though many times restrained has increased greatly so that it has gained the free observance of its customs" (Dio *Roman History* 37.17.1).[5]

A look at the history of the Jews' presence in the capital of the Roman Empire helps us gain a sense of the continuity of that presence. Jews were in Rome as early as the mid-second century B.C.E. Some were expelled from Rome in 139 B.C.E. for proselytism. Pompey the Great brought back to Rome many Jewish slaves after he conquered Jerusalem in 63 B.C.E. Many of these were freed soon afterward, and, granted the rights of Roman citizenship, they settled in Trastevere, on the farther bank of the Tiber. Cicero, defending Flaccus in 59 B.C.E. against charges of misgovernment, appealed to the snobbish elitism of the Roman senate by contrasting his client's Roman qualities with those of Flaccus's adversaries, both Greek and Jew. The Jews seem to have received more favorable treatment under Julius Caesar after Jewish military help under Herod the Great saved Caesar in Alexandria in 47 B.C.E. This led to decrees that the Jews were to be allowed to follow their own customs and traditions in cities of the Roman Empire. Augustus Caesar remained on good terms with the Jews, and Roman writers at the court of Augustus evidenced an awareness of things Jewish and even sometimes a positive attitude. Both Horace and Ovid made witty passing references to the Jews, and Augustus himself is said to have twitted admiringly about Jewish religious customs: "Not even a Jew, my dear Tiberius, keeps the fast on Sabbath as diligently as I have today, for I did not eat two mouthfuls until in the bath after the first hour of the night before I began to be anointed" (Suetonius *Divus Augustus* 76:2).[6]

Jews were expelled from Rome in 19 C.E. and in the reign of Claudius (41–54). Around this time the anti-Jewish writer Apion of Egypt was active as a teacher in Rome and represented the citizens of Alexandria in their case before the Emperor Gaius Caligula against Alexandrian Jews. Apion, like Chaeremon, who was a teacher of Nero, repeated accounts whereby the Jews at the time of Moses were said to have been expelled from Egypt as unclean by reason of leprosy or some other contagious disease (Josephus *Against Apion* 1.219–320) and also that the Jews used ritually to slaughter foreigners in the Temple (2.89–99). However, even at this time the Emperor Caligula was a friend of Agrippa, grandson of Herod the Great and future king of Judea, and the Emperor Claudius defended the rights of Jews in Alexandria. The bitterness of the Jewish war against Rome of 66–73 in Judea did not lead either Vespasian or Titus to change Roman policy toward the Jews. In fact, the Jewish historian Josephus was maintained in Rome and repaid the hospitality with a benign account of Vespasian's and Titus's activities in the Jewish war. After the war, Vespasian imposed on all Jews a special annual tax of two drachmas, officially paid to Jupiter Capitolinus; this theoretically took the place of the half-shekel tax contributed to the Temple while it stood. Ever eager for more revenue, Domitian tried to impose this tax more rigorously on all evaders, but his harsh approach was repealed by his successor, Nerva, in 96. Besides the tax, the Jewish war affected the attitudes of certain Romans against the Jews, for it is clearly not accidental that many of the anti-Jewish slurs occurred in writers who flourished just after the war—Martial, Juvenal, and Tacitus. Of course, for a self-made jingoist like Juvenal, anything un-Roman was to be sneered at. Hadrian's ban against circumcision was lifted as regards the Jews by his successor, Antoninus Pius. So, in general, the Jews in Rome maintained their identity and civic rights, and their continued vitality can be glimpsed in the vibrant paintings and ornate embellishments in the Jewish catacombs in Rome, dating to the third and fourth centuries. A golden glass found in the Torlonia catacombs, now in the Israel Museum in Jerusalem, shows on top two lions guarding an open Torah shrine within which are depicted six Torah scrolls. Beneath this scene are two menorahs, flasks, an ethrog, and a shofar.[7]

The examples adduced suggest a vital and self-confident Judaism within the Roman Empire. Unfortunately, we have almost no evidence to document the Jews' understanding of what it meant to be a Jew in the cities of the Mediterranean world. The synagogue would have clearly been an important focal point for maintaining the ancestral religion. In larger cities there may have been several such meeting places, as, for example, at Rome, where there were ten synagogues, and a shrine in which to place the scrolls of the Torah was found in the synagogues at Dura-Europus, Sardis, and Ostia. But we are in the dark as to how the Law was expounded in these synagogues. No doubt these synagogues would have followed some of the same rules and regulations promulgated by the rabbis, for it was basically the same Torah, or at least the Greek translation of it. Recent work, however, particularly on the place of women in these synagogues, has demonstrated a significant difference from what the rabbis taught.[8] But non-Jewish writers do consistently stress the Jews' observance of the Sabbath, their abstention from pork, and their practice of circumcision, and the frequent depiction of the menorah and other ritual objects attests to an attachment to ancestral traditions.

Since scholars have only artifacts from Jewish life in the Diaspora to go on, not verifiable narrative, legal, or philosophical texts, there have been widely varying interpretations of the lives of the Jews who produced these paintings, mosaics, carvings, and ritual objects. Is the menorah, for example, simply a reminder of Temple life, or does it have a deeper mystical meaning whereby God is light, a meaning found in the work of Philo of Alexandria? The artifacts remain silent. Nevertheless, a writer like Galen, and also Celsus, insisted that Jews held that there was only one creator God. This would have been basic to their worldview, as was the belief that this creator God had chosen the Jews to be his people and had spoken to them in the Torah.

Such a general statement of belief, however, could have been uttered by Jews as widely divergent as Philo of Alexandria and the Qumran Covenanters, whose beliefs we know through the discovery of the Dead Sea Scrolls. Philo, a wealthy, well-educated leader of the Jewish community in Alexandria, saw revealed in Hebrew Scriptures a grand program to lead the soul to the vision of God—"to perceive the order that God created in the world, then to reason to the ruling and creating powers of God, ultimately to the unitary Reason of God, and then, beyond even rational apperception, to unite with the One Who Is. The name 'Israel' for Philo, by an ingenious but incorrect etymology, means 'the man who sees God' (e.g., *On Rewards and Punishments* 44)."[9] The Qumran Covenanters believed with Philo that God rules the world, but they also found revealed in the Hebrew Scriptures that he would wage war on their behalf against their enemies, the forces of darkness, to defeat them. Only by withdrawing from contact with the evil world to dwell in purity could the Covenanters be ready for the final battle. General statements of belief, therefore, interact with social, historical, and economic factors to forge a particular Jewish group's worldview.

JEWS AND CHRISTIANS

Jesus had been a Jew, and his earliest followers were Jews. In the Acts of the Apostles, Paul is said to have first preached in synagogues, and the Council of Jerusalem required that non-Jewish followers of Jesus follow the commandments for foreigners found in Leviticus 18 (Acts 15). The writings of the first and second centuries that are classed as apocryphal writings, such as the *Testaments of the Twelve Patriarchs,* the *Sibylline Oracles,* and the *Martyrdom of Isaiah,* demonstrate how some Christian writers made a few deft touches here and there to make a Jewish writing into their own. In a writing such as *Joseph and Aseneth,* scholars are still not sure if it is a Jewish or a Christian writing. The similarity of worldview is therefore quite strong.

Yet some members of the Christian movement also strove to show how different their group was from other groups within Judaism. The writers of the canonical Gospels highlighted in various ways that the destruction of Jerusalem by the Romans in 70 was the fulfillment of Jesus' prophecy and part of the events leading to the inauguration of a new kingdom. To show that the former Jewish leaders would have no part, the author of the Gospel of Matthew recast two parables to emphasize the violent transition of God's promises away from those leaders in Jerusalem and toward his own community (Matt. 21:41–46, in the parable of the wicked tenants; Matt. 22:7–8, in the parable of the wedding feast).

As more and more Gentiles became Christians and fewer and fewer Jews did, Christians and Jews moved apart. Christian authors began to stress the destruction of the Jews and Judaism as part of the replacement of Judaism by Christianity. Justin Martyr, for example, wrote of a debate he had with a Jew named Trypho and set it just after the bar Kosiba revolt. In contrast to the seemingly amicable framework of a dialogue, the content of the work is a devastatingly hostile attack against the Jews: The Mosaic law has been abrogated (*Dialogue with Trypho* 11); Israel has always been unfaithful, as the prophets said (12); the Jews are incapable of reading the Scriptures properly. In particular, the sufferings imposed on the Jews in the recent bar Kosiba revolt were just. They had been set apart so that they might be punished.

In Leviticus it is written: "Because they have transgressed and despised me, and because as traitors they walked contrary to me, I also will walk treacherously with them, and I will destroy them in the land of their enemies. Then their uncircumcised heart will be ashamed" (Lev. 26:40–41). For the circumcision according to the flesh was given to you from Abraham as a sign so that you might be distinguished from other nations and from us, and so that you alone might suffer what you now rightly suffer; so that your land might become desolate, and your cities burned, and strangers eat the fruits of your land before you, and not one of you set foot in Jerusalem. ... Therefore these things have rightly and justly come upon you, for you put the just one to death, and before him his prophets and now you deal treacherously with those who hope in him, and with him who sent him, Almighty God, the Creator of all things. (*Dialogue with Trypho* 16; PG 6.509–512)

This attack against the Jews continued and escalated in many brands of early Christianity. Lengthy treatises against Judaism abounded and became almost a stereotyped genre. One of the earliest was the lost *Dialogue Between Jason and Papiscus* attributed to Aristo of Pella, followed by the *Dialogue of Timothy and Aquila*, the *Dialogue Between Athanasius and Zacchaeus*, and the *Dialogue of Simon the Jew and Theophilus the Christian*. Tertullian wrote a polemical tract under the title *Against the Jews*, and written accounts were made of public debates between Jews and Christians. Origen, writing around 250, referred to debates he had held with Jews (*Against Celsus* 1.45, 55, 2.31). Around the same time Bishop Cyprian of Carthage provided a list of testimonies from the Hebrew Scriptures with which to confound Jewish opponents. The Christian historian Eusebius of Caesarea, writing in the time of Constantine, saw in the destruction of Jerusalem a significant moment in history: From now on the nation of the Jews no longer lived in Jerusalem, and there were no longer any Jewish bishops there (*Church History* 4.5.2–3, 4.6.1–4).

The Christian Empire and the Jews

The Christians used every rhetorical skill to paint the Jews as enemies. In the second century, Melito of Sardis denounced the Jews as not being the true Israel, as God-killers. "He who suspended the earth is suspended. He who fixed the heavens is fixed. He who fastened all things is fastened on a tree. The Master is insulted. God is murdered" (*Homily on the Passover* 96). The Jewish community at Sardis was well established there, and the Christians were a minority vis-à-vis the larger and more socially acceptable Jewish community. The wall paintings in the synagogue at Dura-Europos attest to a more prosperous group than the much smaller Christian house church in the same city. The abusive rhetoric and shrill tone of Melito's remarks were within the norms of polemic in the Greco-Roman world, but the situation changed when the emperor became a Christian and the Christians became a favored group within the empire. The rhetoric of enmity was placed in a different social setting, where those who had formerly been in a minority now had imperial support.

Yet even behind the legislation concerning the Jews, we can still glimpse a Judaism flourishing within the Roman Empire.[10] In a decree of September 29, 393, the Christian emperors Theodosius, Arcadius, and Honorius stated, "It is sufficiently determined that the sect of the Jews is prohibited by no law. We are therefore gravely disturbed that their assemblies have been prohibited in some places" (CTheod 16.8.9). In a law in 412, the Emperor Honorius decreed:

> Since ancient custom and usage has preserved the day of Sabbath sacred to the abovementioned people of the Jews, we decree that it must also be prevented

that an affair requiring attendance in court oblige a man of the said observance under pretext of public or private businesses, since it would seem that all the remaining time would be sufficient for the public laws, and since it would be most appropriate to a temperate age that privileges once granted not be dishonored. (CTheod 16.8.20)

Until 398 Jewish leaders seem to have enjoyed some legal autonomy and to have been able to use the power of the Roman government to enforce their judicial decisions. Even a law of 398 allowed the Jewish courts some scope for action, particularly if both parties agreed to abide by a court's decision:

Let the Jews, who live under the Roman common law, approach the courts in the usual solemn way in those cases which pertain not so much to their superstition as public court, laws and rights, and let them all introduce and defend lawsuits under the Roman laws; in conclusion, let them be under our laws. Certainly, if some think that, with the consent of the parties and only in a civil matter, they ought to litigate by means of an agreement through those who are like arbitrators among the Jews or the patriarchs, let them not be prohibited by public law from obtaining their decision; let the governors of the provinces even execute their sentences as if they had been given by the sentence of a legal arbitrator. (CTheod 2.1.10)

In 415 Christians were prohibited from being tried in the Jewish patriarch's court (CTheod 16.8.22), but this presupposes that that had been the practice. In addition, the Jews were allowed to establish the prices for their own merchandise:

No outsider to the religion of the Jews shall set prices for the Jews when something is offered for sale: for it is just to entrust to each what is his own. Therefore, province governors shall not allow that a controller or a supervisor be appointed over you. But if someone, except you and your leaders, shall dare to take this office to himself, then they shall hasten to force him by punishment as someone coveting another's property. (CJust 1.9.9)

As Bernard Bachrach comments, "In short, it would seem that the vast edifice of imperial economic control that had been set in place in Diocletian's reign and which had been modified in various ways by his successors did not pertain in a fundamental manner to the Jews."[11] In fact, the legislation implied that it was possible for Jews in the second and third centuries to take part in the municipal government of cities, but ancient custom exempted them collectively. This exemption meant something, for the honor of being part of local government entailed paying for various citywide services, or "liturgies," as they were called.

Membership in the city council required that a person be from or reside in the city, be freeborn and, most important, own property, which usually meant land.[12] The amount of property required varied from city to city. As A.H.M. Jones comments on the decurions, or members of the councils:

To the emperors the decurions were, as Majorian put it: "the sinews of the commonwealth and the hearts of the cities." In the former capacity they collected and underwrote the imperial levies and taxes, repaved the roads, administered the public post, conscripted recruits for the army, managed the mines; and though the government attempted on occasion to find substitutes for them in one or other of their many roles, such experiments were short-lived. As "the hearts of the cities" they maintained those amenities of urban life, in particular the baths and the games, which were in Roman eyes essentials of civilized life.[13]

In 321 Constantine basically repealed exemption of the Jews, "but in order that something of the former custom be left to them as a consolation, we allow them as a perpetual privilege that two or three (in every curia) shall be employed by no nominations" (CTheod 16.8.3). Jewish "clergymen"—patriarchs, presbyters, priests, archisynagogues, fathers of synagogues, and the others who served in synagogues—were exempted from such liturgies in 330 (CTheod 16.8.2), but this exemption was rescinded in 383 (CTheod 12.1.99). A fascinating law from 398 read, "We find that many city positions throughout Apulia and Calabria are insecure, because they belong to the Jewish superstition and consider themselves protected from the necessity of undergoing liturgies by some law proposed in the Eastern regions" (CTheod 12.1.158). This edict from the western part of the Roman Empire suggests that the position of Jews in certain regions was so strong that some towns would actually go under if Jewish citizens did not perform the liturgies. In this way the Jews in the fourth and fifth centuries were treated as the rest of the population was, although they still did not have to perform liturgies inconsistent with their religious practice.

The imperial government in this period needed financial help in running the cities and cut back on all exemptions. Beginning in the sixth century, however, Jews were discriminated against as they were not allowed to serve in government offices but still had to pay for some burdens of such offices (Justinian *Novellae* 45). We can see this sense of the wealth and position of Jews in the correspondence between the Jewish patriarch Gamaliel V and the most famous Greek rhetorician of his day, Libanius, a friend and adviser to the Emperor Julian. Several of Libanius's letters to Gamaliel survive and bear witness to the important position of the patriarch in the society of Antioch. Jerome even mentioned the implacable war Gamaliel waged against a man of consular rank, Hesychius (Letter 57.3). This is often taken to mean that Gamaliel caused Hesychius's death, but Jerome did not say this. What the mention does show is the stratum of society in which Gamaliel moved. His son was educated by Libanius, an education that was not inexpensive.

A later patriarch, Gamaliel VI, held the rank of illustrious honorary *praefectus praetorio* but in 415 was demoted to the rank of *spectabilis* (CTheod 16.8.22). It seems that the patriarch broke several laws: He had built new synagogues; judged cases between Jews and Christians; circumcised non-Jews, both slaves and freeborn; and owned Christian slaves. Yet the emperor made no effort to dislodge the patriarch from his position, merely taking away from him an honorary title while allowing him to retain all the honors that had been previously bestowed.

This recognition of the Jewish patriarch by the imperial government is also seen in the authority to nominate officeholders given to the patriarch in a law of 397 (CTheod 16.8.13) and confirmed in a law of 404 (CTheod 16.8.15); to these was given the power to excommunicate and to revoke excommunication (CTheod 16.8.8). It seems that the imperial government was trying to classify the Jewish religion by analogy to the Christian religion, with the patriarch as undisputed leader. Such a classification logically followed from the steps taken to control conversion to Judaism, as first circumcision and then the joining of a synagogue and participation in Jewish ritual were prohibited (in 329, CTheod 16.8.1; in 353, CTheod 16.8.7; in 383, CTheod 16.7.3). From the second century on, circumcision had been treated as castration (*Digest* 48.8.11): A physician who performed circumcision was liable to execution, and Roman citizens who had been circumcised were to be exiled and have their property confiscated (Paul *Sentences* 5.22.3–4). The very fact that these laws had to be repeated so often suggests at least that they were hard to enforce and that there were converts to Judaism. The same can be said of a law of 388 (CTheod 3.7.2) that prohibited intermarriage between Jews and Christians—such a marriage was put on a par with adultery. There must have been sufficient cases to require the enactment of such a law. There was legislation against Jews stoning Jews who had converted to Christianity (CTheod 16.8.1) and against Jews mocking Christian symbols on the feast of Purim (CTheod 16.8.18), but no action was taken against those who had previously committed these offenses. Bachrach's well-argued conclusion is that there was no anti-Jewish policy in the fourth and early fifth centuries because "it saw the potential cost, in terms of social dislocation, economic decline, and military conflict, that the Jewish *gens* would impose if it were attacked."[14] The Jews were an integral part of the social fabric of the Roman Empire, yet retained their own distinctive identity.

The Rhetoric of Abuse

Despite the importance accorded the Jewish community through imperial legislation, the Jews were the targets of a rhetoric of abuse. The Jews were said to be a deadly and nefarious sect (CTheod 16.8.1), their assemblies were considered sacrilegious (CTheod 16.8.7), and they were called arrogant and audacious (CTheod 16.8.26, 16.9.5). Those who converted to Judaism were said to be polluting themselves with Jewish contagions (CTheod 16.7.3) and contaminated sacraments (CTheod 3.1.5). In this view, Christian slaves owned by Jews, should not be corrupted by the filth of this nefarious superstition (CTheod 16.9.4).

This language of abuse flourished among the Christian leaders of the late fourth century. They were particularly disturbed by Julian's 361–363 attempt, whether out of spite to the Christians or a desire to bolster ancient ethnic religion or both, to rebuild the Temple in Jerusalem. The whole short reign of Julian, a scant twenty months, brought home to the Christians how fragile their access to imperial power was and how one emperor could revert life to a pre-Constantinian era. They did not relish that thought. So Christians delighted in the failure of Julian's scheme, and all kinds of miracle stories abounded to show that God had frustrated the attempt. Fire came down from heaven, earthquakes proliferated, a great cross was seen in the sky, a copy of the Gospel of Saint John was found in a mysterious cave beneath the Temple foundation.[15] But these stories attested to the relief the Christians felt at the failure of the attempt.

It was after Julian that attempts increased, particularly in the reign of Theodosius I, to install Christianity as the religion of the Roman Empire, with increasing restrictions on other religions. As noted in Chapter 1, Ambrose, bishop of Milan, was violently anti-Jewish in his sermon of 389 concerning the proposed restoration of a synagogue that had been burned by Christians. Saint John Chrysostom, bishop of Antioch, tried to convince his fellow Christians that demons dwelled in synagogues and in the souls of Jews (*Homily 1 Against the Jews*). Augustine, in the last years of his life, wrote the tractate *Against the Jews*. In this he continued the method of arguing against them found scattered in his earlier writings—namely, that the Jews understood the Scriptures carnally, not spiritually. They chanted the Psalms "fruitlessly and foolishly," for they did not understand what they were singing (*Against the Jews* 2; PL 42.52). They castigated the Christians for not following the precepts of the Law but did not understand themselves that the commandments had changed (*Against the Jews* 3.6; PL 42.52–54). In an earlier sermon, Augustine had exhorted his congregation to observe the Sabbath spiritually: "Not as the Jews observe it in a fleshly idleness. For they want to have time for their trifles and extravagances. The Jew would do better to do something useful in his field rather than to be disorderly in the theater, and their wives would do better to weave wool than to dance shamelessly the whole day on their balconies" (Sermon 9.3; PL 38.77).

We might glimpse here why the Jewish feasts were so attractive to some Christians but not to Augustine. He linked contemporary Jews to their ancestors who had crucified Jesus: "You in your parents killed Christ. All this time you have not believed and you have spoken against [Christians], but you have not yet perished because you have not yet gone out of the body. Now you have a space for repentance" (*Against the Jews* 11; PL 42.60). In a comment on the psalm verse (69:21) that the Gospel of Matthew had seen as fulfilled in Jesus' death—"They gave me gall for food, and in my thirst they gave me vinegar to drink"—Augustine wrote:

> Those [Jews] who object to us [that we Christians do not observe the commandments] are still bitter from their parents who gave the Lord gall for food, and they are still time-worn from the vinegar that they offered him to drink. There-

fore they do not understand that what follows is fulfilled in them, "Let their table become before them a trap, a retribution, a stumbling-block" (Ps. 69:22). For they themselves have become gall-like and bitter, since they served gall-like, bitter food to the living bread. (*Against the Jews* 6; PL 42.54).

CONCLUSION

Every human construction of a social world and worldview is transmitted and transformed over time, particularly when different cultures meet. The experiences and changes in social and cultural circumstances that Jews underwent both in the homeland and in the Diaspora transformed their worldview. Both Philo of Alexandria and the Qumran Covenanters were devoted Jews, but they exemplified the diversity among Jews in the Greco-Roman world. As Christians, followers of Jesus the Jew, began to chart their course in the complex and variegated culture of the Mediterranean world, most believed, with the Jews, in one God who had spoken through Moses and the prophets. As greater distinction grew between the two communities, so did the polemic between them. Nonetheless, the polemic on the Christian side always retained a dose of irony and uneasiness about its Jewish heritage. The continued, flourishing existence of the Jews was an anomaly to Christian leaders, not the way the world should be, and this anti-Judaism would be part of their worldview. The following chapters explore how the Christians would begin to forge further their own self-definition.

Suggestions for Further Reading

Feldman, Louis H. *Jew and Gentile in the Ancient World: Attitudes and Interactions from Alexander to Justinian.* Princeton: Princeton University Press, 1993.

Gager, John G. *The Origins of Anti-Semitism: Attitudes Toward Judaism in Pagan and Christian Antiquity.* New York: Oxford University Press, 1983.

Goodenough, Erwin R. *Jewish Symbols in the Greco-Roman Period.* 13 vols. New York: Pantheon, 1953–1968.

Ruether, Rosemary R. *Faith and Fratricide: The Theological Roots of Anti-Semitism.* New York: Seabury, 1974.

Segal, Alan F. *Rebecca's Children. Judaism and Christianity in the Roman World.* Cambridge, Mass.: Harvard University Press, 1986.

Shanks, Herschel, ed. *Christianity and Rabbinic Judaism: A Parallel History of Their Origins and Early Development.* Washington, D.C.: Biblical Archeology Society, 1992.

Stern, Menahem. *Greek and Latin Authors on Jews and Judaism.* 3 vols. Jerusalem: Israel Academy of Sciences and Humanities, 1974–1984.

Wilken, Robert L. *John Chrysostom and the Jews: Rhetoric and Reality in the Late Fourth Century.* Berkeley and Los Angeles: University of California Press, 1983.

_____. *The Land Called Holy: Palestine in Christian History and Thought.* New Haven: Yale University Press, 1992.

⊷ FOUR ⊷

The First Steps:
Articulating Alienation

THE CHRISTIAN INTELLECTUALS WHO TOOK the first steps toward defining Christianity were attempting to reshape the symbolized world in which they lived. As mentioned in the first pages of this book, all of us are born into a world whose signs and symbols we learn through the process of socialization.[1] When we change communities—for example, if we go to live in Japan or China—we may have to learn the way people in those societies interact and perceive their world. What the early Christian intellectuals were doing was trying to reinterpret the cultural traditions of the Greco-Roman and Jewish world in light of their allegiance to the Christian community. In a world where kinship relationships were very strong, the Christians were marginals, outsiders to the normal flow of daily living, no longer paying respect to the gods and goddesses who protected household and city. This sense of marginality, of being aliens in this world, strangers within it, would remain entrenched in the Christian self-definition throughout this period. It found expression in the earliest writings by Christians: "Our citizenship is in heaven" (Phil. 3:20); "they do not belong to the world, just as I do not belong to the world" (John 17:16); "here we have no lasting city, but we are looking for the city that is to come" (Heb. 13:14). Christians were a pilgrim people, a people newborn, "not of perishable but of imperishable seed" (1 Pet. 1:23), and so they should behave as aliens and exiles in this world (1 Pet. 2:11). This image of alienation is found in the fourth century in the Syriac Christian writer Aphrahat, who in 337 exhorted, "We should be aliens from this world, just as Christ did not belong to this world" (Sixth Demonstration). Augustine of Hippo's great early-fifth-century work contrasted the city of God with the city of this world. The metaphor Augustine returned to again and again was that of Christians as pilgrims in this world, moving on to their true homeland. This image of themselves as "not of this world" articulated itself in their way of life and also in their cosmological speculations. For if they were not of this world, of what world were they? If they were pilgrims, where were they bound? How should they live in this world?

65

CHRISTIANS AND THE HEBREW SCRIPTURES

Because of their Jewish heritage, Christians first grappled with these questions of origin in defining their relationship to that body of traditional literature handed down among the Jews and consisting of the Law, the Prophets, and the Writings. There was still flexibility as to the precise constituents of this literature, particularly as regards the catchall group the writings, and this was evident in the variation between the Hebrew Bible and the Greek "translation" of it, the Septuagint. Most Christian intellectuals from the second century on used the Greek version. To retain the sense of the traditional literature of the Jews, however, I use the term *Hebrew Scriptures* to refer to this body of literature.

As followers of the Jew Jesus, Christians had to ask whether following him also entailed accepting this traditional literature. If no, then why not? If yes, then how would Christians interpret this literature differently from the many Jews living in the Mediterranean basin? The response of early intellectuals ran the whole gamut—from full acceptance of the Hebrew Scriptures to outright rejection.

Full Acceptance of the Hebrew Scriptures

We do not know a great deal about those Christians who accepted completely the Hebrew Scriptures, in particular the requirements of the Mosaic Law. Most statements about them come from later sources, such as the fourth-century bishop, Epiphanius of Salamis. Epiphanius spoke of groups such as the Ossaeans or Sampsaeans "who follow the Jewish way of life in observing the Sabbath, circumcision and everything the Law requires" (*Panarion* 19.5.1)[2]—likewise the Nazoreans and the Cerinthians. Epiphanius's report of the Cerinthians' argument on following the law is interesting: "They bear this witness, saying again from the Gospel: 'It suffices for a pupil to become as his master' (Matt. 10:25). So what? They say: Jesus was circumcised, so you be circumcised. Christ lived according to the Law, they say, so you also do the same" (*Panarion* 28.5.1–2).

Epiphanius ridiculed this argument as built on sophisms, but the argument would have had great weight in a culture where the master-pupil relationship was extremely intimate and where the pupil modeled himself on his master. During the *Dialogue with Trypho,* written by Justin Martyr in the mid-second century, Trypho questions whether someone will be saved who confesses Jesus as Christ and yet also wants to observe the commandments of the Mosaic Law (47). Justin admitted that in his opinion such a person would be saved unless he or she tried to make others act the same way. Justin thus stated both that there were Christians who observed the Mosaic Law and that they were not accepted by some other Christians. How many Christians followed such practices is simply unknown. Epiphanius located most of his groups in the eastern empire, but Justin Martyr wrote in Rome about a dialogue, the *Dialogue with Trypho,* he located in Asia Minor, so there could have been Christians who observed the Jewish Law anywhere. Such an acceptance of the Jewish Law was, of course, not in line with the metaphor of alienation, of breaking with kinship ties, of starting a new race. For these Christians, the cosmos had been created according to Genesis, and Jesus was described as born naturally from Joseph and Mary and as distinct from an angelic power that had possessed him (Epiphanius *Panarion* 30.1.2–3,14, 51.2.3, 51.3.6, 51.6.7; Irenaeus *Adversus haereses* 1.26.1).

Rejection of the Hebrew Scriptures

Marcion. At the opposite end of the scale was a resounding rejection of Judaism. Marcion adopted this position. Born in Sinope in Asia Minor around 85, the son of a Christian bishop, Marcion moved to Rome, where he taught until his expulsion from the churches there in 144. After this he kept preaching his message until his death in 160. His efforts bore remarkable fruit: Tertullian of Carthage found it necessary to write a tractate against him a full fifty years after his death, and pockets of Marcionites were being debated by Theodoret of Cyrrhus in Syria in the fifth century, although Theodoret's work *Against Marcion* has been lost. In his Letters 81 and 113, Theodoret claimed to have converted eight villages from Marcionism. Marcion clearly inspired followers, and his speaking ability may have been honed by education. Both his wealth (he was reported to have given two hundred thousand sesterces to the Christians in Rome) and his father's standing in the community suggest one of those better-off families that may have been rising on the social scale.[3]

Marcion's own writing, *The Antitheses,* can only be reconstructed from fragments quoted by his adversaries. Most striking is that Marcion considered himself a true disciple of the apostle Paul. Marcion emphasized the polemical statements of Paul against the Mosaic Law. Following Paul, Marcion insisted on the newness of the revelation in Jesus Christ—it has nothing to do with what went before. This sense of newness, perhaps influenced by Paul's language of new creation (Gal. 6:6), led Marcion to distinguish between the God and Father of Jesus Christ and the God of the Hebrew Scriptures. Where Paul said, "The god of this world has blinded the minds of the unbelievers, to keep them from seeing the light of the gospel of the glory of Christ who is the likeness of God" (2 Cor. 4:4; cf. 1 Cor. 8:4–6; Gal. 4:8–9), Marcion interpreted this as referring to the God of Genesis, who had created this world, a being distinct from the God who had sent Jesus Christ. Marcion found other problems in the text of the Hebrew Scriptures: How could the God of Jesus Christ ever have said, "I am the one who forms light and makes darkness, who makes peace and creates evil" (Isa. 45:7)? How could the God of Jesus Christ be as ignorant as the God who walked in the garden and did not know where Adam was (Gen. 3:8–9), so unjust as to have little children eaten by bears because of a few insults (2 Kings 2:23–24)?

Marcion thus called for the radical alienation of the Christian from this world, an alienation also expressed in his strongly ascetic lifestyle. His theology was developed around a series of oppositions, as the title of his work *The Antitheses* suggests, and he was fearless in following through the logic of his position. He systematically rejected much of the previous Christian tradition and accepted only one gospel: an excerpted version of the Gospel of Luke and ten expurgated epistles of Paul. Marcion rejected what he called the Gospels perverted by Judaizers, which contained elements such as the Jewish genealogy of Jesus.

Secret Book According to John. Another work written in this period, the *Secret Book According to John*, combined anti-Judaism and rejection of this world. Irenaeus, bishop of Lyons, referred to it around 180, although whether this is exactly the same version of the text now known from *The Nag Hammadi Library* is unclear. Who wrote the book and where also remain unknown, but it was originally written in Greek. The narrative describes a revelatory discourse of the resurrected Jesus to the apostle John, who in distress wonders how the savior was chosen, why he was sent into the world, and who the parent was who sent him. In response to these questions, a revealer appears to John and basically rewrites Genesis. The first part of the discourse describes the structure of the divine world, the pre-Genesis story. Here the source of all being is described through a series of negations:

> It is immeasurable light, which is uncontaminated, holy and pure; it is ineffable and perfect in incorruptibility: not in perfection, nor in blessedness, nor in divinity; rather as being far superior to these. It is not corporeal, it is not incorporeal, it is not large, it is not small, it is not quantifiable, nor is it a creature. Indeed no one can think of it. It is not something among the existents; rather it is something far superior to these. … It is eternity, as bestowing eternity. It is life, as bestowing life. It is good, as bestowing fondness. It is all these things not as possessing attributes; rather as bestowing them. (*Secret Book* 3:17–4:8)[4]

This ineffable primal source produced something out of its pure intelligence, which initiated the generation of a highly complex divine world whose production is imaged in terms of human generation somewhat along the lines of the theogonies of Hesiod or the Mesopotamian *Enuma Elish*. This divine realm is complete in itself, it is called the entirety (or *plēroma*, a term used in the Pauline corpus at Col. 2:16), and it contains the expanded power of the primal parent of all. The emanation of this spiritual world, the entirety, would have been all that the primal parent would have brought into being had it not been for an act of ignorance by the last element of the entirety to be produced, Wisdom. Wisdom acted in a disorderly fashion and brought forth, because of the power with her, an imperfect product called Ialdabaoth, possibly "begetter of Sabaoth." It is this imperfect, misshapen product, no proper image of its mother, that is to produce this world and that is identified with the creator God of Genesis 1:1.

The rest of the *Secret Book* deals with how this world is created, particularly Adam, who is modeled after an image of the entirety, yet whose body is ruled by the forces of the heavens; how Ialdabaoth is tricked into breathing some of his power, which he had from his divine mother, Wisdom; and how the story of humanity is the struggle for humans to realize that through this divine power they belong properly to the realm of the entirety and not to this poor imitation of a world. The material world is thus an alien realm to that of true spiritual existence, the entirety. By a person's knowing that he or she comes from the divine realm of the entirety and not from this world ruled by fate and the stars, he or she returns to that world. The role of Christ is in fact to reacquaint humans with their origin, to free them from the bondage of their material bodies.

This powerful telling of the tale of humanity's origins is a classic example of cosmological alienation. Genesis is turned on its head: This world is not good—it enslaves humans; humans are not made in the image of the creator of this world—they truly belong to a world different in degree from this world. The God of this world is not beneficent but jealous and evil. Thus, the author symbolically expressed his or her own separation from this world and sense of belonging to a different race, those who were acquainted intimately with the entirety, rather than those who lacked this knowledge and were in ignorance and error. The Christian group to which the author of the *Secret Book* belonged clearly viewed itself as different from (or at least superior to) the rest of the society in which it lived and articulated its sense of self in this mythic fashion. This mythic stance of strong alienation and rejection of the values of this world predominates in what is called "Gnostic" literature, that is, the literature of those who know (from Greek *gnostikos,* which means "leading to knowledge"), who have intimate acquaintance with the divine realm of the entirety.

The Valentinian Gnostics

There are many tellings of the Gnostic myth that nevertheless retain the same basic structure. We can imagine the Gnostics, I believe, as members of small seminar groups or study circles discussing the great problems. The circle of friends who gathered around the philosopher Plotinus seems to have been small—Porphyry listed ten close friends of Plotinus (*Life of Plotinus* 7)—and occasionally others would drop in to listen or to act as guest speakers; discussion would flow back and forth.[5]

There was probably an acknowledged leader as guide of the group. In the second century, Christians would have met in enlarged private houses or rooms, and there may have been several such meeting places in a large city. At Dura-Europos around 240, a Christian meeting place was enlarged by converting two rooms into one, for a capacity of sixty people.[6] Fifty to seventy-five years earlier a small room would have sufficed for the Christians. It is this small scale that we must keep in mind when discussing early Christian teachers.

We must also keep in mind that during the second century there was no canon of authoritative writings accepted by all Christians. As we have seen, Marcion limited his authoritative books to letters of Paul and an abbreviated Gospel of Luke and no Hebrew Scriptures. The community in which the *Secret Book* was read certainly did not respect the authority of the Genesis narrative in any literal sense. One Christian group in Alexandria accepted as authoritative the Hebrew Scriptures and most of the present Christian Scriptures but also read with the same respect the *Gospel According to the Hebrews, Revelation of Peter, Preaching of Peter, Epistle of Barnabas, Epistle of Clement, Traditions of Matthew, Teaching of the Twelve Apostles,* and more. In contrast, some Christian groups were trying to limit what books would be accepted as authoritative. In the western part of the Roman Empire there was a growing consensus that there were only four authoritative Gospels. In the late second century, Bishop Irenaeus argued that this number of four was divinely decreed: (1) in creation there are the four winds and the four zones of the world (north, south, east, and west) in which humans live, and so the number four is appropriate to God's revelation; (2) the description of God's chariot in Ezekiel 1 has four aspects, which correspond to the four Gospels; and (3) God gave four principal covenants to humans—under Adam, under Noah, under Moses, and under the Gospels (*Against Heresies* 3.11.8).

In this world of small Christian study groups lived another powerful personality, Valentinus. He studied in Alexandria and there became acquainted with Greek philosophy, particularly of the Middle Platonist type, for a passage of one of his sermons seems to echo the work of Philo of Alexandria. Valentinus's followers claimed that he learned his Christian teaching from a certain Theudas, who was claimed to be a follower of Saint Paul. Between 136 and 140 Valentinus moved to Rome and taught there until around 165. A persuasive teacher, Valentinus inspired many Christians, and "his followers blossomed into a brilliant international school of theologians and biblical commentators."[7] This teaching spread to almost all parts of the Roman world, and there is evidence that there were still Valentinians in the seventh century.

Valentinus and his school were very close readers of the biblical text. (The earliest commentaries on New Testament books that we have come from this school.) In Valentinus's case, he read through the lens of Greek philosophy, particularly Platonism and Stoicism. In his *Gospel of Truth,* Valentinus frequently alluded to passages from writings that would become part of the canon of the Christian Scriptures. Valentinus and his school thus seem to have respected this move toward accepting some books as authoritative. In the *Gospel of Truth,* Valentinus referred movingly to the parable of the lost sheep in Matthew 18:12 and used imagery from the Genesis story of the garden of Eden and the eating of the fruit of the tree of knowledge (Gen. 2:17) to describe Jesus as in some sense a new Adam:

> It is to the perfect that this, the proclamation of the one they search for, has made itself known, through the mercies of the father. By this the hidden mystery Jesus Christ shed light upon those who were, because of forgetfulness, in darkness. He enlightened them and gave them a way, and the way is the truth, about which he instructed them. For this reason error became angry at him and persecuted him. She was constrained by him, and became inactive. He was nailed to a tree and became fruit of the father's acquaintance. Yet it did not cause ruin because it was eaten. Rather, to those who ate of it, it gave the possibility that whoever he discovered within himself might be joyful in the discovery of him. And as for him, they discovered him within them—the inconceivable uncontained, the father, who is perfect, who created the entirety. (*Gospel of Truth* 18:11–33)

Valentinus stressed strongly the place of Jesus as the one savior who accomplishes this redemptive act by his death on a cross. It is through Jesus that error and ignorance are exposed and that those who belong to the entirety come to knowledge. Valentinus extended the notion of predestination found in Paul's letter to the Romans and in the Gospel of John: "Those whose names he foreknew were called at the end, as persons having acquaintance. ... So that whoever has acquaintance is from above: and if called, hears, replies, and turns to the one who is calling; and goes to him" (*Gospel of Truth* 21:25–22:6). Such a doctrine of predestination, of being receptors of special revelatory knowledge, would appeal to many in a small group such as the Christian movement. It provided for them an encompassing explanation of how the world around them had come to be as it was, of why the Christian revelation was new, and of their privileged position in that world.

The Hidden Meaning in the Text. The cosmological structure found in Gnostic literature such as the *Secret Book* is also found in the writings of Valentinus and his followers, and yet there is a difference. Whereas the author of that document stressed the discontinuity between the divine and this world, Valentinus seems to have allowed more play to the metaphor of this world being modeled after the divine realm. Here Adam's body is described as the modeled form:

And just as fear was among the angels because of that formed figure when it spoke things greater than what was appropriate to its formation, on account of the one who had invisibly placed in it a seed of the essence from above and who was outspoken, so also among the races of worldly humans, human works become objects of fear for those who made them as, for instance, statues and representations and everything that hands make in regard to the name of god. For Adam, formed in regard to the name of human, caused fear of the preexistent human as manifestly the latter was established in him. And they were terrified and quickly hid the work. (Clement of Alexandria *Miscellanies* 2.36.2–4)[8]

There are discontinuity and some trace of continuity here. This sense of artistic model perhaps explains the Valentinian school's approach to the reading of the Hebrew Scriptures. In the previously cited quotation from the *Gospel of Truth,* we can see how Valentinus imaged the death of Jesus in language from Genesis. Jesus becomes the fruit of knowledge/acquaintance of the Father on a tree, fruit that does not cause ruin when eaten. Eating of Jesus does not bring error/death but knowledge. In this way Jesus is assimilated to the fruit from the tree of the knowledge of good and evil, which makes its eaters like God, knowing good and evil (Gen. 2:17, 3:5). But the tree of Genesis brings death, and so in this sense is an antitype, an opposite to the "tree" of Jesus' crucifixion. This way of reading a sacred text, of finding a deeper meaning within the narrative of Genesis than the surface meaning of the text, was one common to philosophers of the Greco-Roman world. In *Life of Plotinus,* written by Porphyry between 301 and 305, is found an oracle that the god Apollo is said to have spoken concerning the career of Plotinus:

Spirit, man once, but now nearing the diviner lot of a spirit, as the bond of human necessity has been loosed for you, and strong in heart, you swam swiftly from the roaring surge of the body to that coast where the stream flows strong, far apart from the crowd of the wicked, there to set your steps firm in the easy path of the pure soul, where the splendor of God shines round you and the divine law abides in purity far from lawless wickedness.

Then, too, when you were struggling to escape from the bitter wave of this blood-drinking life, from its sickening whirlpools, in the midst of its billows and sudden surges, often the Blessed Ones showed you the goal ever near. Often when your mind was thrusting out by its own impulse along crooked paths the Immortals raised you by a straight path to the heavenly circuits, the divine way, sending down a solid shaft of light so that your eyes could see out of the mournful darkness. Sweet sleep never held your eyes, but scattering the heavy cloud that would have kept them closed, borne in the whirl you saw many fair sights which are hard for human seekers after wisdom to see.

But now that you have been freed from this tabernacle and have left the tomb which held your heavenly soul, you come at once to the company of heaven, where winds of delight blow, where is affection and desire that charms the sight, full of pure joy, brimming with streams of immortality from the gods which carry the allurements of the Loves, and sweet breeze and the windless brightness of high heaven. (*Life of Plotinus* 22; LCL)

Here the oracle uses the language of Homer's *Odyssey* (5.370–493), which describes the wrecking of Odysseus's ship and his swimming through the waves to the shore of the Phaiakians. A deeper meaning is found within the sacred pages of Homer, not the physical buffeting of the sea, but the spiritual struggle of the soul to reach the divine realm. This method of interpretation, termed *allegorical,* had been developed as early as the fifth century B.C.E. by pre-Socratic philosophers and had been used by Philo of Alexandria to interpret the Hebrew Scriptures. Philo, as we saw in Chapter 1, had recognized that Genesis 1 and 2 contains two accounts of the creation of Adam and so he had read this, not as evidence of two different sources (the view taken by modern biblical scholars), but as an indication of the deeper meaning that there are two realms: a world of perfect ideas and the sensible world humans live in. So the two creation accounts refer to the forming of human, the perfect type of the intellectual world of Plato's ideas, and of humans, the sensible, clay-formed people we all are. Valentinus, therefore, because of his education, read the Hebrew Scriptures, in their Greek translation of course, in this way.

The Place of the Hebrew Scriptures. Valentinus's evaluation of the Hebrew Scriptures, however, may have been quite complicated. From the work of his pupil Ptolemy, we can gain an insight into how the school of Valentinus read the Scriptures. In a letter to Flora found in the work of the fourth-century heresy-hunter Epiphanius, Ptolemy provided an introductory explanation of Valentinian teaching. Throughout the letter Ptolemy referred to authoritative Christian writings as proof that his more systematized teaching was correct. For example, in discussing allegorical interpretation, Ptolemy wrote, "Both his [Jesus'] disciples and the apostle Paul explained these teachings" (Epiphanius *Panarion* 33.6.6). In closing his letter, Ptolemy indicated what the next lesson would be and that Flora would also learn "to regulate all the discourses by our Savior's teaching" (33.7.9). This sentence is ambiguous— does it mean that Flora will be able to judge all other doctrines by means of the doctrine she will next learn or that all the doctrines of the next lessons will be proven by the Christian Scripture? As Ptolemy said earlier, "We shall offer proofs of what we say by drawing from our Savior's words, by which alone it is possible to reach a certain apprehension of the reality of the matter without stumbling" (33.3.8). Whatever the case, Ptolemy clearly insisted that his teaching was based on the Christian Scriptures and had come down to him by apostolic succession.

How, then, did Ptolemy view the Hebrew Scriptures? He rejected the views both of those who held that the legislator of the Mosaic Law is the devil, perhaps like the author of the *Secret Book* or Marcion, and of those who held that the legislator is the highest God, the source of all existence, like the views of Justin Martyr and Origen. The legislator who speaks in the Hebrew Scriptures is, according to Ptolemy, midway between these two, and therefore the Hebrew Scriptures themselves, like their author, partake of both good, insofar as the legislator resembles the source of all goodness, and imperfection, insofar as its author is imperfect. As for the Mosaic Law itself, Ptolemy argued that there are three sources of the Law: the divine legislator, Moses, and the elders. For Ptolemy, only the law of the divine legislator is important. Within that, he distinguished among legislation that is pure but in need of completion, as, for example, the Ten Commandments; legislation that is interwoven with injustice and imperfection and is to be rejected, as, for example, the law of retribution, which commands an eye for an eye, a tooth for a tooth, a death for a death (Lev. 24:20–21); and legislation that is symbolic and so has to be seen as imaging the spiritual, invisible realm, as, for example, ritual prescriptions such as circumcision so that what is enjoined is not really bodily circumcision but circumcision of the heart. Ptolemy's approach to the Hebrew Scriptures was therefore an extremely complex one and reflected his cosmological speculation. He did not reject this world or the authority of the Hebrew Scriptures entirely, as Marcion and the author of the *Secret Book* had. Rather, he saw it as an imperfect image of the divine world. He had a greater sensitivity to this world as imaging the divine realm and so did not radically reject it.

Qualified Acceptance of the Hebrew Scriptures

A middle ground between entire acceptance and outright rejection of the Hebrew Scriptures is that represented by such diverse Christians as Justin Martyr, Tertullian, Irenaeus of Lyons, and the Alexandrians Clement and Origen. Whereas Marcion had stressed the Pauline image of Christianity as a new creation and the Valentinian school had emphasized the metaphor of Christianity as the reality opposed to the shadow of the Hebrew Scriptures (Col 2:17), these Christian thinkers adopted the metaphor of the Law as preliminary (Gal. 3:24). They believed both that Christianity was something new and that the creator God of the Hebrew Scriptures was the Father of Jesus. These Christians retained both beliefs by introducing the notion of a development in revelation. This "economy of salvation," to use Irenaeus's phrase, meant that God could allow certain practices, such as the patriarchs' polygamy, and certain laws, such as an eye for an eye, as appropriate for an earlier time but not for when the full revelation arrived. Prophecy also came to the fore with this notion. The events and persons of the Hebrew Scriptures were seen typologically, as foreshadowings of the Christian dispensation. Hints of Christianity could also be found throughout God's creation. Justin found allusions to the truth of Christianity in Plato and in Greek narratives about the gods and goddesses. Justin saw intimations of the cross everywhere:

> For look closely at all the things in the cosmos, and see whether they are administered or can be connected without this shape [of the cross]. For the sea cannot be cut through unless this trophy which is called a sail remains intact in the ship; the earth is not plowed without it; diggers do not perform their work, nor artisans likewise, except with this shape. Human shape differs from that of irrational animals in nothing else except this, that it both is upright and can have its hands extended, and it bears on its face lined up from the forehead what is called a nose, through which both there is breath for the living being, and also none other than the shape of the cross is displayed. It is also said through the prophet in this way: "The breath before our face is Christ the Lord." The symbols on your standards and trophies, with which your processions take place everywhere, manifest the power of this shape. You do this, although unknowingly, and display in them the signs of rule and power. You set up the images of your dead emperors on this shape, and you call them gods by your inscriptions. (*1 Apology* 55)

Justin, born at Neapolis in Samaria, settled in Rome and was martyred there around 165. Marcion, Valentinus, and he thus all taught in Rome as Christians at the same time, and so we can realize how flexible the appellation *Christian* was in Rome in the second century. Justin considered it the great mark of God to tell beforehand what will happen (*1 Apology* 12), and Justin's God is, like that of the Platonists, superior to the changeable (*1 Apology* 20). In fact, it is not God himself who speaks to humans in this world but God's Word, or Logos, the mediator between God and this world, whom Justin can speak of as a second God (*Dialogue with Trypho* 58–61). This Logos speaks with Moses from the burning bush in Exodus 3 (*1 Apology* 62–63), and elsewhere, and has sown seeds of truth throughout the world by which humans can come to the truth:

> For Moses is more ancient than all the Greek authors. The philosophers and poets were able to understand and expound everything about the inmortality of the soul, whether about punishments after death, or about the contemplation of heavenly things, or about other similar doctrines, since they took their starting-point from the prophets. Therefore the seeds of truth seem to be among all. However, they are proven not to have understood accurately since they contradicted one another. (*1 Apology* 44; cf. Tatian *Against the Greeks* 31–41)

Justin was a very close reader of the Hebrew Scriptures but had to yield in this respect to the great Origen. He was born in Alexandria of Christian parents around 185 and died in 254 after suffering imprisonment and torture during the Decian persecution. Origen still exhausts anyone who studies his life by his overwhelming assiduousness in studying and in publishing. The sheer volume of his output is staggering—he produced by dictation some two thousand works—and yet he combined this with an active role in the Christian community. His work on the text of the Hebrew Bible by itself would have been enough to secure his fame. He arranged in six columns (hence the six versions are called the *hexapla*) the Hebrew text, a transliteration of the Hebrew into Greek, the Greek translations by Aquila and Symmachus, the Septuagint, and the translation by Theodotion, and he marked where the text of the Septuagint, the Greek translation most used by the early church, diverged from the Hebrew. He, too, found problems in interpreting the text:

> It must be said that the inspired character of the prophetic words and the spiritual nature of the law of Moses became clear when Jesus resided here. For before the arrival of Christ it was not at all possible to furnish clear examples that the ancient scriptures were divinely inspired. But the arrival of Christ led those who dared to suspect that the law and the prophets were not divine to the clear proof that they were written by heavenly grace. (*On First Principles* 4.1.6).

Origen recognized that the style of the Scriptures is horrible (*On First Principles* 4.1.7, 4.3.6) and that often the literal meaning of a passage is meaningless:

> Now what thinking person will believe the first and the second and the third day, and the evening and the morning to have taken place without the sun and moon and stars? ... And to come to the legislation of Moses, many of the laws, so far as the goal of observing them individually, appear irrational, and others are impossible. A case of an irrational law is the prohibition to eat vultures, since nobody even in the worst famine was forced to go as far as [to eat] this animal. ... Moreover, to one who inquires carefully about the famous Sabbath, the command, "Each of you shall sit in your houses; let none of you go out from his place on the Sabbath day," is impossible to observe according to the text, since no living creature is able to sit for a whole day and not move from his seat. (*On First Principles* 4.3.1–2)

Origen thus saw problems in the Hebrew Scriptures and also in the Christian Scriptures. However, he did not resolve them by appealing to the work of different gods, as Ptolemy had done, or by rejecting the authority of the whole Hebrew Scriptures and expurgating the Gospels, as Marcion had. Rather, Origen insisted that the one perfect God had written the whole Hebrew Scriptures but in such a marvelous way that they would benefit all readers:

> One ought therefore register the thoughts of the holy writings on one's soul in a threefold way, so that (1) the one who reads more simply may be edified by the flesh, as it were, of the scripture, the name we give to the obvious interpretation; (2) one who has advanced somewhat may be edified by its soul, as it were; (3) one who is perfect ... by the spiritual law. ... For just as humans are composed of body, soul and spirit, in the same way also is the scripture, which was ar-

ranged by God to be given for the salvation of humans. (*On First Principles* 4.2.4)

Breaks in the narrative structure, irrational and impossible laws, all these were placed by God in the Scriptures:

> But since, if the usefulness of the legislation and the sequence and elegance of the narrative were immediately to be obviously manifest throughout, we would not believe that anything other than the obvious meaning could be meant in the Scriptures, the Word of God arranged for certain snares, as it were, and obstacles and impossibilities to be interwoven into the law and history, lest, drawn altogether away by a strongly attractive style, we might either completely reject the doctrines since we learned nothing worthy of God, or, by sticking to the letter, not learn its more divine meaning. (*On First Principles* 4.2.9)

God is an exceedingly devious teacher. The negatives of the Hebrew Scriptures are found to be positive. Here is a wholesale acceptance of the Hebrew Scriptures but in a distinctively Christian way. We could not find in the Scriptures anything to contradict the Christian creed Origen followed, only what would help Christians understand that creed so that they would know not only what is believed but also the reasons for and interconnections among the various parts of the creed (*On First Principles* 1.Preface). This acceptance of the Hebrew Scriptures was concomitant with acceptance that this world had been created by the one, just, and good God, impassible and incorporeal, beyond and behind whom there are no other gods. As Irenaeus of Lyons would put it:

> For all the apostles taught that there were two testaments for the two peoples; but that it was one and the same God who arranged both for the profit of those humans (for whose advantage the testaments were given) who were beginning to believe in God. We proved that from the very teaching of the apostles in the third book. The first testament was not given idly, or uselessly, or by chance, but (1) it inclined those to whom it was given to the service of God, for their profit (for God does not need the service of humans); (2) it disclosed a type of heavenly things, because humans were not yet able to see through their own vision what pertains to God; (3) it prefigured the images of those things which are in the Church, so that our faith might be steadfast; (4) and it contained a prophecy of things to come, so that humans might learn that God has foreknowledge of all things. (*Against Heresies* 4.32.2)

These final Christian thinkers, therefore, did not found the distinctiveness of Christianity on different divinities or on the rejection of the authority of the Hebrew Scriptures. They maintained, as did the Jews, the divine inspiration of the Hebrew Scriptures and, as did most of the Greek intellectual tradition, the continuity of this world with the divine realm. The newness they claimed for Christianity was the newness of Christ: The Hebrew Scriptures could properly be understood only as pointing to Christ; the Jesus who had

lived marked the appearance on earth of the Word of God, who was mediator between the one God and this created world. Many questions still remained: Did Christians maintain the monotheism of the Jews? Origen already used terms such as *two Gods* in discussing the creed. How far could
the Christians use the Greek philosophic triad of hypostases? What Christian modifications would need to be made to the model? Justin Martyr,
Clement, and Origen were indeed steeped in Platonism through their education and so understood Christian doctrine in these terms. What further steps
would need to be taken to distinguish Christianity from its Greek philosophic environment?

WAY OF LIFE

In one area the Christians had already distinguished themselves—in their
way of life. As we saw in Chapter 1, the Greek medical authority Galen cri-
tiqued the Christians' cosmology, but he is also said to have written admiringly of their way of life. In a passage preserved only in Arabic sources,
Galen is quoted as saying:

> [The Christians] sometimes act in the same way [as those who philosophize].
> For their contempt of death [and of its sequel] is patent to us every day, and like-
> wise their restraint in cohabitation. For they include not only men but also
> women who refrain from cohabiting all through their lives; and they also num-
> ber individuals who, in self-discipline and self-control in matters of food and
> drink, and in their keen pursuit of justice, have attained a pitch not inferior to
> that of genuine philosophers.[9]

The belief that Christians had entered a new creation had in the beginning
of Christianity caused problems about how to live. We have only to read
Paul's first letter to the Corinthians to become aware of these: Should
women let down their hair like men (1 Cor. 11:2–16)? Should couples have
sex or not (1 Cor. 7)? Could a person have sex indiscriminately, for example,
with a father's wife (1 Cor. 5:1), regardless of social taboos? What kind of
food should be eaten?

The Eucharist

Very early on the Christians had distinctive rituals that set them apart from
others—the initiation ritual of immersion, or baptism, the communal meeting for a commemorative meal. The Roman governor Pliny in 112 described
as an outsider what Christians did at their meetings:

> [The Christians] affirmed, however, the sum of their guilt or error to be this:
> that they were accustomed to meet on a fixed day before dawn, to sing antipho-
> nally a hymn to Christ, as to a god, and to bind themselves by an oath, not to
> some wickedness, but not to commit acts of fraud, theft, or adultery, not to fal-

sify their word, not to refuse to return a deposit if called upon to do so. When they had done these things, they used to depart and then come together again to take food—but food of an ordinary and harmless kind. They stopped doing this after my edict in which, according to your orders, I had forbade secret societies. (*Letters* 10.96.7)

Around 150 Justin Martyr outlined both baptismal and eucharistic liturgies. Justin's description of the eucharistic meal has, of course, quite a different flavor from that of Pliny. He described the eucharistic service that took place after the baptism of new Christians, which, he later said, was the same as what took place each Sunday:

When we finish the prayers, we greet one another with a kiss. Then, bread and a cup of water and mixed wine are brought to the one presiding over the brethren. He takes them and offers praise and glory to the Father of all through the name of the Son and of the Holy Spirit, and he gives thanks for a long time for those things honored by him. When he finishes these prayers and thanksgiving, all the people present assent, saying "Amen." This word "Amen" means in the Hebrew language "So be it." When he who presides has given thanks and all the people assented, those called by us deacons give to each of those present to partake of the bread, wine and water for which thanks have been given; and they carry it also to those not present.

This food is called by us the Eucharist. No one else is allowed to partake of this except one who believes what has been taught by us to be true, who has been washed by the water which is for the forgiveness of sins and for rebirth, and who lives just as Christ handed down. For we do not understand these to be ordinary bread and ordinary drink, but just as Jesus Christ, made flesh by the Word of God, had flesh and blood, so we have been taught that the food over which thanks has been given by the prayer of the word, and by which our flesh and blood is nourished by transformation, is both the flesh and blood of that Jesus made flesh. (*1 Apology* 65–66)

Christians and Their Bodies

To give a full picture of how early Christians lived would require asking, among other things, about the occupations they pursued, their wealth and status, their level of education, whether they served as soldiers or refused military service, whether they were slaves or owned slaves. As I noted in the Introduction, these kinds of questions are not the focus of this book. What is important in an intellectual history of the worldviews of early Christians is a discussion of how Christians viewed their bodies because the body has always been a symbolic boundary marker. It distinguishes individuals as well as groups from one another. The body has always been an available symbol for society—"the body politic." Dionysius of Halicarnassus, writing toward the end of the first century, had Menemus Agrippas resolve the quarrels among factions in Rome in 494 B.C.E. with this image: "A community in some measure is like a human body. For each of them is composite and of many parts; and each of the parts in them neither has the same strength nor produces the same services" (*Roman Antiquities* 6.86.1). The ritual of the eating of the Passover lamb resonates with images of the unity of the believing community (Exodus 12:3–10). The cutting up of the concubine's body in Judges 19 reflects the disintegration of communal unity in early Israel. Paul frequently invoked the image of the body to describe the unity-in-variety of the Christian community (1 Cor. 12; Rom. 12).

But what if some, like the Christians, wished to opt out of the larger social body, if some insisted that they did not belong to this worldly kingdom? The apostle Paul, expecting the world to end soon, advised:

> I mean, brothers and sisters, that the appointed time has grown short; from now on, let even those who have wives be as though they had none, and those who mourn as though they were not mourning, and those who rejoice as though they were not rejoicing, and those who buy as though they had no possessions, and those who deal with the world as though they had no dealings with it. For the present form of this world is passing away. (1 Cor. 7:29–31)

This world did not pass away, but the Christians still imaged themselves as outsiders to it. Besides their distinctive rituals and meetings, how were Christians to distinguish themselves from their neighbors? The distinctive bodily signs of the Jews were circumcision and kosher food laws, but as the second century wore on, only a minority of Christians were so distinct. How would a Christian's body signify a gulf between him or her and the surrounding world?

As Peter Brown so concisely states, the early Christians lived

> in a society that was more helplessly exposed to death than is even the most afflicted underdeveloped country in the modern world. ... In such a situation, only the privileged or the eccentric few could enjoy the freedom to do what they pleased with their sexual drives. Unexacting in so many ways in sexual matters, the ancient city expected its citizens to expend a requisite proportion of their energy begetting and rearing legitimate children to replace the dead.[10]

We might pause over the word *citizens* in this quotation and remind ourselves of the makeup of ancient society. The Greco-Roman world abounded in slaves, but children born of slaves could not become citizens. Slaves were the property of their masters, which meant that masters had sexual rights over their slaves. Greco-Roman society was also a society of clear social status, where a person did not marry someone of a lesser station. We can see how Augustine of Hippo in the fourth century, a Christian, though not yet a Catholic Christian, lived with a woman for thirteen years. This "concubine" bore him a child, Adeodatus, but when the chance came for Augustine to marry a young heiress, he took it even though, as he said, his heart was crushed, for he loved his concubine dearly (*Confessions* 6.15.25). As Pope

Leo the Great responded in the fifth century to a question concerning those who left the women by whom they had children and took wives: "Because a wife is one thing, a concubine another, to eject a maidservant from one's bed and take a wife of assured free-birth is not bigamy but an advance in decency" (Letter 167; PL 54.1205).

Christians lived in this complex, status-laden world of marriage and children. Although from early on Christian authors such as Justin Martyr insisted that the Christians married only to beget children and did not indulge in promiscuous intercourse, such teaching was clearly an ideal to be striven for. As Robin Lane Fox notes, "How could a woman remain virtuous when the whole organization of her social existence conspired against her? She had only to go to the public baths, where men and women bathed naked together. ... [The early councils] presuppose Christians who still turned to slaves and prostitutes, boys and other men's wives, who had sex with animals and even (on one interpretation) encouraged Christians to do the same."[11]

One fascinating piece of advice for married Christians is found in the writings of the late-second-century author Clement of Alexandria. Clement found his inspiration in the ethical philosophy of the Stoics, with their ideal of a life freed of the passions, where their Logos/reason would make proper decisions undisturbed by any movement of emotion. Clement brought this notion into the bedroom, charging that couples approach intercourse in full consciousness that the act was being done only for the begetting of children in accordance with the plan of God (*Miscellanies* 2.23, 3.7). Not only must a Christian, for Clement, be scrupulous not to eat or drink too much, not to laugh too boisterously or sleep too long; he or she must also strive to minimize pleasure in the sexual act. All must be done composedly, serenely. In a world where infant mortality and the death rate were high and where the Christians could undergo persecution at any moment, such a desire to control emotions is understandable. Clement sought to prepare his charges to face death with serenity, and the tight checks he placed on their emotions in other areas prepared for that final test. His advice is fascinating not only in itself but also because it was devoted to Christian married households and assured them that married Christians could be leaders of Christian communities. Christians were to be self-controlled, but they would not differ as regards marriage from others in Greco-Roman society.

Such was not the case for other vocal groups within the Christian movement. They saw marriage as being part of this world and so sought to remove the Christians from it. As Galen showed, the Christians were known as a group among whom some abstained from intercourse throughout their lives. In arguing to the Emperor Antoninus Pius that Christians led decent lives, Justin Martyr emphasized Christian self-control:

> But first of all, either we do not marry except to rear children, or we refuse to marry and we exercise complete self-control. Further, to convince you that we do not have a secret rite or licentious sexual intercourse, one of us sent to Felix, the governor of Alexandria, asking him to permit a surgeon to take away his [the Christian's] testicles. For the surgeons there said that they were forbidden to do this without the permission of the governor. When Felix was not at all willing to sign [this permission], the youth remained by himself, and found his own and his associates' conscience sufficient. (*First Apology* 29)

What a depth of human emotions resonates in this laconic statement. Even Clement's composed Christians seem to have lived in a different world. And a different world it was. Sayings rejecting marriage and attributed to Jesus circulated among second-century Christians: "When Salome inquired: 'How long will death prevail?' the Lord answered: 'As long as you women bear children. ...' They say that the Savior himself said: 'I came to destroy the works of the female,' meaning by 'female,' desire, and by 'works,' birth and death" (Clem *Miscellanies* 3.45.3, 3.63.2).

Narratives circulated telling the deeds of the apostles, such as the acts of Paul, Judas Thomas, and Peter, but the message they contained was the rejection of marriage and the exaltation of virginity. Nothing could be quite so chilling as the alternatives found in a story about Peter:

> Since a gardener had a virgin daughter who was his only child, he besought Peter to pray for her. When he had prayed, the apostle in turn told him that the Lord would perform what was fitting for her soul. Immediately the girl fell down dead. But that old man in despair did not know how great was the heavenly grace. He misunderstood, namely, the divine favor, and he asked Peter that his only daughter be raised up. But when she had been raised, after a few days a man, a believer who was possessed, pressed to stay in the old man's house and corrupted the girl, and the two of them were never seen again.[12]

Modern readers might cheer on the young girl for her romantic affair and elopement with the stranger as she left her overbearing father, but not so ancient Christians. Nor would they have been moved by the poignant speech of Charisius, whose wife, Mygdonia, had left him and renounced sex at the preaching of the apostle Thomas:

> I beseech you, O man: I have never done any wrong against you or someone else or against the gods. Why have you hurled so great an evil against me? Why have you brought such confusion on my house? ... If, as you say, there is after our departure from this world some life and death in another world, and also condemnation and victory and a court of judgment, I, too, will go in there to be brought to trial with you. If the God whom you preach is just, and applies punishments justly, I know that I shall obtain satisfaction in my dealings with you. For you have injured me, although you were not wronged by me. ... Therefore ... per-

suade Mygdonia to be with me just as she was, before she saw you! (*Acts of Thomas* 128)

The Christian readers would not have been persuaded. They knew that they had left this world of city, family, and sex and transferred to a new paradisiacal kingdom where there would be no marrying or giving in marriage.

This emphasis on sexual chastity, or what the Christians at times simply called virginity, and on the renunciation of marriage was increasingly to become the distinctive hallmark of excellence among the Christians so that the spiritual leaders par excellence became the monks and the celibate bishops. Such a stress on virginity was rare among the Jews and the adherents of the Greco-Roman religions, yet the grades of perfection in the Christian life came increasingly to be measured in terms of the absence of sexual activity. When Jovinian in the late fourth century argued for the equality of all baptized persons, regardless of their sexual status—"Virgins, widows, and married women who have been once washed in Christ, if they do not differ in other deeds, have the same merit" (Jerome *Against Jovinian* 1.3)—he was roundly condemned by Ambrose of Milan, Siricius of Rome, Augustine of Hippo, and Jerome. By the fifth century, celibacy was a firmly entrenched factor in Christian life, distinguishing it from other religions of the Greco-Roman world and marking Christianity as a community not quite of this world.

CONCLUSION

Among the early Christians, there were divergent voices attempting to articulate how the Christians should see themselves in this world. Out of those surveyed in this chapter, we can begin to see how many Christian leaders came to adopt a fascinatingly ambivalent attitude toward this world. The God who had created this cosmos was the creator God of Genesis, but his commands as given in the Mosaic Law did not have to be obeyed; they had to be interpreted in light of the Christian movement. The Christian God was the God of the Jews, and he was not. And one command the Christians felt they did not have to obey was the command to be fruitful and multiply (Gen. 1:28), as this movement claimed that there was another world besides this world waiting for those who believed, a world where there would be no more marriage and giving in marriage (Luke 20:34–36), no more birth and death. A person could begin to anticipate this life by living like the angels, by renouncing use of the sexual organs. Once again, an ambivalent position: As we see in Chapter 6, Christian leaders would not condemn marriage, but they would save their accolades for the virginal life, a life in this world but alien to its biological rhythms of birth and regeneration. But first we explore how Christians related the creator God of Genesis to Jesus, their Savior. Where did ultimate power reside in the Christian cosmos?

Suggestions for Further Reading

Brown, Peter Robert Lamont. *The Body and Society: Men, Women and Sexual Renunciation in Early Christianity.* New York: Columbia University Press, 1988.

_____. *The World of Late Antiquity, A.D. 150–750.* New York: Harcourt Brace Jovanovich, 1971.

Droge, Arthur J. *Homer or Moses? Early Christian Interpretation of the History of Culture.* Tübingen: Mohr, 1989.

Grant, Robert McQueen. *Gods and the One God.* Philadelphia: Westminster, 1986.

Greer, Rowan A., and James L. Kugel. *Early Biblical Interpretation.* Philadelphia: Westminster, 1986.

Layton, Bentley. *The Gnostic Scriptures.* Garden City, N.Y.: Doubleday, 1987.

⊰ FIVE ⊱

The Source of Power

IN APPROPRIATING THE HEBREW SCRIPTURES, the Christians had also appropriated the creator God of Genesis as the God of their cosmos. Yet the Christians further claimed that it was Jesus who had power to save them. How did these two powers, the power to create and the power to save, relate to each other? How did Christians envisage the cosmos? Was there a gulf between the creator and the created, or was there a descending chain of realities (as we saw in discussing the view of Plotinus in Chapter 2) through which the source of all power interacted with the cosmos? What did the divine part of the Christian cosmos look like?

In his attack against Christianity, the second-century writer Celsus stated that the Christians had claimed the unthinkable in holding that God had come down to this material world.[1] Celsus was arguing from his own presuppositions, but they were presuppositions that he shared with most thinkers of the period and pointed to the problems that dominated and would dominate much of the intellectual discussion both of Christians and pagans. On the human level, the problem was how the mind interacts with the body. Porphyry related how he questioned his teacher Plotinus for three days on end while seeking to solve this puzzle. How can the incorporeal, eternal mind exist in a body? Plotinus, and Porphyry after him, seem to have held that the mind, through a power or energy that it puts forth external to itself, is able to come into contact with the corporeal body. This power is present in the body and plays a role similar to that played by form in matter in Aristotle's scheme or to soul as understood as the moving force of the nervous system. Here we see the same sense of mediation between the mind and body as was already noted in Chapter 2 in referring to the cosmic design of levels of being found in the intellectual heirs of Plato. There we saw how some Platonic thinkers spoke of two gods, one turned in on itself and one directed to outward activity, like the demiurge of Plato's *Timaeus*.

In a tradition where the epithets *god* and *divine* could be applied to a variety of beings of different ranks, such an unbroken chain of levels of being caused no puzzlement. But how could a tradition that insisted on one creator absorb such a cosmological scheme? Philo of Alexandria, a contemporary of

Jesus, incorporated much of Platonic thought into his worldview, although
Philo was primarily a commentator on the Hebrew Scriptures. Philo spoke
of a Logos figure in describing the creation of the world. Earlier the Book of
Proverbs had spoken of a feminine figure, Wisdom (*hokmah*, who was in
Greek *sophia*), as a veritable helpmate to God (Prov. 8:22–30), and this notion had been even further strengthened in the Wisdom of Solomon, where
Wisdom is described as God's consort and the one who decides the practical
details of creating (Wisd. of Sol. 8:3–4). As a confirmed misogynist, Philo
preferred to speak of the masculine Logos. For Philo, the Logos is the instrument God uses in creation, the place where the purely intelligibles reside. In
commenting on the creation account of Genesis 1–2, Philo distinguished between two creation accounts: one in Genesis 1, which describes the creation
of the ideal human made in the image of God, and one in Genesis 2, which
portrays the moulding out of clay of an individual, sensible human being like
ourselves. The Logos, then, as that which holds the intelligible world, seems
similar to the active, outward-looking being of other Platonists. He is, and
he is not. Rowan Williams rightly points to the metaphoric quality of Philo's
language about the Logos. Philo, according to Williams, distinguished between God as he is in himself, utter simplicity, and as he is in his world-re-
lated aspect, his Logos.[2] For Philo, there is no separate existent being called
the Logos.

But within the Christian tradition, Christ was called by Paul the power
and the wisdom of God (1 Cor. 1:24) and had clearly assumed a cosmic role,
as "the image of the invisible God, the first-born of all creation for in him all
things in heaven and earth were created" (Col. 1:15–16) and as the Logos
who was in the beginning with God (John 1:1). The first description by a
non-Christian, Pliny, of what Christians did stated that they sang hymns to
Christ as to a god (Pliny *Letters* 10.96), and the author of the Gospel of John
showed sensitivity to the claim that Christians worshiped two gods (John
5:17–47). How were Christians to envision the relationship of Christ to
God?

THE CHRISTIAN DIVINE REALM

The Christian school of thought that was founded by Valentinus seems to
have been conversant with the works of Philo but was also influenced by
other intellectual traditions. I have already discussed part of the Valentinian
system in Chapter 4; here I concentrate on its teaching about the Logos. Re-
constructing this teaching, however, is not an easy task. Apart from fragments, the only arguably extant work by Valentinus is "The Gospel of
Truth," a Christian sermon with no specific description of the divine realm.
The preacher tells how the Father, the unknowable God, sent his Word or
Son to those who were ignorant so that they would come to have knowledge

(*gnosis*) of the divine realm. Jesus' crucifixion is seen as the focal point of Christian faith (*Gospel of Truth* 18:10–34).

An opponent of Valentinus and his school, Irenaeus, bishop of Lyons, provided around 180 an incomplete summary of Valentinus's view on the divine realm and a more extensive view of that of Valentinus's student Ptolemy. The system of this Ptolemy is extremely complex. A preexistent, perfect eternity—uncontained, invisible, everlasting, and ingenerate—"thought to emit from himself a source of all things and to place this emission which it had thought to emit like sperm, in the womb of Silence who coexisted with it. When the latter received this sperm, she became pregnant and bore Mind, like and equal to the emitter and alone containing the greatness of its parent. This Mind they also call Only-begotten, Father, and Source of all things" (Irenaeus *Against Heresies* 1.1.1).

From this mind and its consort, truth, emanate another pair, Logos and life, then the pair human being and church. Five pairs of aeons emanate from Logos and life, six pairs from the human being and church to provide finally the fullness or the entirety of thirty silent and unrecognizable aeons. The first pairs are masculine and feminine nouns, which can all find resonances in the Christian Scriptures: at 1 Corinthians 2:16, Paul said, "We have the intellect [nous] of Christ"; in the Gospel of John, Jesus is the Logos (1:1), the truth, and the life (14:6); in Ephesians, Jesus is the new human being (2:15) and is "the head over all things for the church, which is his body, the fullness/entirety [*pleroma*] of him who fills all in all" (1:22–23). These terms have been transferred to become part of the entirety, which the Valentinians posited as the divine realm. Within the drama of redemption that Ptolemy composed, there are two restorative actions which correspond to a disturbance within the entirety itself and to what had been emitted outside the entirety because of that disturbance. The aeons within the entirety are set in order by a Christ and a Holy Spirit, and the restored fullness of the aeons emits an emanation "the most perfect beauty and star of the Fullness, a perfect fruit, Jesus, who was also named Savior, Christ, and, after his Father, Logos and All, because he is from the All" (Irenaeus *Against Heresies* 1.2.6).

The few fragments of Valentinus's that survive reveal him as a mystical poet, and that poet's vision clearly is at work in the portrayal of the redemptive drama. The very variety of descriptions to which Irenaeus attested—"Sometimes they say this, at other times this other" (*Against Heresies* 1.11.1)—suggests poetic fluidity rather than logical treatise, with multiple characters to play their roles. Valentinus presented a new Christian theogony that, in contrast to Hesiod's, placed Christian redemptive history at its center. As with other great insights, however, Valentinus's was quickly turned into a system even by his own followers. Just as Plato hated the poets, so more traditional and more philosophical Christian leaders and teachers intensely disliked the Valentinian description of redemption. They particularly disliked the way images of physical conception, where sperm was emitted into a womb, were transferred to the divine realm. Valentinus's drama was made into a philosophical system, and rejected as unsuitable to describe the deity. Yet Valentinus had linked cosmology and redemption and had posited the existence of a whole divine realm between the first source/first father/first principle and this human realm, and it was this fullness that had orchestrated the redemptive drama of the cosmos.

Theodotus

When we read through the lists of heresies compiled by writers such as Irenaeus of Lyons or Hippolytus of Rome, we notice other second-century Christian groups—the followers of Carpocrates, the followers of Cerinthus, the Ebionites—that insisted that Jesus was a man born normally to Joseph and Mary and that later a divine power descended on Jesus. The followers of Theodotus, a leather worker in Rome, held that Jesus was born of a virgin but a divine power called Christ descended on him later. Theodotus seems to have held an interesting position: In contradistinction to Carpocrates and Cerinthus, he insisted that this world was created by God; he accepted the gospel narratives of Jesus' birth from a virgin but held that some superior power, which he called Christ, came on Jesus at his baptism. This Christ, he insisted, never became God.

> A certain Theodotus, from Byzantium, introduced a new sect saying, on the one hand, what is consonant in part with what the true community [holds] concerning the source of the cosmos, as he confesses that everything was made by God, but, on the other hand, he says, drawing from the school of the gnostics, Cerinthus and Ebion, that the Christ appeared in such a manner [as they do]. Now he says that Jesus was a man born of a virgin according to the will of the father and that he lived like all men and became very virtuous; that later, at his baptism in the Jordan, he contained the Christ which came down from above in the form of a dove. Wherefore the powers were not active in him before it is declared that the spirit came down upon him, which spirit he [Theodotus] calls the Christ. He never wants the Christ to have become God, but some of his followers at the descent of the spirit, others after his resurrection from the dead. (Hippolytus *Refutation of All Heresies* 7.35)

In Theodotus we thus find the tension generated by insisting on one God as creator of this world and accepting the gospel narratives but avoiding the term *Logos*. The result is an intermediate being. This intermediary figure is not a means of explaining the relationship of God to the world but of explaining the special powers wrought by the man Jesus.

The *Alogoi*

Other Christian groups in the second century seem to have been hesitant to accept an intermediate figure like the Logos of the Gospel of John. Both

Irenaeus and Hippolytus reported a group that rejected the Gospel of John, with its depiction of Jesus as the Logos. Known only through the lenses of later writers, this group, if it was an organized group at all and not rather Christian communities of various localities, stressed the human character of Jesus and opposed any hint that Jesus was a divine being who just seemed to appear on earth. John's Gospel was said to contradict the other Gospels since it left out the human birth and progress of Jesus (Epiphanius *Panarion* 51.17.11–18.1) and had a different chronology, with its account of several Passovers during Jesus' ministry (51.22.1). As members of this group dismissed any talk of Jesus as Logos, they were contemptuously nicknamed by their opponents the *alogoi*, that is, opponents of Jesus as Logos but also the "irrational." This group was described sympathetically by Irenaeus and Hippolytus as it accepted so much of the synoptic Gospels' view of Jesus. Yet it was clearly reluctant to go the further step and embrace Jesus as the Logos.

Monarchians and Sabellians

A more radical approach to the problem of Christ as mediator was taken by Christians such as Noetus, Epigonos, Praxeas, Cleomenes, and Sabellius. We know of these Christians only through their opponents' writings against them, and their statements were quickly solidified into a system, most often in the east called Sabellianism, and as such pilloried. Hippolytus summarized Noetus in this way:

> Noetus says "that the Father and the God of all things is one. When he had made all things, he becomes nonapparent to humans when he wishes, but he appears when he wishes, he is unseen whenever he is not seen, but seen whenever he is seen; unbegotten when he is not begotten but begotten when he is born of a virgin, impassible and immortal when he does not suffer or die, but he suffers and dies when he goes forth to suffering. This is father and son, named according to the times and to circumstances. (Hippolytus *Refutation of All Heresies* 10.27)

Thus, Noetus and others like him held that there is only one God and that this God appears to humans at various times and in various ways and has appeared in Jesus and suffered and died somehow. Noetus and Praxeas took seriously the belief that God died for humans, a belief found earlier in the homily of Melito of Sardis:

> But now, in the middle of the street and in the middle of the city, at midday with everyone looking on, a just man's unjust murder took place. So he was lifted up on a lofty tree and an inscription attached to indicate who was being murdered. Who was it? To tell it is hard; not to tell it most fearsome. Yet listen, trembling before him on whose account the earth trembled. He who suspended the earth in place is suspended. He who fixed the heavens is fixed. He who fastened all things is fastened on a tree. The Master is insulted. God is murdered. (*Homily on the Passover* 94–96)

No doubt this view was held by the Christians—but both Tertullian and Origen dismissed it as the belief of uneducated Christians.

> The simple, indeed (much less will I call them ignorant and uneducated), who are always the majority of believers, are startled at the arrangement (of the Three in One) because the very rule of faith directs them away from the world's many gods toward the one and true God, since they do not understand that He must be believed to be one indeed but with his arrangement. They forthwith pronounce that two or three gods are preached by us, and they take for granted that they are truly worshipers of the one God. (Tertullian *Against Praxeas* 3)

But the majority of Christians may have been such simple people, to use Tertullian's condescending phrase. The Monarchians, as they were called since they insisted on one God who was the monarch of the universe, saw the appearance of God in Jesus as a continuation of God's appearances in the Hebrew Scriptures. They insisted that God himself had appeared to humans, that there was no need for an intermediary figure like the Logos (Tertullian *Against Praxeas* 18). Pope Callistus of Rome denounced Hippolytus for believing in two gods, whereas Hippolytus maintained that Callistus made only a nominal distinction between Father and Son:

> [Callistus] says that the Logos himself is Son, and he is Father; that the names are different, but the undivided spirit is one; that the Father is not one thing and the Son another, but they are one and the same; and that all things are full of the divine spirit, both those above and those below; that the one spirit, which became incarnate in the virgin, is not different from the Father, but one and the same; that the saying "Do you not believe that I am in the Father and the Father in me?" (John 14:11) is explained in this way: what is seen, which is the man, is the Son, but the spirit contained in the Son is the Father. "For," says [Callistus], "I will not proclaim two Gods, Father and Son, but one. For the Father, who was in himself, took hold of flesh and divinized it, by uniting it to himself, and made it one; so that one God is called Father and Son, and that this person, being one, cannot be two." So the Father suffered along with the Son; for he does not wish to assert that the Father suffered, and is one person, but wishes to avoid blasphemy against the Father. (Hippolytus *Refutation of All Heresies* 9.12.16–19)

This denial of any suprahuman mediating figure between a unique God and his dealings with this world and the claim of only nominal distinction between God the Father and his Son—Sabellius even coined the word *huiopater,* "fatherson," for God—was quickly denounced by many Christian writers, Tertullian and Hippolytus among them. Although it was easy to point to scriptural passages that stressed the independent existence of the Son, a comprehensive statement of how Christians were to understand the relationship between God and Jesus still needed to be worked out.

Justin Martyr

Another group of second-century Christian writers was also wrestling with the question of Christ's relation to the Father, rejecting the Monarchian solution but approaching the problem more restrainedly than the Valentinians. These writers followed more in the steps of Philo, but for them the Logos becomes a separate existent being. In a stylized account of a dialogue with a Jew, Justin Martyr wrote:

"Friends," I said, "I will give you another proof from the Scriptures that at first, before all creatures, God gave birth from Himself to a certain rational [*logiken*] Power, which is called by the Holy Spirit also Glory of the Lord, sometimes Son, at other times Wisdom, or Angel, or God, or Lord, or Logos. One time when he appeared in human form to Josue, the son of Nun (Josh. 5:14–15) he says that he is Commander in Chief. For he can be called all these names both from serving the Father's will and from existing by will from the Father. ... The word of wisdom confirms what I say, that he is this god begotten from the Father of all things, and he is the Logos and Wisdom and Power and Glory of the begetter, saying through Solomon: 'If I have announced to you daily events, I shall remember to recount events from eternity. The Lord created me at the beginning of His ways for His works.' [Then follows an abridged version of Prov. 8:22–36.]

"Friends, the word of God, through Moses, said the same thing, when it revealed to us that God, with the design of making humans, spoke to this one whom it indicated saying: 'Let us make humans according to our image and likeness; let them rule over the fishes of the sea, and the birds of the air, and over the beasts, and the whole earth, and every creeping creature that creeps upon the earth. And God created man, according to the image of God did He create him; male and female He created them. And God blessed them, saying: Increase and multiply, and fill the earth, and subdue it' (Gen. 1: 26–28).

"But so that you will not change the meaning of these words and say what your teachers say—either that God was speaking to himself when He said, 'Let us make,' just as we, when we are about to make something, often say to ourselves, 'Let us make'; or that God said 'Let us make' to the elements, that is, to the earth and the others from which we think the human was composed—I will again state the words spoken by the same Moses from which we are obliged to recognize indisputably that He spoke with someone distinct in number and who was rational. These are the words: 'And God said: Behold Adam is become as one of us, knowing good and evil' (Gen. 3:22). Does he not reveal a number of people, at least two, living together when He says 'as one of us'? For what the school of thought mentioned by you asserts, I would not say to be true, nor are their teachers able to prove, namely, that he spoke to angels, or that the human body was a thing made by angels. But this offspring, truly emitted from the Father, was living with the Father before all things were made, and the Father is talking with him, as the word through Solomon indicated, saying that this same offspring, who is called Wisdom by Solomon (Wisd. of Sol. 6–7), was begotten by God and is the Beginning before all the things that were made." (*Dialogue with Trypho* 61–62)

The relationship between the Father and the Son is put succinctly by another second-century writer, Athenagoras:

> If it occurs to you, because of your excellent wit, to consider what is meant by the Child, I will say briefly that he is the first offspring of the Father, not as having come into being [for, from the beginning, God, who is eternal mind himself, had the Logos in himself, as from eternity he possesses reason (*logikos*)], but as coming forth to be the form and activity of all material things, which were like an inert nature and unseeded ground, with denser mixed up with lighter. (*A Plea for the Christians* 10)

In these writers the relationship of the Father to the Son is seen primarily in terms of the relationship of the Father to the created world. For Justin, the Son/Logos mediates in creation and revelation. In Athenagoras, the Logos is eternally within the Father but comes forth to create the material world. In these writers, the Platonist scheme of a staggered universe surfaces, with the Logos somehow occupying a middle ground between the Father of all and this material world, the channel of communication between the two. Discussing God's appearance to Moses at the burning bush, Justin remarked, "The God who said to Moses He was God of Abraham, of Isaac and of Jacob will not be the creator of the cosmos. ... Nobody even of the slightest intelligence would dare to say that the Creator and Father of all things left everything beyond heaven to appear in a little piece of earth" (*Dialogue with Trypho* 60). Justin clearly distinguished between the creator God and his Logos, who acts as his messenger to earth. Justin, like Celsus, would not have the creator God leave heaven.

Origen

A major attempt at a synthetic presentation of the Christian faith was made by the great Christian thinker Origen of Alexandria. He opposed those who saw only a nominal distinction between the Father and the Son and those who held that the God of the Christians was different from the creator of this world. A fascinating example of his position is found in the record of an examination he made of Bishop Heracleides.

This discussion with Heracleides took place during a conference of bishops and in the presence of all the faithful, most probably during the 240s in the Roman province of Arabia at the place where Heracleides was bishop. Disorders had arisen in this church, and the conference had been called to deal with them. The problem was the relation of the Father and the Son.

> **Origen said:** ... I beseech you, father Heracleides: God is the almighty, the uncreated, the God over all who made all. Is this acceptable?

Heracleides: It is. For so I believe.

Orig.: Christ Jesus being in the form of God (Phil. 2:6), being other than the God in whose form he existed, was he God before he came into the body or not?

Herac.: He was God before.

Orig.: Was he God before he came into the body or not?

Herac.: Yes, he was.

Orig.: Another God than this God in whose form he himself existed?

Herac.: Obviously he was of some other and he was in the form of that one who created all things.

Orig.: Therefore he was God, the Son of God, the only-begotten of God, the firstborn of all creation, and we should not scruple to say that in one way there are two Gods, that in another way there is one God?

Herac.: What you say is clear, but we say that God is the almighty, God without beginning, without end, who contains all things but is not contained by anything; and that his Word is the Son of the living God, God and man, through whom all things were made, God according to the spirit, man according to the fact that he was born of Mary.

Orig.: You do not seem to have answered what I asked. Make it clear, then, for perhaps I did not understand. Is the Father God?

Herac.: Certainly.

Orig.: Is the Son other than the Father?

Herac.: How can he be Son if he is also Father?

Orig.: The Son, while he is other than the Father, is he himself God?

Herac.: He himself is also God.

Orig.: And do two Gods become one?

Herac.: Yes.

Orig.: Do we confess two Gods?

Herac.: Yes. The power is one.

Orig.: But since our brethren are shocked [if one says] that there are two Gods, we must pay careful attention to what we say, and show in what respect there are two and in what respect the two are one God. Now the holy Scriptures have taught that many things which are two are one. And not only things which are two, but they have also taught that in some cases more than two, or even a much greater number, are one. What is now before us is that, when we detect a problem, we should not pass it by, but for the sake of the more unsophisticated to chew on it like meat, and to put the doctrine in the ears of our hearers little by little. Therefore, many things which are two are said in the Scriptures to be one. What passages of Scripture? Adam is one person, his wife another. Adam is other than his wife, and his wife is other than her husband, but it is said straightaway at the creation that those two are one: "For the two shall be one flesh." It is therefore possible that two beings can sometimes be one flesh. But watch me carefully, because it is not said about Adam and Eve that the two will be one spirit, nor that the two will be one soul, but that they will be one flesh. Again, the righteous person who is other than Christ is said by the apostle to be one with Christ: "For he that is joined to the Lord is one spirit" (1 Cor. 6:17). Is not one of a deficient nature or of a low and inferior nature, while Christ is of a more divine and more glorious and more blessed nature? Are they therefore no longer two? But really the man and the woman are "no longer two but one flesh," and the righteous person and Christ are "one spirit." So in relation to the Father and God of the universe, our Savior and Lord is not one flesh, nor one spirit, but what is higher than flesh and spirit, namely, one God. The word "flesh" is required when humans are joined to one another; the word "spirit" when a righteous person is joined to Christ. But when Christ is united to the Father neither the word "flesh," nor the word "spirit" is applied, but the word more honorable than these—the word "God." So we understand the phrase "I and the Father are one" (John 10:30). We pray as among those who maintain the duality and as among those who hold to the unity. In this way we do not fall into the opinion of those who have separated from the Church toward the illusion of monarchy, destroying the Son by the Father and who virtually destroy also the Father. Nor do we fall into the other unholy teaching which denies the divinity of Christ. (*Dialogue with Heracleides* 120–128)

Here we see Origen insisting both that the Son and the Father are two distinct beings and that this is not the same as teaching two equal principles. Origen remained very much in the tradition of Justin Martyr and others who saw the Logos as the mediating principle of creation. Origen, too, stressed the absolute transcendence of God: The absolute simplicity of the Father requires a Son who in his multiplicity can account for the diversity in the created world. Origen avoided the use of the term *homoousios* to describe the relationship between Father and Son, as for him it had a smell of Valentinianism and meant the coordinate members of the same class, beings sharing the same properties.[3] Alongside this clear subordination of the Son to the Father, however, runs a strand in Origen's thought that insists that the Son is not outside the sphere of the deity. Origen stressed the correlative quality of the terms *Father* and *Son*. Since there is no change in God, he is always Father and so always has a Son with him. In later works, Origen seems to have minimized the gulf between Father and Son.[4] Here we can see how Origen began to think of the Son's relationship to the Father not only as a mediation between God and the created world but also as a relationship in and of itself without reference to creation.

In discussing the redemption of humans, Origen made fascinating comments about the role of the human soul of Jesus. To appreciate the teaching of Origen, however, we have to note Origen's understanding of how the world came to be as it is. Origen passionately believed, as opposed to Marcion, that the God of this creation had created it justly, was a just God. How then could this just God have created rational creatures who were different from one another? Did not justice demand equal treatment? Origen therefore suggested that originally God through his Logos/reason had created all rational creatures equal. The present ranking of rational creatures into the four major types of angels, powers of wickedness, the animating spirits of the heavenly bodies, and human souls resulted from a free and responsible choice of each rational creature. This would have been the original fall, one result of that was that some souls became embodied, that is, human.

> Therefore, when the scriptures concerning Esau and Jacob are attentively examined, it is found that there is "no injustice with God" so that before they were born or had done anything, I mean in this life, it was said that "the elder shall serve the younger," and as it is found that there is no injustice in the fact that Jacob supplanted his brother even in the womb, if we understand that from the merits of a previous life [Jacob] was worthily loved by God so that he merited to be set before his brother. So also the same thing is found concerning the heavenly creatures, if we note that their diversity is not originally a principle of creation, but that from previous causes a different duty of service is prepared by the Creator for each one in proportion to the worthiness of his merit. This comes from the fact that each, because a mind or rational spirit created by God, has prepared for himself, in proportion to the movements of his mind and the inclinations of his intelligence, a greater or less amount of merit, and has made himself either lovable or even hateful to God. (*On First Principles* 2.9.7)

Exempt from this fall of rational creatures was the human soul of Jesus. This was the rational creature who clung to God.

> For since [the only-begotten Son of God] is the invisible image of the invisible God, he granted invisibly to all rational creatures a participation in himself, so that each, in proportion to the loving affection with which he clung to him, would take so much participation from him. But since, in proportion to the faculty of free will, there was variety and diversity in each soul, so that one was bound to its author with a warmer and another with a weaker and meager love, that soul concerning which Jesus said, "No one takes from me my soul," clung to God inseparably and indissolubly from the beginning of the creation and afterward, as to the wisdom and the word of God and to the truth and to the true light, and all of it receiving him wholly, and yielding itself into his light and splendor, was made with him preeminently one spirit, just as the Apostle promises to those who ought to imitate (that soul), that "he who joins himself to the Lord is one spirit." Since this substance of the soul, then, mediated between God and the flesh (for it was not possible for the nature of God to mingle with a body without a mediator), the God-man is born, as we said, with that substance to which it was not contrary to assume a body acting as a medium. But also it was not against nature for that soul as a rational substance to receive God, into whom, as we said above, it had already wholly yielded as into the word and wisdom and truth. Wherefore, because either all the soul was in the Son of God or received into itself all of the Son of God, that soul with the flesh it assumed is rightly called the Son of God and the power of God, Christ and the Wisdom of God; and again the Son of God, "through whom all things were created," is called Jesus and the Son of man. (*On First Principles* 2.6.3)

Origen thus had a twofold scheme of mediation: In the creation of this world, the Logos to some extent stood between God the Father and the created world; in regard to the redemption wrought by Christ, the preexistent immortal human soul of Jesus was the mediating link between the Logos and the material world. Such a schema enabled Origen to make sense of numerous biblical passages. As regards the Logos's relationship to the Father, passages such as John 14:6, "The Father is greater than I," and Proverbs 8:22, "The Lord created me," where Origen understood "create" in an extended sense, supported his notion of subordination, while those such as John 10:30, "I and the Father are one," were easily accommodated into a unanimity of purpose. As regards Jesus, passages that expressed change or development could be interpreted as referring to the soul of Jesus. The hymn in Philippians 2, which speaks of the exaltation of Jesus, was seen as reflecting the exaltation of the human soul of Jesus.

Origen was one of the most prolific writers of his time. He taught in both Alexandria and Caesarea and visited Rome. The very greatness of his intellect combined with his winning personality ensured that his legacy would be a lasting one. He achieved a masterful synthesis of the biblical data, but it was a fragile synthesis. Although major emphases of his worldview were accepted, not all aspects were, particularly as regards his notion of the preexistent souls that only later "fell" into material bodies.[5] Methodius of Olympus, writing later in the third century, saw in this a latent dualism within Origen's thought that would have restricted the freedom of God the Father.

Arius

The fragility of a Christian consensus about the mediating role of Christ came to the fore early in the fourth century in what is known as the Arian controversy. The history of this controversy is extremely complex, and I discuss only the major actors here. It was a period during which there was a high level of violence over religious differences, and much of that violence "was inspired at the level of the urban elite, among whom the local ecclesiastical leadership from time to time was rent apart by rivalries, unable within itself to bring such rivalries to an end, and tempted to seek a deciding power through appeal to the masses."[6] The urban elite was a combative class, and Rowan Williams suggests that some such rivalry may have lain behind the debate between the priest Arius and his bishop, Alexander, in Alexandria.[7] Sides were quickly taken by the bishops of the various cities, and Arius himself was almost forgotten.

What was Arius's concern? His objection to his bishop's teaching was based on the sense that Alexander was affirming two equal principles. The flashpoint for the debate, perhaps based on earlier Alexandrian theology, came to be the temporal relationship of the Father and the Son. If they both have always existed, then there must be two Gods, said Arius, and he rejected such a notion. He characterized Alexander as teaching "God eternal, the Son eternal, the Son at the same time as the Father, the Son exists with the God ingenerately, eternal, born without origin, God is not prior to the Son in thought or in time, God eternal, the Son eternal, the Son is from God himself" (quoted in Epiphanius *Panarion* 69.6.3).

Now Alexander did hold that the Son has a "mediating only-begotten nature," but his emphasis lay on the eternal correlativity of the Son, as we saw in Origen. Arius repudiated that aspect of Origen's thought, perhaps under the influence of Methodius. For Arius, the Logos is the mediator between God and creation. Such a mediator is necessary because of the absolute simplicity and unknowableness of God. When this monad freely decided to create this world, he first formed the mediator, the Logos, through whom the world would be made. This Logos is not like the other creatures, but it was created and below God. Arius rejected the Valentinian system when, in his profession of faith, he denied that the only-begotten Son is an emission. Arius thus continued the tradition of seeing the Logos within the framework of creating this material world. Like Origen, he, too, read Scripture as a whole, attempting to reconcile difficult passages. For him, Proverbs 8:22, which speaks of the creation of the Son, gives the clue to understanding the relationship of the Logos to God, whereas texts that speak of the Logos as Son are to be seen as metaphorical, along the lines of John 10:31–36. Because Arius saw the Logos as a being lower than God, he did not feel the need for another mediating figure between the Logos and the human body of Jesus. The Logos itself is the animating principle of the body of Jesus. As a reduced God, as a being less than the utterly simple God, the Logos is able to be enfleshed; he is able to suffer.

From an abusive letter in which the Emperor Constantine replied to an earlier letter from Arius and quoted from that letter, Richard Hanson has been able to reproduce some of Arius's position.[8] It is difficult to gain complete understanding from fragments, but Hanson convincingly argues that Arius spoke of one God whom Arius did not wish "to be involved with the suffering of insults." The one God must not be lessened in any way. Rather, the Logos, as a being foreign to the Father, is able to take on exile in the body "towards the administration of the divine forces."[9] This reconstruction of Arius's thought on the incarnation of the Logos dovetails nicely with what later supporters of Arius held. Hanson finds the heart of Arianism to consist in this: "The Arians want to have a God who can suffer, but they cannot attribute suffering to the High God."[10] As the Arian Asterius preached:

> Therefore, just as when you hear that [the demiurge] made coats of skin and that he was walking around and that he was looking and asking, "Where are you?", and that he undertook human deeds and emotions, you do not say, "He is [merely] a human"; so when you hear that the maker of Adam was crucified, that he was hung up, that he was nailed in the flesh, do not say, "A mere man," but God in the flesh making his own the suffering and the death of the flesh.[11]

Herein lies the very Christian dilemma of Arius and those who thought like him: They saw the suffering of God on behalf of humanity as the central point of the Christian message, and yet they also passionately believed, as Celsus had, that the notion of a source of all existence involved the notion of impassibility. How were these two notions to be reconciled? The Arians' solution was to see the Logos as mediator, below the first God but above all creatures. As such, the Logos is the means by which all other creatures come into being and is able to be enfleshed and suffer and die. The formal statement of the great missionary bishop Ulfilas, who was an Arian, is worth quoting:

> He never hesitated to preach openly and clearly both to those willing and unwilling that there is one sole true God the Father of Christ according to the teaching of Christ himself, knowing that this sole true God is the sole ingenerate, without beginning, without end, eternal, celestial, lofty, exalted, the highest source, superior to any excellence, better than any goodness, limitless, incomprehensible, invisible, boundless, immortal, imperishable, incommunicable, incorporeal, uncompounded, simple, immutable, undivided, unmoving, needing nothing, unapproachable, unsevered, undominated, uncreated, unmade, perfect, existing in singularity, incomparably greater and better than everything. When he was alone, not to create division or diminution of his Godhead but to show forth his goodness and power, by his sole will and power, impassibly impassible, imperishably imperishable, and immovably unmoved he created and begot, made and established the only-begotten God.[12]

For the Arians, therefore, the utterly simple being who is God at some point of his own free will decided to create this universe, and to do this he fashioned a Logos who was subordinate to him. When the need for redemption arose, this second God, or Logos, assumed flesh to suffer and redeem humanity.

The Creed of the Council of Nicea

Although the Arian position seems to have achieved a wide popular following, most Christian bishops could not go along with the views of Arius. They believed that the Son is subordinate to the Father but is also truly or fully God. The Son is the image of the Father, and talk of the Son as a being foreign to the Father was not acceptable.[13] At the Council of Nicea in 325, then, Arius was condemned, primarily on the grounds of holding that the Son is a creature by saying there was a time when he did not exist. One cannot say that the Son was made out of nothing, as can be said of creatures, or that the Son was made out of some other existent being, as though there were something else besides God at the beginning. Rather, the Son came from the *ousia* of the Father and was *homoousios* with God.

I have left these last terms untranslated because much of the ensuing debate concerned itself with how this term *ousia* and the compound form *homoousios* were to be understood. We can already get a sense that the problem of using language about God looms large. Since humans deal with material things and their language reflects this, how can language be stripped of material associations? Take the phrase "from the *ousia* of the Father." How are we to understand the preposition *from*? In a context of generation, does it imply physical generation, as the system of the Valentinians suggested? In fact, the Valentinians seem to have used the term *homoousios*, and this term came to have a Gnostic ring about it and to imply "belonging to the same order of being." If the term is not to be used in a Valentinian sense, must it imply some physical separation as cutting a piece of cloth from another? Arius had already placed himself in a bind, for, not wishing to hold that there was some other material alongside God out of which God fashioned the Logos, he had stated that the Logos was made out of nothing. But that resulted in the counteraccusation that Arius made the Logos the same as all other creatures, for all creatures are said to be made out of nothing in 2 Maccabees 7:28, accepted by Christians then as Scripture. Again, in holding that there was a time when the Logos was not, denying the argument from the correlativity of the terms *Father* and *Son* and affirming that God is first God and only later is he Father, Arius laid himself open to charges, whether justified or not,[14] that he was using time-bound material concepts in discussing the Son's generation. Language therefore became a central concern.

Within the creed formulated at Nicea, *ousia* is synonymous with another term, *hypostasis*. Within the Neoplatonist context, hypostasis means something like "realization turning into appearance," as "distinct reality." It is found in the Septuagint and the Christian Scriptures, significantly at Hebrews 1:3, where the Son is said to be the impression of God's hypostasis. Some writers preferred to use hypostasis rather than *ousia* because it occurred in the Bible. From his analysis of the use of the terms before the Council of Nicea, Hanson concludes that some writers regarded hypostasis and *ousia* as synonyms; that some used hypostasis and ignored *ousia*; that some used hypostasis to mean "distinct existence" and *ousia* to mean "nature"; and that writers could not be sure how either of these terms should be used.[15] *Homoousios*, as we have noted, had been used by the Gnostics to mean "belonging to the same order of being" and had been used by Sabellius to reject any distinction between the persons of Father and Son. There was a sense that it involved some kind of division of an *ousia*. In general, the term carried enough baggage to merit suspicion among some and seems to have been adopted by the Council of Nicea in its most basic sense of holding that the Son and the Father are on the same level of being.

Athanasius

Once the quarrel in Alexandria between Arius and Bishop Alexander had been elevated into a quarrel among bishops and then into an imperial con-

cern, Arius faded into the background and died in 336. The main protago-
nist against Arius was Alexander's successor in 328, Athanasius of Alexandria. Athanasius was single-minded in his opposition and, as he lived until
373, kept the issue going against all kinds of imperial pressure, as we saw in
Chapter 1. Part of his problems he brought on himself. A ruthless and
dogged man, Athanasius was convicted by a council for disgraceful behavior, and no eastern bishop after 335 communicated with him for twenty
years.

Athanasius, as heir to Alexander, insisted against Arius on the correlativity of Father and Son: "When the Arians argue that transitory, created
things could not bear God's unmediated hand, Athanasius replies that this
idea makes out God to be incompetent and in need of an assistant, and he
asks why on the Arian hypothesis there should have been only one mediator,
why not an infinite series."[16] Athanasius insisted on the gulf between creator
and created and on the Son belonging to the creating realm. The distinction
between Father and Son was known, not through the process of creation,
but through that of redemption. As long as it was maintained that the Father
and Son belonged to the same level of existence, Athanasius was not afraid
to use many formulas to express this ontological unity: exact image of the
substance, peculiar offspring of the substance, like in all respects, like in substance.[17] He seems to have held that *homoousios* includes a sense of deriva-
tion—it refers only to the relation of the Son to the Father, and not vice versa.[18] So even a term like *homoousios* is to some extent not sufficient in and
of itself but has to be balanced by other expressions, such as the relation of
the light to the ray or the spring to the stream, to ensure that the Son is seen
as coming from the Father.

This emphasis on the essential similarity between Father and Son forced
Athanasius to interpret drastically certain passages of Scripture. He found
two texts in the Gospel of John as central to his belief: John 10:30, "I and the
Father are one," and John 14:9, "He who has seen me has seen the Father."
"For him St. John's Gospel is at the very centre of the Christian faith; the
Synoptics, on which the Arians relied heavily for their picture of Christ, he
sometimes found an obstacle, presenting tiresome evidence which had to be
explained away."[19]

Texts such as Proverbs 8:22, Hebrews 3:2 ("faithful to him that made
him"), and Philippians 2:6–11—all these he referred with enormous ingenu-
ity to the human body of Christ (*Against the Arians* 1.37). Whereas the Arians stressed that the Logos is a god capable of suffering and so is a lesser god
within the whole structure of the cosmos, Athanasius insisted that both Father and Son are impassible and that the Son is the way in which the uncre-
ated realm chooses to reveal itself.

For this purpose, then, the incorporeal and incorruptible and immaterial Word of God comes to our region, although indeed he was not far from us before. For no part of creation was left devoid of Him, but He has filled all things throughout all things while he was present with his own Father. But he comes down with benevolence toward us and in visible appearance. For (1) he saw the race of rational creatures perishing, and death ruling among them by corruption; (2) he saw also that the threat which was to control transgression [became] the corruption over us, and that it was inappropriate that the law should be dissolved rather than fulfilled; (3) he saw also that it was unbecoming that those things of which he was the fashioner were being spoiled; (4) he saw further that it was the excessive evil of humans that had little by little brought it to an unendurable level; (5) he saw, finally, that all humans were liable to death. Therefore he took pity on our race, and had mercy on our weakness, and came down to our corruption and, not admitting the dominion of death—so that what had come to be should not perish and the work of his Father toward humans be undone—he took to himself a body, and that no different from ours. ... For being powerful, and Fashioner of everything, He prepared for himself in the virgin a temple, namely, the body, and made it His own as an instrument, becoming known in it and dwelling in it. (*On the Incarnation of the Word* 8; PG 25.109)

What then must God do? Or what must be done except renew again what was according to the image, so that through that humans might again be able to know Him? But how could this happen unless the very Image of God, our Lord Jesus Christ, should come? For through humans it was not possible, since they were made according to an image; but neither by angels, for not even they are images. Therefore the Word of God came by Himself so that, as He was the Image of the Father, He might be able to rebuild the human according to the image. (*On the Incarnation of the Word* 13; PG 25.120)

Here we see the characteristic emphasis on the Word as belonging to the realm of God, as being the image of God in a way different from all others. We also see how for Athanasius the body of Jesus is an instrument. Athanasius, like most of his contemporaries, never thought of Jesus as having a human mind and soul. After 362, Athanasius formally admitted that Jesus did have a human mind and soul, but he never seems to have integrated it fully into his vision of Jesus. Could Jesus have been afraid (Mark 14:34), in Athanasius's view? Any human emotion displayed by Jesus, Athanasius asserted, was displayed for humanity's sake, not because Jesus was actually afraid. "For it is possible for them to see how the one who performed the miracles is the same as the one who showed that his body was passible in permitting it to weep and hunger and for the properties of a body to appear in it" (*Against the Arians* 3.55; PG 26.437). Athanasius thus squarely placed the mediating sphere of activity in the incarnation of the divine Word, but at the expense of downplaying the suffering of God.

This sense of the impassibility of the Logos even when enfleshed—"God is not weak"—was pushed to extremes by Hilary of Poitiers, a sympathizer to Athanasius:

> For since these kinds of suffering affect the infirmity of the flesh, yet God the Word made flesh was not able to be changed from himself by suffering. For to suffer and to be changed are not the same thing. Because suffering of every kind changes all flesh by sensation, by pain, and by endurance. But the Word made flesh, although He subjected Himself to suffering, was not, however, changed by the passibility of suffering. For He was able to suffer, but he was not able to be passible, because passibility is a sign of a weak nature, whereas suffering is the endurance of what is brought against one. Since God is unchangeable and yet the Word was made flesh, what was brought against him found in Him the material for suffering but without the weakness of passibility. (*On the Councils* 49)

> Although a blow struck this man Jesus, or a wound penetrated, or ropes bound [him], or he was lifted on high, all these things delivered indeed the violence of suffering, but did not cause the pain of suffering. ... The Lord Jesus Christ indeed suffered as He was struck, as he was lifted on high, as he was crucified, as he died; but the suffering which attacked the body of the Lord was not indeed suffering, but did not eliminate the nature of suffering. As [the suffering] raged with its duty of inflicting punishment, the bodily strength took the force of the punishment raging against it, but without the sensation of the punishment. ... He had indeed a body to suffer, and He suffered; but He did not have a nature to feel pain. (*On the Trinity* 10.23)

This is indeed a subtle distinction between suffering and passibility and a strange sort of body that suffers without the sensation of pain, a body like a block of wood. Yet Hilary felt it necessary to posit such a distinction to safeguard the immutability of God if the Word is consubstantial with the Father.

The Creeds of the Fourth Century

This debate about how to describe the Christian view of the divine realm raged throughout the fourth century and even further as Arian churches remained outside the Roman Empire. All Christians now believed that the Son is like the Father; the question was, How like? Athanasius believed that the Son is like in *ousia,* but since for him, as for the Council of Nicea, *ousia* was a synonym for hypostasis, he could not fail to give the impression that he saw no distinction between Father and Son. His opponents held that the Son is like the Father in all things save in *ousia,* and so the Son is less than the Father. So we find a plethora of creeds formulated during this period. The Dedication Creed of 341 said:

> Following the evangelical and apostolic tradition, we believe in one God the Father Almighty, fashioner and maker and administrator of the universe, from

whom are all things. And in one Lord Jesus Christ his Son, the only-begotten God, through whom [are] all things, who was begotten before the ages from the Father, God from God, whole from whole, sole from sole, perfect from perfect, King from King, Lord from Lord, living Word, living Wisdom, true Light, Way, Truth, Resurrection, Shepherd, Gate, unmoved and unchangeable, precise image of the Godhead, and of the substance [*ousias*] and will and power and glory of the Father. ... And in the Holy Spirit, who is given to those who believe for comfort and sanctification and perfection, just as our Lord Jesus Christ bequeathed to his disciples, saying [quotation of Matt. 28:19], obviously [in the name] of the Father who is truly Father and the Son who is truly Son and the Holy Spirit who is truly Holy Spirit, because the names are not given loosely or idly, but signify precisely the appropriate hypostasis and order and glory of each of those named, so that they are three in hypostasis but one in concord. (Found in Athanasius *De synodis* 23; PG 26.721–724)

This creed attacked both those who would not see the Son as the "precise image of the *ousia* of the Father" and those who held no distinction among the persons, apparently an implicit attack on the Nicene Creed.[20] The Fourth Creed of Antioch, written shortly after the Dedication Creed by unknown framers, was much more a formula to satisfy everybody:

It leaves out the word *ousia* and its compounds altogether; it makes no attempt to establish the distinctness of the 'Persons' in an anti-Sabellian manner. ... It leaves open to anyone to believe that the Son is a creature, as long as it is acknowledged that he is begotten. ... But the fact remains that it was destined to be used for nearly fifteen years as the basis for all other creeds which were designed to be ecumenical.[21]

A meeting of bishops at Serdica in 343 set up to reconcile the eastern and western bishops only produced more division than ever. In 359 another creed, often called the Dated Creed because it was the only creed that gave its own date, was drawn up:

We believe in one sole and true God, the Father Almighty, creator and fashioner of all things: And in one only-begotten Son of God who before all ages and before all beginning and before all conceivable time and before all comprehensible substance was begotten impassibly from God, through whom the ages were arranged and all things came into existence, begotten as only-begotten, sole from the sole Father, like to the Father who begot him, according to the Scriptures, whose generation no one knows except the Father who begot him. ... As for the word *ousia*, because it was naively placed by our fathers and produced a scandal as it was unfamiliar to the people and because the Scriptures do not contain it, we have resolved that it be removed, and that there should in the future be absolutely no mention of *ousia* in reference to God, because the Scriptures make no mention at all of *ousia* concerning the Father and the Son. But we say that the Son is like the Father in all respects, as the holy Scriptures also say and teach. (Athanasius *De synodis* 8; PG 26.692–693)

But such a plea for dropping further discussion only provoked more. Did the phrase "like in all respects" include *ousia* or not? Did it mean "like in will" but not in *ousia*? The Council of Seleucia in 359 recommended that Christians should not say *homoousion* ("of the same substance"), *homoiousion* ("like in substance"), or *anhomoion* ("unlike"), but *homoios* ("like") (Epiphanius *Panarion* 73.25.4–5). On the very last day of 359, the Creed of Nice was signed. This creed was basically the same as the Dated Creed, but with one notable change in its last paragraph:

> But as for the word *ousia* because when it was naively placed by the Fathers, though unfamiliar to the people, produced a scandal, and because the Scriptures do not contain it, we have resolved that it should be removed and that there should in the future be absolutely no mention of it, because the Scriptures make no mention at all concerning the *ousia* of the Father and of the Son. *Nor should hypostasis be uttered concerning the Father and Son and Holy Spirit.* But we say that the Son is like the Father, as the Holy Scriptures say and teach. *And let all the heresies, those which have already been previously condemned, and those which, if they have recently appeared, are opposed to the creed set out here, be anathema.* (Found in Athanasius *De synodis* 30; PG 26.748)

Here the phrase "in all respects" had been dropped, and this creed could have been accepted by the Arian party. Both *ousia* and *hypostasis* were ruled out of court in the discussion. Until some way could be found to define what God is as three as distinct from what He is as one, suspicions of Sabellianism, which maintained only a nominal, not a real, distinction in the one God, would always appear. A step toward resolving this problem was taken at a council that met in Alexandria in 362. The Letter to the Antiochians that resulted from this meeting began to address the confusion between *ousia* and *hypostasis*. It did not fully resolve the problem, but it clearly recognized that some people were using these words differently. The letter also attacked those who held that the Savior has a body that lacks a soul or mind. The linkage of these elements showed a recognition that to place the Logos as of the same substance as the Father required a discussion of what the incarnate Logos is like.

It was left to the great Cappadocian theologians, Basil of Caesarea, Gregory of Nazianzus, and Gregory of Nyssa, to resolve in some way the semantic intricacies. As Hanson indicates, Basil sometimes used hypostasis as equivalent to *ousia,* but he normally used hypostasis when referring to the distinction of the persons within the Godhead and *ousia* or its synonyms when discussing "substance" in God.[22] Ambiguities still remained, and do remain. What exactly is the relation of *ousia* to hypostasis? At times Basil and Gregory of Nazianzus spoke of the relationship as that of general to particular, like humanity as the *ousia* in three humans as the hypostases, but both were also aware of the limitations of this analogy. Basil was firm in rejecting the notion that there is some substance prior to or underlying the Father and Son and argued that *homoousios* has a derivative sense, just as Athanasius did. "What are akin with each other are not called consubstantial [*homoousia*] as some people suppose, but when both the cause and that which has its existence from the cause are of the same nature they are called consubstantial" (Letter 52.2; PG 32.393). The Holy Spirit, Basil argued, should not be seen as a subclass under the genus Godhead.

> What, however, they call subnumeration, and according to what meaning they hold this word, is not easy to perceive. For everyone knows that it was brought among us from the wisdom of the world; but let us investigate if it has something to say relative to what is before us. For some who are skilfull in respect of profane things say that some nouns are common and extend widely in signification, while others are more specific, and that some have a more particular meaning than others. For example, essence is a common noun, attributed to all things alike, both animate and inanimate; animal is more specific, attributed to fewer than the former, but to more than those considered under it, as the nature of rational and irrational things are contained in it. Again, human is more specific than animal, and man than human, and the individual, Peter, Paul, or John, than man. So do they then mean by subordination the division of the common into its subordinates? But I would not believe that they would be so far deranged as to say that the God of the universe, like some common quality which is conceivable only by reason and has existence in *hypostasis,* is divided into subordinates, and that then this subdivision is called subnumeration. (*On the Holy Spirit* 17; PG 32.144)

Gregory of Nazianzus also pointed out the limitations of analogy and the need to use a number of analogies, rather than one, to try understanding the relationship of Father to Son. Thus, the Cappadocians cleared up the semantic difficulty but kept alive the mystery of generation within the Godhead. We know of the hypostases in God because of God's revelation of himself, but the *ousia* of God remains beyond our ken.

With the Cappadocians and the Council of Constantinople in 381 came an end to a time-honored tradition that saw in the Son and the Holy Spirit instruments created by an unknowable God to produce this cosmos. The relationship of the persons is internal to the Godhead, not external. There is no mediator between the Godhead and the cosmos in creation, only in revelation. The revelation of the Son is most apparent in Jesus Christ. But the question then arose, How is the Logos present in Jesus?

THE DIVINE-HUMAN NEXUS

Within the Greek religious tradition, the Olympian gods appear among humans as mortals to help or hinder. When the goddess Athena wishes to encourage Telemakhos in Book One of the *Odyssey,* "she bent down to tie her beautiful sandals on, ambrosial, golden, that carry her over water, or endless land on the wings of the wind. ... Flashing down from Olympos' height she went to stand in Ithaka, before the Manor, just at the doorsill of the court. She seemed a family friend, the Taphian captain, Mentes, waiting, with a light hand on her spear" (1.96–105).[23] The ambiguity of the goddess's presence among mortals is reflected in the dialogue between Telemakhos and Athena: "But tell me now, and put it for me truly—who are you? Where do you come from? Where's your home and family? What kind of ship is yours, and what course brought you here? Who are your sailors? I don't suppose you walked here on the sea" (1.169–173). To this the gray-eyed goddess answers truly that she is Mentes and gives a detailed account of her travels, never once letting on that she in fact came by foot across the sea. Only when she leaves, "as a bird rustles upward," does Telemakhos realize that a goddess has been his guest.

Within the Hebrew Scriptures, too, unexpected guests can in fact be divine, as at Genesis 18, where Abraham entertains three men who turn out to have been the Lord. The motif of the helper from the divine world is most fully worked out in the Book of Tobit. In this delightful story from around the third century B.C.E., when Tobias, the son of Tobit, is looking for someone to accompany him on a trip, he happens to run into an angel, who, when asked where he comes from, tells Tobias he is an Israelite and later gives his name as Azarias, the son of the older Ananias. Only at the end of the narrative is it revealed to Tobias and Tobit that Tobias's companion was in truth Raphael, one of the seven angels who stand in attendance on the Lord.

A Body Only in Appearance

When discussing the visit of someone from the divine realm, people had some models with which to correlate such a visit. Some early Christians assimilated the story of Jesus to stories in which a divine being appears in mortal form. The second-century *Acts of John* recounts how the apostle John was weeping while Jesus was being crucified. Suddenly, however, Jesus appeared to John and chided him for believing that the body being crucified was Jesus.

> Often when I was walking with [Jesus] I wanted to see if his footprint appeared on the ground, for I used to see him lifting himself up from the ground, but I never saw [a footprint]. (*Acts of John* 93)

> When he was hung [on the Cross] on Friday, at the sixth hour of the day a darkness came upon the whole earth. Now my Lord was standing in the middle of the cave and lit it up and he said, "John, for the crowd below in Jerusalem I am being crucified and pierced with lances and reeds, and am being given vinegar and gall to drink. But I am speaking to you. Listen to what I say." (*Acts of John* 97)[24]

Such a model of Jesus' sojourn on earth had been attacked earlier by Ignatius of Antioch: "For [Jesus] suffered all these things on account of us so that we might be saved. He truly suffered as he truly raised himself, not as some unbelievers say, that he suffered in semblance [*to dokein*], but they are the ones who are in semblance. Just as they think so shall it happen to them that they will be incorporeal and like daimons" (*To the Smyrneans* 2). Ignatius insisted that Jesus was truly born and that he ate and drank—he was not in semblance (*To the Trallians* 9.1).

The opponents of Ignatius and their model of interpreting Jesus' life have been called Docetists, from the Greek *dokein*, "to appear." A docetic interpretation of Jesus' life may even have been fostered by the Gospel of John, where Jesus does not eat food offered to him but declares that he has food to eat that the disciples do not know about and that food is the work of the one who sent him (John 4:31–34) and where Jesus dies when he decides to do so (John 19:28–30, 10:18). Against such a view of the gospel was written the First Letter of John: "Every spirit that confesses that Jesus Christ has come in the flesh is from God and every spirit that does not confess Jesus is not from God" (1 John 4:2–3).[25] The Gospel of Luke also reacts against any understanding that the risen Jesus does not have a real body or is a ghost like those of condemned criminals, who must roam the earth. Instead, Jesus asks to be touched and then requests something to eat and eats broiled fish in the disciples' presence (Luke 21:37–43). Although there were Christian proponents of this model for interpreting Jesus' life, the prevailing opinion was that Jesus was a real human being, not a divine being in disguise.

Jesus as Hero

Another model for interpreting Jesus' life was provided by those lives of humans who had been elevated to the rank of immortals or lives of humans who had later been called gods. Such a model is found in the lives of the great heroes Heracles and Alexander, the deification of Demeter understood as the result of her discovery of grain, and the deification of Dionysos as a result of his discovery of wine. The Roman emperors, too, were recognized as gods after their deaths. This model for interpreting a human life is the one Porphyry used to assert that Jesus was a pious man whose life was rewarded by the gift of immortality, and it is a model so well known that it can be parodied, as in Seneca's *The Pumpkinification of Claudius* and in Lucian of Samosata's *The Passing of Peregrinus*.

This model, that in response to an extraordinary life a human could be elevated to the divine world, could be used to interpret such passages as this, found in the Acts of the Apostles 2:22–36:

> Jesus of Nazareth, a man attested to you by God with deeds of power, wonders, and signs that God did through him among you, as you yourselves know—this

man, handed over to you according to the definite plan and foreknowledge of God, you crucified and killed by the hands of those outside the law. But God raised him up, having freed him from the pains of death, because it was impossible for him to be held in its power. ... Therefore let the entire house of Israel know with certainty that God has made him both Lord and Messiah, this Jesus whom you crucified.

Some Christians saw in the narrative of Jesus' baptism an account of the adoption of Jesus as God's son. The words of the coronation Psalm 2:7, "You are my son," were seen as a formal declaration of Jesus' status and a bestowal of the Holy Spirit as a sign of that adoption. However, as we have already seen, that view did not prevail. By the end of the third century, most Christians believed in one God, yet a God who had a Son who had really appeared in a physical body, had been truly born, had truly died, had truly risen.

Apollinaris of Laodicea

The Arian controversy had brought to the attention of the Christians the difficulties inherent in such a simple declaration that Jesus is truly God, truly man. We have already noted how the Arians saw the Logos as replacing the human soul and mind in Jesus and that in reaction to that position, the Letter to the Antiochians of 362 insisted that Jesus has a human soul and mind. A further spur to reflection was provided by the teaching of Apollinaris of Laodicea. Apollinaris was a longtime friend of Athanasius and shared his views concerning the relationship of the Son to the Father. In fact, he may have influenced Basil of Caesarea to accept the use of *homoousion* to describe that relationship. But in discussing the way the Logos, *homoousios* with the Father, is present in Jesus, Apollinaris maintained, like the Arians and most Christian thinkers of the time, that the Logos takes the place of the human mind in Jesus. As the human mind/logos makes humans what they are, that is, *logikoi*/rational animals, so the divine Logos takes the place of the human logos and makes Jesus what he is. "Humans are of the same essence [*homoousioi*] with irrational animals according to their irrational body, but insofar as they are rational [*logikoi*], they are of a different essence. So God also is of the same essence [*homoousios*] with men according to the flesh, but is of a different essence insofar as he is Logos and God" (Frag. 126).[26]

But this logically means that Jesus is by nature different from other humans. "So Christ, having God as his spirit—that is, his mind—together with soul and body, is rightly called 'the human from heaven'" (Frag. 25). "He is not a human but is like a human, because he is not of the same essence [*homoousios*] as a human according to his most important part" (Frag. 45). He is human insofar as a human being is an intellect in flesh, but his intellect in fact is the Logos. Thus, in Jesus there is no conflict of will, and the mind of

Christ is changeless, not "taken prisoner by sordid calculations, but is a divine mind, immutable and heavenly."[27] For Apollinaris, then, the nature of Christ holds the mediating position between the Godhead and humanity. "O new creation and divine mixture! God and flesh made one and the same nature!" (Frag. 10). Such a doctrine was quickly repudiated. In the pungent phrase of Gregory of Nazianzus, "What was not assumed was not redeemed." But the precise language in which the relationship of the Godhead to the human nature in Christ was to be stated was still lacking.

Theodore of Mopsuestia

The debate flared up again in the late 420s between Cyril, bishop of Alexandria, and Nestorius, bishop of Constantinople. Much of this debate was entwined in personality and political conflict. The Council of Constantinople of 381 in its third canon had stated that the bishop of Constantinople was "to have the prerogatives of honor after the bishop of Rome, because that city is the new Rome." This canon put the bishop of Constantinople ahead of the bishop of Alexandria and in some sense reduced Rome to a political priority. Neither Rome nor Alexandria was pleased. The intrigues and machinations of the next decades were in part an attempt to subvert this canon. Cyril of Alexandria was more astute than Nestorius and was able to bring about his condemnation.

The theological issues in the debate arose out of polemics against the Arians. I noted earlier in this chapter how the Arians used scriptural passages that speak of Jesus as weak, hungry, and suffering to show that the Logos as subject of these emotions must be lesser than the impassible God. Athanasius combated this logic by distinguishing the way in which actions can be predicated of the Logos. The Logos hungers and suffers, but He does so, not according to his own nature as divine, but according to the human nature that he has assumed. Athanasius protected the divinity of the Son, but a little at the expense of his humanity.

Christian thinkers in Antioch took a different tack in arguing against the Arians. Where Athanasius maintained the same subject but distinguished the mode of predication, these theologians held that the Logos is not the subject of the human actions and suffering of Christ but rather of the man Jesus. They maintained that there are two subjects of action within the one Savior. Theodore of Mopsuestia, of whom Nestorius was a disciple, was the interpreter of Scripture at Antioch. Theodore stated that there was to be no confusion of the divine and human natures and that the person of Christ had to be acknowledged as undivided. When describing the union in Christ, Theodore maintained that it cannot be a union of essence or of active operation since that means that either God should dwell this way in all creatures or that God is limited to be with and operate in only some creatures. Rather, it is fitting to say that the indwelling comes to be by favor. Favor is the noblest and most honorable will of God, which he brings into effect when he is pleased with those who are zealous to be dedicated to him, because he has a good and noble opinion about them. (*On the Incarnation* 7; PG 66.973)[28]

"And Jesus increased in age and in wisdom and in grace with God and humans" [Luke 2:52]. He increased in age as time went by; in wisdom as he gained understanding in proportion to the advance in time; in grace as he pursued virtue consistent with his knowledge and insight, from which virtue the grace of God was added to, and in all these ways he advanced in the sight of God and humans. Humans saw this growth, but God not only saw it but also testified to it and assisted in what was taking place. (*On the Incarnation* 7; PG 66.980)

Theodore thus insisted that Jesus grows in virtue and wisdom like other humans but is also different from other humans: "For he was deemed worthy of the indwelling of the Spirit in a way surpassing other humans, and was deemed worthy of this not like other humans. For he received the whole grace of the Spirit in himself, but he supplied to others a partial share in the whole Spirit" (*On the Incarnation* 7; PG 66.980). Theodore therefore stressed that Jesus is a human subject. Theodore analyzed the way that God is said in the Scriptures to indwell the saints and then extrapolated with due caution to the case of Jesus:

Therefore, whenever [God] is said to indwell either in the apostles or in righteous persons generally, he makes his indwelling as favoring the righteous, as pleased with those who are duly virtuous. But we do not say that the indwelling took place in [Jesus] in this way, for we could never be so mad, but *as in a son;* for in this way favoring him God indwelt. But what is "as in a son"? In dwelling in this way, he united the one occupied as a whole to himself and adapted him to share with himself in all the honor which the indweller, being Son, shares by nature, so as to unite into one person according to the union with him and to share with him all his authority, and in this way to achieve everything in him, so as to complete both judgment and examination of the world through him and his coming, of course keeping in mind the distinction in what is characteristic according to nature. (*On the Incarnation* 7; PG 66.976)

Even with all his caution, Theodore still spoke of the human as a subject to be adapted, to share. The image of union was that of a union of wills, which can be seen clearly in the analogy he used to describe this union:

In every way, then, it is clear that the name "mixture" is useless, inappropriate and unsuitable, since each of the natures remains undissolved from itself. It is also clear that the name "union" is suitable, for through it the natures brought together produce one person according to the union. So, when the Lord says about man and woman, "Wherefore they are no longer two, but one flesh" [Matt. 19:6], we may reasonably say, in accord with the logic of union, "They are no longer two persons but one," although obviously the natures are separate. Just as there, when it is said that the flesh is one, the phrase does not do outrage to the number two, for it is clear in reference to what one is said, so also here [in the case of Christ] the union of the person does not do outrage to the distinction of natures. For when we distinguish the natures, we say the nature of God the Word is complete and his person is complete (for one cannot say hypostasis without a person). Moreover, the nature of the human is complete, and likewise his person. But when we look at the combination, then we say of one person. (*On the Incarnation* 8; PG 66.981)

Nestorius, as a disciple of Theodore, used the same type of exegesis in preaching against Arians in Constantinople. In the course of this anti-Arian polemic, he found it unsatisfactory to call Mary, the mother of Jesus, Theotokos, or "Mother of God," for Mary as a woman could not bear God; Nestorius seems to have felt that the use of this title would provide ammunition for the Arian claim that the Logos is less than God. Nestorius insisted that the two natures in Christ remain unaltered and distinct in the union so "[that] what belongs to the sonship and lordship are not sundered and that what belongs to the natures might not run the danger of confusion in the disappearance within a single form of the sonship" (Letter 2 to Cyril of Jerusalem; PG 77.52). Such preaching about Mary not being *Theotokos* scandalized Nestorius's congregation.

Cyril of Alexandria

Cyril of Alexandria, ever on the lookout to discomfort the patriarch of Constantinople, responded to this situation by drawing on his theological tradition of anti-Arianism. He insisted that "the Logos united to himself hypostatically flesh animated by a rational soul, and became a human being in an unutterable and incomprehensible way and bears the title 'Son of Man'" (PG 77.45). Cyril went further than talking of a union in hypostasis. Appended to Cyril's second letter to Nestorius was a list of anathemas. The third read, "If anyone in the one Christ divides the persons [*hypostaseis*] after the union, combining them by a sole combination according to worth, or according to authority or domination, and does not speak rather of a meeting according to a natural union, let him be anathema" (PG 76.300).

This anathema contained both a positive description of the union (it is a natural union) and a negative one (it is a combination in accordance with worth or effected by authority or domination). The negative description seems aimed at the work of Theodore of Mopsuestia, as the words *combination* and *worth* show. It is interesting to note Cyril's comment on Luke 2:40, a text that is similar to Luke 2:52, which we previously saw Theodore comment on:

For what is written about him in a human way manifests the manner of his emptying (Phil. 2:6). For it is not in the realm of the possible for the Word brought forth by the Father to support such a thing in his own nature, but when he became flesh, i.e., a human like us, then he was born of a woman according to the flesh and it is said that he submitted to human attributes. For the Word, being God, could have mounted his own flesh in the dimensions of a full-grown human straight out of the womb, but to do that would have been close to miracle-mongering. Therefore he gave to the customs and laws of humanity to hold sway even over his own flesh. So he might be said to advance in wisdom, although he did not receive an addition of wisdom insofar as God is understood to be completely perfect in all things and absolutely not lacking any honors appropriate to the divinity. But God the Word little by little extended the manifestation of his wisdom together with the age of his body. So the body advances in age, the soul in wisdom. For divinity receives neither increase, for the Word of God is completely perfect. He had reason to connect the increase in wisdom with the increase in age, for according to the measure of the age of the body, the divine nature revealed its own wisdom. (*Commentary on the Gospel of Luke;* PG 72.508)

Note how Theodore had Jesus increase in wisdom as he grew older, as all humans do, whereas Cyril had the Word manifest the wisdom that he already had.

The Formula of Reunion

Theodore and Cyril both held to a union of two natures in the person of Jesus. Cyril even conceded, in the Formula of Reunion signed in 433, that "as to the phrases concerning the Lord in the Gospels and Epistles, we know that theologians regard some as common as referring to one Person, and others they distinguish as referring to two natures. They teach that those which are appropriate to the divine nature [are said] in reference to the Godhead of Christ, and that those which are humbler [are said] in reference to his Manhood" (Letter 39; PG 77.177). But the two metaphors used by the two authors, a natural union for Cyril and a marriage union for Theodore, showed both sides grasping to explain the union. The natural union was the closest kind of union—without each part the object could not be what it was in itself. A modern metaphor might be that water is the combination of hydrogen and oxygen; without oxygen there is no water. But Cyril's phraseology was at times suspect: He used the phrase "one incarnate hypostasis of the Word," which he derived from Apollinaris of Laodicea, and his insistence on a natural union made him subject to some of the same criticisms that Apollinaris's views had received. Theodore's image was more suited to the uniting of two independent subjects, and his insistence on the unparalleled nature of the union in the person of Christ still did not dispel doubts that somehow he was talking about the Logos adopting an already existing human. Behind all this discussion lay the enormous difficulty for later Platonic thinkers in describing how, in the makeup of humans, an incorporeal mind can inhabit a corporeal body.

The Formula of Reunion tried to satisfy all parties, but it contained the phrase "out of two natures a union has been made." This led to further difficulties, for Eutyches, an archimandrite in Constantinople, later argued that there were two natures before the union but only one after and concluded that Christ's humanity was not therefore humanity in the normal sense of the term. The Council of Chalcedon in 451 spoke therefore of a union *in* two natures, not *out of* two natures. The semantic distinction that had helped resolve the Arian crisis, the distinction between *ousia* and *hypostasis,* was used in this crisis also, for now it was defined that in Christ there was one person/ hypostasis in two natures.

CONCLUSION

This chapter has explored the worldview the Christians articulated for themselves in the fourth and fifth centuries. They set out what the divinity was and how it interacted with the cosmos. In discussing the divinity, Gregory of Nazianzus wrote:

> Existing separately they are one, and separated they exist connectedly, even if to speak in this way is paradoxical; they are to be worshiped just as much because of their relation to each other as each individually is perceived and accepted; a perfect Trinity, consisting of Three perfects, a Monad set in motion bcause of its abundance, a Dyad surpassed (for God is beyond the duality of matter and form by which bodies are made), a Trinity bound because of perfection. For the Trinity first surpasses the combination of a Dyad, so that the Godhead does not remain constricted, but it does not flow out infinitely, because the former is not honorable and the latter undisciplined; the former is wholly Jewish, and the latter Greek and polytheist. (*Orat.* 23.7; PG 35.1160)

The Christian God was distinguished from that of the Jews and that of the Greeks. But the Christian description of divinity, for all its disassociation with Judaism, remained very much the one creator God of the Hebrew Scriptures. The thrust of Athanasius and the Cappadocian theologians was to insist that there was a huge gulf between creator and created and that no being could exist in between. There was either God or not-God, i.e., a creature. The basic cosmic worldview therefore remained essentially the same as that of the Hebrew Scriptures: opposed to a plethora of many gods or intermediate beings between the one God and the cosmos and supporting a view in which God could deal directly with his creation.

The Chalcedonian Christians, in presenting their view of the mediator, Jesus Christ, by their rejection of Apollinaris of Laodicea and by their dislike of the metaphor of natural union also rejected the idea of an intermediate being between God and humans. Jesus is God and man, not something different from either. Peter Brown writes eloquently on how the emergence of the holy man in late antiquity coincided with the downgrading of temples as the places where the gods meet humans; the temple had received a human face.[29] Nowhere is this truer than of Jesus—he becomes the temple where God dwells, as the Formula of Reunion stated. This image also harks back to the Hebrew Scriptures—to the tent of meeting in the desert wandering, and to the Temple at Jerusalem, an image already exploited in the Gospel of John, where the Logos "tented among us" (John 1:14). The worldview of the Christians, formulated in different terms because of the Jesus event, remained structurally the same as that of the Hebrew Scriptures.

Suggestions for Further Reading

Gregg, Robert C., and Dennis E. Groh. *Early Arianism: A View of Salvation*. Philadelphia: Fortress, 1981.

Hanson, R.P.C. *The Search for the Christian Doctrine of God*. Edinburgh: Clark, 1988.

Kannengiesser, Charles. *Arius and Athanasius: Two Alexandrian Theologians*. Brookfield, Vt.: Gower, 1991.

Kannengiesser, Charles, and William L. Petersen. *Origen of Alexandria: His World and His Legacy*. Notre Dame, Ind.: University of Notre Dame Press, 1988.

Kelly, J.N.D. *Early Christian Creeds*. London: Longman, 1972.

_____. *Early Christian Doctrines*. San Francisco: Harper and Row, 1978.

Stead, Christopher. *Divine Substance*. Oxford: Clarendon, 1977.

_____. *Substance and Illusion in the Christian Fathers*. London: Variorum, 1988.

Williams, Rowan. *Arius: Heresy and Tradition*. London: Darton, Longman and Todd, 1987.

Winslow, Donald F. *The Dynamics of Salvation: A Study in Gregory of Nazianzus*. Cambridge, Mass.: Philadelphia Patristic Foundation, 1979.

Young, Frances M. *From Nicaea to Chalcedon: A Guide to Literature and Its Background*. Philadelphia: Fortress, 1983.

SIX

The Human Condition

THE DIVINE WORLD OF THE CHRISTIANS, as articulated by Christian leaders in conciliar creeds, was a fascinating, creative combination that attempted to balance the belief in the one creator God of Genesis with the belief that there are three actors in the divine drama of redemption, a Father who sends his Son, who sends his Spirit to guide the Christians. The combination also tried to safeguard the incomprehensibility of God, while maintaining that humans can say something about the divine world. Thus, one part of the Christian worldview was mapped, but what of the world that humans lived in?

The Christian baptistery at Dura-Europos, which dates from the mid-third century, is a rectangular room, at one end of which stands a stone font shaped like a sarcophagus. The vault above it is a star-studded blue; behind the font is a painting of the Good Shepherd carrying a sheep on his shoulders, while his flock goes before him. Right under the Good Shepherd is a much smaller, narrow depiction of Adam and Eve, both frantically trying to hide their sexual organs. Here we see themes that were central in the Christian articulation of what life in this world would be and that echoed the vision of the apostle Paul: Baptism is a death to this life and the beginning of a new life (Rom. 6–8); Christ is the new Adam, for the first Adam was not a life-giving spirit (1 Cor. 15:45), and Christ inaugurates a new creation (2 Cor. 5:17; Gal. 6:15). From early on, the Christian view of the world was in tension with the creation story in Genesis. In exploring this Christian worldview, we must keep before us two resonances to the word *genesis:* not only the original generation, or coming-into-being, of this world, its cosmology, but also the generative, or birth, process by which humans come into this world.

THE REJECTION OF GENESIS/GENERATION

Earlier chapters noted how some Christians—followers of Marcion and certain of the Gnostics—held that the old creation was so bad because it was made by an inferior god. Christians of this persuasion believed they belonged to a completely different order of being than those who inhabited the material world. There were also Christians who maintained that humans had been divided from the beginning of time into groups and that some were powerless to change for the better or the worse.

As Kurt Rudolph describes the view of humans found in Gnosticism:

> The gnostic anthropology is reflected in the division of men into two or three classes: the "spiritual" (pneumatic), the psychic, and the "fleshly" (sarkic, from Greek *sarx* "flesh, body") or "earthly" (choic, from Greek *choikos* "earthly"), also called "hylic" (Greek *hyle,* "matter"). "There are three men and their races to the end of the world: the spiritual (pneumatic), the psychic and the earthly (choic)," it is said in the anonymous treatise, which accordingly also distinguishes three Adam figures: the first or pneumatic, the second or psychic and the third or earthly. All three have indeed originated in succession, but they are united in the one first man; they form the three constituents of every man. The one which in each case predominates determines the type of man to which one belongs. Strictly only the pneumatic and the hylic stand in opposition, since the psychic belong to the latter and are reckoned among the "ignorant." Only the pneumatics are gnostics and capable of redemption. This intermediate position of the "psychic" can also be explained from a historical situation: in Christian Gnosis these were held to include the mass of ordinary Christians, who stood between the heathen and the gnostics and were the target for missionary effort.[1]

Along with this rejection of the material world went a rejection of the Genesis account of the propagation of the human race through sexual intercourse. Sayings attributed to Jesus were circulated in the Gospel of the Egyptians, which read, "I came to destroy the works of the female" (Clement of Alexandria *Miscellanies* 3.63). "When Salome asked the Lord: 'How long shall death be in force?' he replied: 'As long as you women bear children'" (*Miscellanies* 3.45). Such sayings, although Clement of Alexandria bravely tried to interpret them otherwise, argued that the process of marriage was bound up with death. Clement also reported the words of one Julius Cassianus:

> For in his book *Concerning Self-Control or Concerning Eunuchry* [Julius Cassianus] says in these very words: "Let no one say that, since we have these parts so that the female body is arranged this way and the male that way, the one to receive, the other to implant, sexual intercourse is allowed by God. For if this equipment was from the God toward whom we hasten, he would not have said that eunuchs are blessed; nor would the prophet have said that they are 'not a fruitless tree,' applying the image of the tree to the man who by his own choice castrates himself of such a notion." Still fighting for his godless opinion he adds: "How would someone unreasonably censure the Savior if he reformed us and freed us from error and from the intercourse of these appended and shameful parts?" (*Miscellanies* 3.91–92)

Clement found that Julius Cassianus was one of many "who with words fair-sounding through self-control commit sacrilege against both the creation and the holy Creator, the almighty only God, and teach that there is no need to take upon oneself marriage and child-bearing nor to bring others to the world in their place who will be ill-starred, nor to supply death with food" (*Miscellanies* 3.45).

Here the Christians around Julius Cassianus were akin to the Gnostic groups explored in Chapter 4: They rejected the creator God of Genesis. They also rejected the whole process of generation and birth commanded in Genesis 1–3. This stance against marriage by some Christian groups is also found, without the strong Gnostic overtones of Julius Cassianus, in the fourth-century Messalians, a group that believed demons still hold power over a person even after baptism and that only intense and ceaseless prayer can diminish the passion and desire by which the demons keep control. As a result, the Messalians refused to work and lived on alms.[2]

The Manichees, another group that appeared in the third and fourth centuries, became very influential.[3] The worldview of the Manichees was a decidedly dualistic one. The movement had been founded in Persia by Mani, who had been martyred for his faith in 276. Mani had set out to found a world religion incorporating elements from Zoroastrianism, Christianity, and Buddhism. Filled with missionary zeal, his followers were found from Carthage in North Africa all the way to China. Persecuted and hunted down by the Roman emperors, Christian and non-Christian alike, they still survived. Within the Manichaean system, there had originally been two opposing principles of good and evil, light and darkness. Evil had attacked good and overcome it, chewing up the light particles so that they became scattered throughout the whole of the dark realm. The purpose of the present life, therefore, was to gather together the light particles, to prevent further scattering of them, and to have these light particles returned, via the moon, to the home of lightness, the sun. The Manichaean movement was made up of two tiers: the "perfect" and the adherents of the sect. The perfect ate only light-bearing vegetables such as melons and radishes, not the dark-filled meat. These perfect ones were ascetics who did not engage in sexual intercourse, for that too involved the encasing of light particles in the realm of darkness. Each human thus was divided within him- or herself into light and dark particles, and each individual was thus not responsible for his or her actions.

THE ACCEPTANCE OF GENESIS

Against such teachings most Christian writers strenuously reacted, for these beliefs attacked the goodness of God's creation through an attack on marriage. In general, Christian leaders stressed that humans have free will to choose how to live and that marriage, like creation itself, is good. For them, the God who created this world is also the God who redeemed the Christians. But what was wrong with the old creation? Why had it needed to be redeemed?

The evidence that something was askew in the cosmos lay before anyone's eyes—pain, suffering, injustice. How had the world come to be like that? As one of the basic questions in religion, it received, and receives, various answers. Hesiod told the tale of the curious Pandora, who disobeyed her husband's command not to open a box and so let loose on the world all evils, an answer with a decidedly misogynistic twist. Plato also gave such a twist in his ironic treatment of the differences between humans. At first all would be created the same. Those who mastered their sensations and lived well would return to his original state and live an appropriately happy life; but anyone who failed to do so would be changed into a woman at his second birth. Or even lower, he would be changed into some sort of beast (*Timaeus* 90–92).

The sense that all is not as it should be in the cosmos pervades the apocalyptic literature of Second Temple Judaism. Such literature frequently traces the present woeful state of the cosmos to some primordial event, whether it be the lustful descent of the wicked angelic figures to the daughters of men, as in 1 Enoch 1–36, or the primordial war between the forces of chaos and order, as in Daniel 7, where the beasts of the chaotic sea are judged and destroyed.[4] The Christians also possessed within the Hebrew Scriptures at Genesis 1–3 a story that tells how this world, which was very good in God's eyes, became full of pain and suffering and hierarchy between humans. From the apostle Paul on, Christians would repeatedly return to that story to contrast the disobedience of Adam and the pain it had brought with the obedience of Jesus and the health it had brought.

Christians and Free Will

Most early Christian writers were exhorting their hearers either to become Christians or to be better Christians. Within that context, they stressed the freedom of the individual to choose, to swim against the tide, and to turn her or his back on social ties. The Gospel of Luke exhorted:

> Whoever comes to me and does not hate father and mother, wife and children, brothers and sisters, yes, and even life itself, cannot be my disciple. (14:26)

> Do you think that I have come to bring peace to the earth? No, I tell you, but rather division! From now on five in one household will be divided, three against two and two against three; they will be divided: father against son and son against father, mother against daughter and daughter against mother, mother-in-law against her daughter-in-law and daughter-in-law against mother-in-law. (12:51–53)

Justin Martyr, in his *Dialogue with Trypho,* referred to the effects of the Genesis story in order to exhort his hearers to repent:

> So Jesus did not submit to be born and to be crucified as if he needed them, but for the sake of the human race which since Adam had fallen under death and the deceit of the serpent, each having sinned by his or her own fault. For God wanted both angels and humans to do whatever he had enabled each to be able to do out of free purpose and to be free, and he created them this way. If they chose to do what pleased him, he would preserve them immortal and free from punishment; if they sinned, he would punish each one as he determined. (88)

Within this exhortative context, emphasis was placed on the penalties that had flowed from the disobedience of Adam, and hearers were encouraged not to disobey as Adam had. The option of obeying was open to all. This stress on the freedom of the individual recurs throughout the writings of the Greek fathers. The sin of Adam has weakened humans, has brought on their mortality, ignorance, desire, but a human can overcome that sin. Such an emphasis was also part of an attack on those who held that humans can do nothing on their own to overcome fate or destiny. The second-century Syrian Christian writer Bardaisan wrote against the idea that humans are prisoners of an unalterable fate:

> Now as to what Awida said: "Why did not God make us so that we would not sin and be found guilty?" If a human were so made, he would not exist for himself, but would be the instrument of whoever moved him. It is clear, that whoever moves something as he wishes moves it either for good or for evil. So then how would a human differ from a harp on which someone else plays, or from a chariot driven by another? ... But God in his goodness did not will to so create humans, but through liberty he raised them above many things and made them equal to the angels. ... By this liberty a human justifies himself, conducts himself divinely, and is joined with the angels, who also possess free will. (PS 1.2.543–548)

Christian leaders always had to encourage their followers to do better. This insistence on the ability of men and women to choose to lead better lives can be found in John Chrysostom's fourth-century sermon on Romans 7:14:

> "Sold under sin." For with death, he says, the crowd of passions also entered in. For when the body became mortal, it then received necessarily desire, and anger, and pain, and all the others, which required much training so that they would not deluge us and drown reason in the depth of sin. For they themselves were not sin, but their unbridled excess brought this about. So, to take one of them as an example, desire is not sin, but when it degenerates into excess and does not want to keep within lawful marriages but rushes after other men's wives, then the deed becomes adultery, but not by reason of the desire, but by reason of its excess. (*Homily* 13.1; PG 60.507–508)

The passions have to be mastered. Lack of mastery leads to sin and injustice. Of particular interest is the way John Chrysostom interpreted Romans 5:19 for his congregation:

> For as by one man's disobedience many were made sinners, so by the obedience of one shall many be made righteous.
>
> What is said seems indeed to contain no small question, but if anyone pays it close attention, this too will be easily solved. What then is the question? The saying that through the disobedience of one many became sinners. For the fact that, when one sinned and became mortal, those who came from him were so also, is not unreasonable. But what kind of logical sequence is it that another became a sinner from that one's disobedience? For one could conclude that such a person will not incur punishment if he indeed did not become a sinner by himself. What then does the word "sinners" mean here? To me it seems to mean liable to chastisement and condemned to death. Now [Paul] had shown clearly and frequently that when Adam died we all became mortal. But the question is why this happened. ... But if any of you were to seek to learn, we should say this: not only do we not suffer loss by this one's death and condemnation if we control ourselves, but we even profit by having become mortal. First, because we do not sin in an immortal body; secondly, because we get numberless occasions for training. For death, both when present and when expected, persuades one to be moderate, to be self-controlled, and to be restrained, and to give up all evil. But along with these, or rather before these, it has introduced other greater blessings. For from there come the crowns of martyrs, and the prizes of the Apostles. ... For if we wish, not only death, but even the devil himself will not be able to harm us. Besides this, one can say that immortality awaits us, and after we have been chastised a little while, we shall enjoy the future goods without fear. We will have been instructed as if in a school in this present life by sickness, tribulation, temptations, poverty, and the other seeming horrors, so that we will be appropriately prepared to receive the future blessings. (*Homily* 10.2–3; PG 60.477–478)

Here we see that for Chrysostom sinning means undergoing the penalties of disease and suffering associated with being in a mortal body, but he insisted that a person can overcome these. Particularly important is the metaphor of this life as a school.

Human Genesis

Along with the question of whether humans are created with free will or not remained the problem of how to regard this world, where the normal course of human life is birth, marriage, parenthood, and death. How were Christians to incorporate these elements into their belief that this cosmos has been redeemed by Christ, who brings about something new in creation? Running throughout the writings of the early Christian leaders are two overriding emphases: a view of life as a training ground for Christians, a school, and a view of life as a deserved punishment for sin.

Life as a School. The question of what had gone wrong with the first creation still remained. In the last citation from John Chrysostom, we begin to glimpse how the Greek fathers read the story of Genesis: The disobedience of Adam resulted in humans receiving mortal bodies. The previous chapter already noted how Origen conceived of the original fall as that of rational, disembodied souls that turned away from God; as a result, some became enfleshed. This allegorical reading of the Genesis story was not the only reading that Origen gave of it, but in that form it was quickly repudiated.[5] However, the description of humans in Eden continued to be compared to that of the angels. This interpretation is expressly found in Chrysostom's sermons on Genesis, in which he asserted that Adam led an angelic life, and in Gregory of Nyssa's response to the question "If procreation only appears after Adam's sin, how would souls have come into being if the first humans had remained sinless?"

> Now in these matters again the really true answer, whatever it may be, will be clear only to those who, following Paul, have been initiated into the ineffable secrets of Paradise. But our answer is as follows. When the Sadducees once spoke against the teaching about the resurrection, and brought forward to prove their own opinion the case of the oft-married woman who had been wife to seven brothers, and then asked whose wife she will be after the resurrection, our Lord answered their argument so as not only to instruct the Sadducees, but also to make manifest to all those after them the mystery of the life in the resurrection: "For in the resurrection," he says, "they neither marry, nor are given in marriage; for they cannot die anymore, for they are equal to the angels, and are the sons of God, since they are the sons of the resurrection." Now the grace of the resurrection promises us nothing else than the restoration of the fallen to their former state; for the awaited grace is a kind of return to the first life, drawing the one cast out of Paradise back to it. If then the life of those restored is akin to that of the angels, it is clear that the life before the transgression was a kind of angelic life; because of this our return also to the former condition of our life is compared to the angels. But yet, as has been said, although there is no marriage among them, the armies of the angels are in countless myriads, for so Daniel described [them] in his visions. Therefore, in the same way, if no alteration and displacement from the status equal to angels had happened to us because of sin, we would not have needed marriage to multiply. Whatever the mode of increase in the nature of angels is (unspeakable and inconceivable by human speculations, except that it at all events exists), this mode would have been in effect also among humans, who were "made a little lower than the angels," increasing humanity to the human limit determined by its maker. ...
>
> Now that we have examined these matters in this way, we must return to our former discourse: how God devised for his work the distinction according to male and female after the construction of the image. I say that our previous investigation will be useful in considering this. For He who brought all things into being and by his own will formed the human as a whole in reference to the di-

vine image, did not wait to see the number of souls completed to its proper fullness by the small additions of those coming after, but he understood all at once
all the human nature in the fullness of his knowledge, and he honored it with the
exalted status equal to the angels, since he foresaw by his power of vision the
choice not to go straight toward the beautiful and, because of this, the choice to
fall away from the angelic life. So that the multitude of human souls might not
be lessened since it fell from that mode by which the angels were increased to a
multitude, God invented for [human] nature a way to increase appropriate to
those who had slipped into sin, implanting in humankind instead of the angelic
nobility of nature that bestial and irrational mode of succession from one another. (*On the Making of Man* 17; PG 44.188–189)

We can glimpse the disdain of so many of the Greek fathers toward human sexuality glaring through this description of the division of the sexes.
But we can also see that for Gregory this life, with all its vicissitudes and
pains, is an alternative plan on God's part, an aspect of the schooling that
humans have to undergo to regain their angelic state. This vision of human
life, a vision derived from that of the ascetics, for whom the monastic life is
"the angelic life," lays emphasis on the need for human struggle to overcome
the desires of the beastly part in all of us and does not condemn those desires
as evil but as something to be controlled. Sin lies in not mastering them, not
in having them. From this line of thought, then, the other great Cappadocian, Gregory of Nazianzus, expounded on how injustice had come into the
world:

Let us imitate the highest and first law of God, who rains on the just and the unjust and makes the sun rise on all equally. He spread out for all the animals the
open land, and the springs, rivers and woodlands; he furnished air to winged animals, water to those whose life was in water, and the primary resources for living were enough for all, not held by any domination, not hedged around by law,
not kept apart by any boundaries. Rather, he set them up as common and ample
and needing nothing more. He honored the equal status of the nature by an
equality of the gift, and showed the wealth of his goodness. But humans squir-
reled away gold, and silver, and expensive and unnecessary clothes, and radiant
stones or any other such thing, which betoken war and rebellion and the worst
tyranny. Then they raised their eyebrows superciliously, they denied mercy to
their unfortunate kinsfolk, and they were not willing to help toward necessities
out of their superfluity. What illiberality! What stupidity! If for nothing else,
they should at least consider that poverty and wealth, freedom as we call it and
slavery and other such names came later to the human race, like a general epi-
demic rushing in along with the evil, since they are its inventions. But in the beginning, as the Gospel says (Matt. 19:8), it was not so. He who formed man at
the beginning sent him away free and independent, ruled only by the law of his
command and rich in the luxury of Paradise. He wanted this also for the rest of
the human race, and freely gave it through the one seed of the first human. On
the one hand were freedom and wealth, and the observance of the command; on
the other, the transgression of the command, true poverty and slavery.

But afterward came envy, rivalries, and the treacherous tyranny of the serpent, which was always seducing by luxurious pleasures and inciting the more arrogant against the weaker, and so what was akin was broken apart into alien groups, and arrogance took hold of the law and split apart natural nobility. But as for you, look with me at the original equality of rights, not at the later distinction, not at the law of the powerful, but at the law of the Creator. Give as much aid to nature as you can; honor the ancient freedom. Be reconciled to yourself as you cover the dishonor to the race. Prevent the plague and relieve the poverty. (*Homily 14 On the Love of the Poor 25–26*; PG 35.889–892)

Although there are the seeds for radical social action in this homily, Gregory, as all the church fathers, was no radical reformer of the status quo; he simply desired amelioration of the glaring inequities of his society. But he found the origin of this injustice in humans' lack of control of their desires, particularly the lust for power and possessions. According to these writers, then, Adam's disobedience brought about this painful life in mortal bodies and brought with it the means of propagating the race through sexual intercourse.

Within this Christian emphasis on life as a school and a training ground also arose the question of how to view the newborn child, who is not yet capable of exercising his or her free will. In arguing strongly against the Gnostics and those like Julius Cassianus who held that generation/birth is evil, Christians like Clement of Alexandria insisted that the newborn child is not evil:

If generation is evil, let the blasphemers say that the Lord who took part in generation/birth took part in evil, and that the virgin begot him in evil. Woe to these evil people! They blaspheme the will of God and the mystery of creation when they slander generation/birth. (Clement of Alexandria, *Miscellanies* 3.102)

Jeremiah says, "Cursed be the day in which I was born, and let it not be rejoiced over." However, he is not saying that generation as such is cursed, but he is discouraged at the sins and disobedience of the people. Then he adds, "Why was I born to see toils and pains and my days lived in shame?" For example, all those who preach the truth are persecuted and in danger because of the disobedience of their hearers. Ezra the prophet says, "Why did my mother's womb not become a tomb, so that I might not see the distress of Jacob and the toil of the nation of Israel?" (4 Ezra 5:55). Job says, "No one is pure from dirt, not even if his life is one day" (Job 14:4). Let them say to us how the newly born child has become a prostitute, or how the child which has done nothing has fallen under the curse of Adam. Their conclusion, it seems, is to say that generation/birth is evil, not only the generation of the body, but also that of the soul on account of which the body even exists. And when David says: "In sin I was born and in unrighteousness my mother conceived me," he says prophetically that Eve is his mother, but "Eve became the mother of the living." So if he was conceived in sin, he himself, however, was not in sin, and surely he himself is not sin. (*Miscellanies* 3.100)

Here we can see Clement trying to deal with the powerful poetry of the prophets and Job when understood literally. We must also remember that the Greek manuscripts Clement was using were unpunctuated. Modern editions of Job, for example, break up the sentence and punctuate it differently so as to translate, "Who can bring a clean thing out of an unclean? No one can. Even if his life last but one day, his months are numbered by you." Such a translation would have made it easier for Clement to insist on his distinction that the body may be unclean, but the soul is not. The soul, for Clement, as the seat of reason and free will, cannot be born sinful. The Greek Christian writers, in fact, consistently made a clear distinction between an adult who sins of his or her own will and an innocent child who is not yet conscious and so cannot yet choose right or wrong:

> Let this be so, one might say, about those who seek baptism. But what do you say about those who are still infants, and have no awareness of the loss or of the grace? Are we to baptize them, too? Certainly, if any danger is imminent. For it is better to be sanctified unaware than to die unsealed and uninitiated. ... But concerning the others, I give as my opinion that they should wait till the end of the third year, or a little less than that or more than that, when they are able both to hear and to answer something about the mysteries so that they receive some formation at least, even if they do not understand it. Then they sanctify both bodies and souls by the great sacrament of perfection. For this is how the matter stands: at that time they begin to have to render an account of their lives, when reason is attained, and they learn about the sacrament, for they are not held accountable for sins of ignorance by reason of their age; and [at that time] it is more advantageous on every account to be fortified by the font, because of sudden dangerous attacks and more violent forces. (Gregory of Nazianzus *Oration* 40 28; PG 36.399)

In this homily Gregory was encouraging people to be baptized, and yet he precluded any sense of original guilt as a reason for early baptism. Gregory of Nyssa formally addressed this question of the early death of infants in a letter written in his old age to a questioner, Hierius:

> But as you wish with thoughtful attention to know the purpose of each event that occurs for the other factors in the divine arrangement, so you also want to know why one person's life extends to a great old age, but another shares only so much of life as to draw one breath of air and straightaway stops living. ... What then is the wisdom in this? A human being enters through birth into life, draws in the air, begins life with a cry, serves nature with a tear, and leaves this life of sorrows before sharing in any of the pleasures of life, before his senses are attuned and he is still loose in the joints of his limbs, tender, relaxed, unset; in short, before he is human (if the gift of reason is proper to humans, and he was not yet capable of reason). Such a one has nothing more than the one confined in the mother's womb except that he has been in the air, and at that time dies, either exposed or suffocated, or ceasing by itself to live because of its weakness.

What should one think about him? What position should one take about those who so die? Will such a soul behold its judge? Will it stand with the rest before the bench? Will it undergo the trial of those who have lived? Will it receive the retribution according to merit, either by being condemned to fire according to the words of the Gospel, or by being refreshed in the pure water of blessing? But I do not know how one ought to think such things about such a soul. The word "retribution" means that something must have been given before; but the material from which to give anything has been taken away from someone who has not lived at all. Because there is no tribute, one cannot properly speak of retribution. (*On Infants' Early Deaths;* PG 46.165–169)

Gregory then went on to ask that if such infants cannot be condemned and are raised to the future blessed life, would it not be better not to live? Are they not better off? He answered, "We say that the soul of one who has passed through every virtue, and the soul of one who has never lived, are equally outside the evils which come from wickedness. We do not, however, think that the course of life of each of them is similar" (PG 46.180–181). The difference for Gregory lies in the notion that this life is a school: Those who have not studied cannot comprehend in the same way as those who have been schooled. However, they will still be part of that future, blessed life, but they will not have the same level of appreciation.

John Chrysostom explicitly stated that infants are baptized, "even though they do not have sins, so that there may be added [to them] holiness, righteousness, sonship, inheritance, brotherhood, to be members of Christ, to become the dwelling place of the Spirit" (*Homily* 3.6).[6] Chrysostom stressed that Adam was the first to sin, but Chrysostom did not envision a handed-on guilt. "See that we do not again become subject to this contract. Christ came once for all; he found our ancestral bond which Adam wrote. He brought in the beginning of obligation; we increased the loan by sins after these" (*Homily* 3.21).

One interesting interpretation of the problem is found in Didymus the Blind, *Against the Manichaeans*. Didymus used the phrase "sin by succession" but did so in a context totally different from that of a sin contracted by Christian babies. Explaining the phrase found in Romans 8:3 that God sent his Son "in the likeness of sinful flesh," Didymus explained:

Again, if [Jesus] had assumed a body from sexual intercourse, being in no way different, he would have been thought to be liable to that sin to which are all who are from Adam by succession. But if some people were to say: if sinful flesh is what is born from sexual intercourse of a man and a woman, then marriage is evil, let them hear: before the coming of the Savior who takes away the sin of the world, all humans just as they did everything else with vice, so they also kept marriage sinfully. Wherefore the bodies born from such a marriage must be considered. And so, since the sexual intercourse of Adam and Eve took place after the sin, therefore it is called sinful flesh. For being immortal before the transgression, when he transgressed he became mortal, and so the succession holds mortality. Therefore the Savior has the likeness of sinful flesh, except his flesh did not see corruption (Ps. 15:10). But after the Savior had come, just as there was a removal of sin from other deeds, so also from marriage. Therefore now those who live according to the Gospel are able to keep an honorable marriage and an undefiled bed, as Paul writes to the faithful "Marriage is honorable and the bed undefiled, but God will judge fornicators and adulterers" (Heb. 13:4). For he distinguishes the honorable marriage and those using it from fornicators and adulterers, and does not wish it to be fornication or adultery. Whence neither is marriage sin. (*Against the Manichaeans* 8; PG 39.1096)

Here Didymus clearly attributed the mortality of human bodies to the transgression of Adam and Eve but did not speak of a transmitted sin to the soul and did not see any transmission of sin to babies after the coming of the Savior, for marriage itself is not sinful. So Clement of Alexandria, John Chrysostom, Cyril of Alexandria, Theodore of Mopsuestia, and Theodoret of Cyrrhus all interpreted 1 Corinthians 7:14, which states that the children of the marriage between a Christian and a non-Christian are not unclean, but holy. For Clement, "I hold that the seed also of the sanctified is holy" (*Miscellanies* 3.46). Cyril of Alexandria in his commentary on 1 Corinthians wrote, "For he says that the unbelieving husband will be made holy in the wife so that even your children will be holy, since the sanctification in the believers completely conquers somehow the uncleanness of those who do not yet believe" (PG 74.876).

This tradition of viewing life as a training ground in virtue was summed up by John Cassian, who had been a disciple of the monks in Egypt and later of John Chrysostom in Constantinople and finally settled down to a monastic life just off the coast of France. His writings were framed as dialogues between famous monks in Egypt. In discussing sexual temptation, he wrote what he reported to have heard the abbot Daniel say:

That this battle has been placed in our members for our advantage we also read in the Apostle: "For the flesh lusts against the spirit, and the spirit against the flesh. But these two are opposed to one other so that you do not do what you want." You have here, too, a contest deeply rooted somehow in our bodies, with the management of the Lord taking care of it. For whatever is present in everybody generally and without any exception, what else can be concluded except that it is assigned as if naturally to the very substance of humans after the fall of the first man. What is found to be born and to grow with everybody, how can it not be believed to have been placed there by the will of the Lord, not to harm them but to take care of them? He tells us the reason of this conflict, i.e., of flesh and spirit, is this: "that you do not do whatever you want." So God took care that we could not fulfill something, i.e., that we could not do whatever we want. If we were to be able to do whatever we wanted, that must have been harmful to us. Therefore, this conflict, placed in us by the management of the Creator, is in some way to our advantage, and challenges and urges us on to a better state. If it were taken away, without a doubt a destructive peace would follow. (*Conferences* 4.7; CSEL 13.102)

Life as Deserved Punishment: Origen. One Christian writer who saw this life as involving something more than a school was Origen, although he was also very emphatic on the training in this life. Origen was very influenced by a series of biblical texts that speak of the uncleanness attaching to birth as well as by the church practice of baptizing infants. Commenting on Luke 2:22 ("When the time came for their purification according to the law of Moses") Origen wrote:

> Therefore did Jesus need cleansing, and was he unclean or stained with some uncleanness? Perhaps I might seem to speak rashly, but I am moved by the authority of the Scriptures. See what is written in Job: "No one is clean from uncleanness, not even if his life were of one day." He did not say "no one is clean from sin," but "no one is clean from uncleanness." But uncleanness and sin do not signify the same thing. ... Every soul which is clothed with a human body has its uncleannesses. ... Therefore it behooved that those things which were wont to purify uncleannesses from the Law be offered for our Lord and Savior, who was clothed with unclean garments and assumed an earthly body. Moved by the opportunity of the place, I examine again what is frequently asked among the brethren. Infants are baptized for the remission of sins. Whose sins? or when did they sin? or how can that reason for the washing exist in infants unless according to that meaning about which we spoke a little before: "No one is clean from uncleanness, not even if his life on earth was of one day" (Job 14:4)? And because through the sacrament of baptism the uncleannesses of the birth are taken away, therefore infants are baptized; for unless someone is reborn from water and the spirit, he or she is not able to enter the kingdom of heaven. (*Homilies on Luke* 14.5; GCS 35.96–98)

Here Origen spoke of the body being unclean and of entrance into a body bringing about uncleanness. Yet he was concerned to deny that Jesus has contact with sin. In a homily on Leviticus 12:1–2, which deals with the ritual for the purification of a mother after childbirth, Origen held that this uncleanness does not apply to Jesus because Mary was a virgin (*Homilies on Leviticus* 8.2, 12.4; GCS 29.394–395, 29.461). Yet in his commentary on Romans, Origen stated:

> The body of sin, therefore, is our body, because it is not written that Adam knew Eve and bore Cain unless after sin. Thence it is also commanded in the Law (Lev. 12:8) that a sacrifice should be offered for an infant who has been born, two turtledoves or two pigeons, of which one is a sin offering and the other a burnt offering. For what sin is this one pigeon offered? Surely a just-born infant is not already able to sin? However, he has a sin for which a sacrifice is commanded to be offered, a sin from which no one is denied to be clean, not even if his life were of one day (Job 14:4). David also is believed to have said

[concerning this sin] what we have recalled above: "In sins my mother conceived me" (Ps. 50:7). For according to the narrative no sin of his mother is mentioned. For this [sin] the Church also received the tradition from the apostles to give baptism even to infants. For they, to whom the secrets of the divine mysteries were entrusted, knew in everybody were innate uncleannesses of sin, which must be washed away through water and the Spirit. (*Commentary on Romans* 5.9; PG 14.1017)

In his battle against the Gnostics, however, Origen insisted that each person is responsible for his or her own sins and rejected any attempt at holding that the fate of an individual is predetermined. In a question about what sin infants have committed, Origen left himself space for the notion that all rational creatures except the soul of Christ sin before their entry into bodies and that this very entry is an uncleanness. However, there does seem to be a sense that Adam's sin somehow infected all humans.

The Western Tradition. *Tertullian and Cyprian.* In the eastern part of the Roman Empire, Christian leaders battled against groups that denied that humans have free will, that said marriage is to be rejected as sinful, and that the offspring of sexual intercourse are sinful. In opposition to these beliefs, they forcefully stated that the Christian God is the creator of this world and that therefore marriage, while perhaps not part of God's original plan, is good and that the children who come from marriage are innocent of any sinful guilt. Their life on earth is bound up with misery, pain, and suffering as a punishment for Adam's disobedience but is also a school for learning how to master desires.

The Christian leaders in the western Roman Empire faced different problems, particularly in the church of North Africa. W.H.C. Frend argues that North African Christians were primarily concerned about the nature of the church and its membership: "The North Africans affirmed the absolute value of the purity of the church and integrity of its membership, however exclusive they might be."[7] The church was not to have spot or wrinkle, stressed Tertullian (*Modesty* 18); for Cyprian, quoting the Song of Songs 4:12, the church was an enclosed garden (Letter 69.2). Such a gulf between the church and those outside led to a major emphasis on the rite of initiation into the church: baptism. In discussing the question of the baptism of infants, Cyprian asserted:

> But, moreover, if the remission of sins is given even to those who have sinned most gravely and to those who sinned greatly against God previously and then afterward believed, and no one is kept away from baptism and from grace, how much more should an infant not be kept away, one recently born who has not sinned at all, except that, born fleshly according to Adam, he has contracted at the moment of birth the contagion of the earliest death? Such an infant draws near more easily to receive the remission of sins by the very fact that it is not its

own sins which are remitted, but the sins of another. (Letter 64.5; PL 3.1054–1055)

The language of impurity, uncleanness, contagion, suggests some kind of miasma attaching to infants. That notion had been more fully developed earlier by Tertullian. He believed that the soul is a body, albeit a more refined body than the flesh. "For [souls] are nothing if they have no bodily substance" (*On the Soul* 7.3). Following ideas of the Stoics, Tertullian held that God is a body (*Against Praxeas* 7.8). From this premise, Tertullian concluded that the soul does not exist before the body, that in fact the soul is somehow handed on from the seed of the father:

(1) How then is a living being conceived? Is the substance of both body and soul brought together at the same time, or does one of them precede the other? We indeed say that both are conceived, made ready, and perfected at the same time, just as they are produced together, and that in the conception no moment intervenes by which any order could be assigned. ... (6) Finally, as more endangering modesty than proof, do we not feel, in the very swell of ultimate passion, when the generative fluid is ejected, that something of the soul has also departed and so we feel weak and without vigor, and with a loss of vision? This will be the ensouling seed from the dripping of the soul, just as that bodily fluid is from the dregs of the flesh. (7) The most trustworthy examples are those from the primordial period. The flesh in Adam was from slime. What else is slime except a thick liquid? From that will be the generative fluid. The soul is from the breath of God. What else is the breath of God except the warm exhalation of the spirit? From that will be what we exhale through that seminal fluid [of the soul].
(8) Since, therefore, in that first creation two different and distinct elements, slime and breath, condensed into one man, both mingled substances mixed their seeds also in one and from that came the model for propagating the human race. So now two seeds, although different, flow forth united together, and together are thrust into in the furrow and field, and together they produce a man from both substances. Again, in this man is present a seed according to his own species, just as it has been determined for all generative situations.
(9) Therefore, from one man is this whole lavishness of souls, as nature observes the command of God: "Increase and multiply." For, in the preliminary statement of one work, "Let us make man," the whole posterity was predicted in a plural form: "And let *them* have dominion over the fishes of the sea." That is not extraordinary, for the promise of the crop is in the seed. (*On the Soul* 27)

Here the well-read Tertullian strikingly adapted the medical theories of his day, which recommended "that the act of intercourse itself, if conducted in the right frame of mind—in effect, with correct decorum—would have a positive effect on the character and sex of the ensuing child, and certainly that the neglect of such decorum might produce offspring worthy of shame and pity."[8] Tertullian, like Origen, was also no doubt influenced by a close reading of Leviticus, with its stipulations for the purification of newborn children. He further insisted that the act of intercourse handed down the twisted soul of Adam. Although aware of the effect of cultural influences, he nevertheless claimed, "40.1 So every soul is assessed to be as it was in Adam until it has been reassessed in Christ, unclean until it has been so reassessed, sinful, too, because unclean, receiving the shame also of the body from their union. ... 41.1 Therefore, the evil of the soul, besides what a vile character builds upon it by accrual, precedes from the blemish of the origin and is in some way natural" (*On the Soul* 40.1, 41.1).

Nevertheless, Tertullian still did not insist that infants be baptized, and so the notion of a guilt attaching to infants for which they can be justly punished is not present in his thought. When discussing who should be baptized, he wrote:

> And so, according to the circumstances and disposition, and also the age, of each person, the delay of baptism is more profitable, but especially in the case of little children. For why is it necessary—if [baptism itself] is not so necessary— for the sponsors also to be thrust into danger? ... Let them come, then, when they are maturing, when they are studying, when they are being taught where they are coming. Let them become Christians when they are able to know Christ. Why does the innocent time of life hasten to the remission of sins? (*On Baptism* 18.4–5)

Ambrose. Ambrose, bishop of Milan from 374 to 397, followed in the tradition of Tertullian and Cyprian in stressing the sharpness of the boundary that lay between the church as an inviolable holy community and outside society.[9] As noted in Chapter 1, during Ambrose's life the emperors were taking increasing measures to end pagan cults and to eradicate heresies. Within this time of antitheses, Ambrose used the language of sin and wickedness to describe all that was outside the church. In commenting on Psalm 49:15, which, as translated in the Latin version as Psalm 48:8, reads, "What shall I fear on the evil day? The iniquity of my heel will surround me," he wrote, "That is, since my mouth speaks wisdom and the meditation of my heart is prudence, what am I able to fear on the day of judgment, except perhaps that the iniquity of my heel be cleansed? Our own iniquity is one thing; another that of our heel in which Adam was wounded by the teeth of the snake and left by his wound the inheritance of human succession guilty, so that we all limp by that wound" (*Enarrato in Ps.* 48.8; PL 14. 1214–1215).

In commenting on the next verse, Ambrose went on to say that the iniquity of Adam is more an inclination to sin than some state or condition of being accused. But elsewhere he used the language of iniquity to describe the condition of all Adam's descendants. In discussing Psalm 40:8 (in the Latin Bible Psalm 38:29), "Deliver me from all my iniquities," Ambrose wrote, "He who prays to be loosed from all iniquities is not confessing the fault of one offense. For he knows that, unless the Lord pardons, no one who is born under sin can be saved, whom the very inheritance of a guilty condition constrains to guilt" (CSEL 64.205). In writing about the death of his brother, Ambrose remarked, "I fell in Adam, I was thrown out of Paradise in Adam, I died in Adam. How shall [Christ] call me back, unless He finds me in Adam, so that as I was accountable for the offense and under obligation to death in [Adam], so now I might be justified in Christ?" (*On the Death of His Brother* 2.6; CSEL 73.254).

The notion of a guilty inheritance, of a corporate participation in Adam's sin, is also found in an anonymous Latin author called the Ambrosiaster writing in Rome at the end of the fourth century. Commenting on Romans 5:12, a crucial text in the discussion of original sin since the Greek text *eph ho*, which means "because," was translated into Latin as *in quo*, "in whom," so that the phrase "because all sinned" became "in whom all sinned," the Ambrosiaster wrote:

> In whom—that is in Adam—all sinned. ... It is clear that all sinned in Adam as if in a lump. For since he was corrupted through sin, all whom he bears are born under sin. Therefore from him all are sinners because we are all from him. For he lost the favor of God when he transgressed, having become unworthy to eat of that tree of life so that he would die. Death, however, is the separation of soul from body. There is another death: this second [death] is said to be in gehenna and we do not suffer [it] through the sin of Adam but, through its opportunity, [this second death] is obtained by our own sins. From which [death] the good are immune, only they are in the lower regions but higher up as if in a free [status], because he was not able to ascend to the heavens. For they are held by the judgment given in Adam. (CSEL 81.165)

Here the Ambrosiaster stated that good people, if unbaptized, still remain kept away from heaven, confined to "the lower regions," because of the judgment given in Adam. On Romans 7:14, the Ambrosiaster commented, "Sold under sin. That is, to be sold under sin [is] to draw origin from Adam, who first sinned, and to become subject to sin by one's own sin just as Isaiah the prophet said, 'You are sold by your sins' (Isa. 50:1). For Adam sold himself first and through that all his seed is subject to sin, for which reason humans are weak in observing the precepts of the law unless strengthened by divine help" (CSEL 81.233–234).

But Cyprian, Ambrose, and the Ambrosiaster all also held that infants are innocent[10] and that each human has to bear the responsibility for his or her individual actions. In the last quotation from Ambrose, we can see that the debt to be paid for guilt is death but that this is not the same as eternal punishment. According to the Ambrosiaster, the second death in gehenna is obtained by a person's own sins. A married layman, he further combated ascetics who held opinions against the good of marriage:

> What therefore has been blessed by God, why is it asserted to be an unclean and defiled work, unless because they in some way infer that God has hands? For

they would not rebuke this, unless they understood God incorrectly. For because they fear to attack God directly, they accuse him through the work invented by him. For when the work displeases, the author is attacked. (*Questions of the Old and New Testament* 127.5; CSEL 50.400)

Augustine of Hippo. All these concerns resounded particularly in the work of Augustine of Hippo. Augustine had grown up in the atmosphere of the North African church, with its long tradition and debate over what constituted a holy church. Cyprian of Carthage had argued that only baptism given within the orthodox church is valid. After the Decian persecution of 249–251, Christians confronted the problem of whether to readmit to communion those who had lapsed. Cyprian allowed readmittance after penance, but his decision concerning lapsed priests and bishops gives an insight into his worldview. A priest who had lapsed was in a state of impurity: "Flee from such men as far as you can; with a care for health, avoid those who cling to pernicious contacts" (*On the Lapsed* 34). "Let not the people delude themselves as if they could be immune from the contagion of sin, when they communicate with a sinful priest and give their assent to the unjust and illegal episcopacy of their leader, since they are warned through the prophet Osee, and the divine Censor says, 'Their sacrifices shall be like the bread of mourning: all that eat them shall be defiled'" (Letter 67.3; PL 3.1060).

The power of the sacrament depended on the ritual holiness of its minister. The position taken here by Cyprian and his council led to further difficulties in the next persecution fifty years later. The question of who had lapsed and how they were to be treated resurfaced. This time the leader who emerged for the more rigorist party was Donatus, a priest from a small town in Numidia. Donatus, a charismatic personality who led his movement as bishop of Carthage from 313 to 347 and who died in exile shortly thereafter, held closely to the views of Cyprian. The formal issue at debate was the consecration of Caecilian as bishop of Carthage in 311. Had one of the consecrating bishops, Felix of Aptunga, been impure because he had handed over the sacred Scriptures during the time of persecution? The issue was complicated by personal rivalry as well as socioeconomic tensions between the less wealthy Numidia and the rich Carthage. Several imperial investigations cleared Caecilian and the consecrating bishop, but the schism had taken hold. When Augustine was consecrated bishop of Hippo in 396, the debate was over eighty years old, and the Donatists were a formidable force in Christian affairs.

Augustine, a monumental figure and towering intellect, explored with great insight the major issues of Christian faith; his writings shaped western Christianity. He has been the subject of minute scrutiny, and every facet of his long life has been intimately investigated, even by himself, for he left us an autobiography up to his baptism in 386, his *Confessions*. A bright boy from a not-too-well-off family living in a small town in Numidia, Augustine was aiming for success—he studied in Carthage, moved to Rome, and then to Milan, where the emperor resided—when he left behind plans to wed a wealthy heiress and was baptized and became a celibate "servant of God."

Paralleling this physical itinerary was an itinerary of the mind and soul in Augustine's view of himself, and it is on that inner itinerary that I wish to focus. Augustine lamented that in his early search for God he could conceive of nothing that was not material, just like the Stoics explored in Chapter 2. God is a more refined physical substance that expands all through creation. A major breakthrough for Augustine came when he read some books of the Platonists. Suddenly he realized that it was possible to conceive of a noncorporeal reality:

> 7.1 I was so thick-witted and even opaque to myself that I was thinking that whatever was not stretched out or diffused or compacted or swollen through some dimensions or could be contained or could contain something was absolutely nothing. ... So I was thinking that even you, O Life of my life, large throughout infinite dimensions, penetrated the whole bulk of the world and beyond it in all directions through immense dimensions without limit, so that the earth and the sky and all creation held you and they came to an end in you, but you never ended. ...

> 7.10 Urged on [by these books of the Platonists] to return to my own self, I entered into my inmost self with you as leader. I was able to because you became my helper. ... 7.17 For I searched from where it was that I could assess the beauty of bodies either on earth or in the heavens, and what it was I had available to me so that I could honestly judge things subject to change and say, "This ought to be this way; that should not be this way." Therefore, searching out from whence I might judge when I so judged, I found above my own changeable mind a changeless and true eternity of truth. So gradually, from bodies to the soul sensing through the body, and then to its inner power to which the senses of the body reported exterior things—this is as far as animals are able to go—then further to the reasoning faculty to which whatever is taken from the bodily senses is referred to be judged. This power, recognizing that in me it was changeable, lifted itself to understand itself and withdrew its thinking from its customary mode and took itself away from the conflicting flocks of images so that it might find what light had touched upon it since beyond any doubt it shouted out that the changeless was preferable to the changeable, and therefore it had known the changeless itself. For unless it knew it in some way it would in no way have so securely preferred it to the changeable. So it came, in the stab of a flickering glance, to that which is. (*Confessions* 7.1, 10, 17)

This notion of an incorporeal, spiritual reality on which this material reality depends was to remain with him for the rest of his life. It also affected deeply his reading of the Scriptures. Previously he had thought the ideas contained in the Hebrew Scriptures crude and uninformed, containing many contradictions; armed with his new sense of spiritual reality, he was able to see under the guidance of Ambrose of Milan how to read the Scriptures spiritually.

Now this intellectual itinerary was also an itinerary away from Manichae-ism. While in Carthage, Augustine had become a follower of this fringe Christian group and remained an adherent for nine years. The commitment of these Manichees attracted Augustine, even though he did not follow their strict mode of life, which leads us to another element of Augustine's autobi-ography: a move from an active sexual life to a life of celibacy. Augustine lived with a woman for thirteen years and had a son by her. He left her in fa-vor of a more advantageous marriage, but that, too, he gave up when he was baptized. For him, baptism and sexual renunciation went hand in hand. In the great passage portraying his difficulty making the final commitment to become a Christian, the debate is framed in terms of a debate between conti-nence and lust, as if there were no intermediary between sexual abstention and fornication (*Confessions* 8.11). Earlier, Augustine had hoped to set up an ideal philosophers' commune, but he was prevented from doing so be-cause some of his companions were married and their wives did not approve. These facets of Augustine's autobiography form a backdrop for his view on the origin of injustice and evil in the world. Combined with a sense of the role that the Donatist schism played in the North African church, they pro-vided the milieu in which Augustine's thought developed.

Before leaving the *Confessions,* however, let us look at one other aspect: the work's organization. Augustine revolutionized the biographical canons of his time. In these, once the hero or heroine had made a decision, his or her life was one of complete holiness. In *The Life of Saint Anthony,* for example, the reader sees Anthony deciding to leave home and follow the life of the monk, the temptations of the devil overcome in the tombs, and then a mar-velous, revitalizing account of Anthony's ability to work miracles, to have insight into his companions' hearts, to lead a holy life (2–10). For Augustine, however, his conversion came, not as a result of his insight into the noncorporeal nature of God, but as a result of a cataclysm within his own soul, where he felt himself as a puppet torn in two directions before God's grace thrust him to safety and conversion. According to normal hagio-graphic standards, that should have been the end of the story, or, at most, should from then on have portrayed Augustine as triumphantly leading his flock against the heretics and schismatics. But no. In Book 10 of the *Confes-sions,* Augustine went on to speak of his continuing struggles against sins and temptation—should he eat that extra piece of fruit or not? How could he keep his mind undistracted by rabbits running in the fields? In this book, he formulated the saying that later became famous: "Give what you com-mand, and command what you will."

There was no triumphal ending to his story; it remained a prayer to God for help, even as bishop. As such, it would have given encouragement to the groups of ascetic Catholics who had sprung up in North Africa as they saw Augustine combating daily temptations. It would also have been a powerful weapon in his argument against the Donatists. Although they were concerned mainly with the ritual purity of the sacraments, Augustine skillfully shaped the debate into a question of whether any church can be really pure, and he pointed to instances of not so morally pure conduct by the Donatist leaders themselves. Being a priest or a bishop did not automatically mean a person was saved and not a sinner; being baptized did not automatically mean salvation. Augustine insisted that the sacraments are the visible signs of God's church, but there is also an immense undercurrent of psychological forces at play. From his years as priest and then bishop, Augustine knew that not all his congregation were saints—the newest enthusiastic convert might find himself or herself in church with one of the biggest and most ruthless land-grabbers; as bishop, Augustine had to arbitrate between brothers wrangling over an inheritance. His own clergy were not above sexual misconduct. As he formulated the matter in the *City of God* (1.35), no one can be sure of what will happen in this world: Those who are today the fiercest enemies of Christianity may tomorrow be converted, and vice versa.

Augustine was most influenced in this understanding by his new reading of the letters of Saint Paul in the heat of the debates against the Manichees. When Augustine had first debated against the Manichees after his conversion to Catholic Christianity, "his criticism of Manichaeism had been a typical philosopher's criticism of determinism generally. It was a matter of common sense that men were responsible for their actions; they could not be held responsible if their wills were not free; therefore, their wills could not be thought of as being determined by some external forces, in this case, by the Manichaen 'Power of Darkness.'"[11] Augustine had trotted out this argument successfully against Fortunatus in a public debate on August 28, 392, but Fortunatus had relied heavily on a dualistic reading of the letters of Paul (where, for example, Paul spoke of a conflict between spirit and flesh [Rom. 7:14–25; Gal. 5:16–21]) to support his theory that in humans there are two wills. This scriptural basis worried Augustine, and he began to study ever more closely Paul's letters. His subsequent reading of Paul did stress the tension between flesh and spirit, not dualistically but psychologically. Augustine now saw the fourfold schema of Romans 7—before the law, under the law, under grace, the end of the world—as taking place in each human. Without the constant help of God's grace, a human's fractured and divided will cannot effect the good it wants: "For I do not do what I want, but I do the very thing I hate" (Rom. 7:15). There are not two wills in humans, as the Manichees held, but one will impaired by the flesh and past habits. Only the grace of God the Physician can reinvigorate this sickened will to choose effectively the good. Augustine's debates with Manichaeism and with Donatism, as well as his own experience of living in a less than perfect church, led him therefore to stress that humans must rely totally on God, not on any human support or sense of human holiness.

The last three books of the *Confessions* are also fascinating for the light they shed on Augustine's development. They reveal to us Augustine the preacher, who as bishop had to sit every day a few paces away from his congregation and expound the Scriptures to them. In these three last books, we see how Augustine, who framed the whole of the *Confessions* as a prayer to God, found God's answer to his prayer, God's part in the dialogue, in the Scriptures, which are God's Word speaking. As we follow Augustine's focus on each word of the first sentence of Genesis 1, we can glimpse how far Augustine went in his ability to read the Scriptures spiritually, not corporeally. The days when he believed that if humans are made in God's image, then God must have hands and feet and a human shape were far gone. His very spiritual reading of Genesis was in itself an answer to his Stoic and Manichaean past. In an earlier commentary on Genesis, Augustine had asserted that Adam had a spiritual body and that the "coats of skin" with which Adam and Eve clothed themselves were in fact corporeal bodies (*On Genesis Against the Manichaeans* 2.21; PL 34.212–213).

Elizabeth Clark shows decisively, however, that Augustine began to read Genesis 1–3 in a very different manner shortly after writing the *Confessions*.[12] The change was a result of the Jovinian debate. At the end of the fourth century, one finds in the writings of Pope Siricius and Ambrose of Milan a clarion call to virginity. As Peter Brown argues:

> To Siricius, the issue seemed clear: service at the altar was only for those who were prepared henceforth to be perpetually free from at least one of the many stains of worldly life: the stain of intercourse. ... Siricius' views coincided with those of Ambrose in that both rested on the unquestioning acceptance of a notion of hierarchy. Both asserted the existence of distinct grades of perfection in the Christian life, and both believed that these distinctions could be measured in terms of the degree of a person's withdrawal from sexual activity. On this scale, the virgins came first, the widows second, and the married persons third.[13]

Against this movement, Jovinian, a respected ascetic, asserted that all Christians were equal, that baptism, not sexual continence, was the deciding factor. The response to this assertion was immediate. Ambrose, Jerome, and Augustine all wrote in opposition to Jovinian. In response to two followers of Jovinian, Ambrose argued against what he saw as a call to pleasure seeking and equated their teaching with that of the caricatured stereotype of all hedonists, Epicurus:

> Epicurus himself, whom these persons think should be followed rather than the apostles, the champion of pleasure, even if he denies that pleasure is the importer of evil, does not deny that certain things come from it from which evils are generated; in short, the life of the luxurious which is filled with amusements does not seem to be reprehensible, unless it is disturbed by the fear either of pain or of death. ... But this is refuted by Holy Scripture, which teaches us that plea-

sure was instilled into Adam and Eve by the snares and allurements of the serpent. If, indeed, the serpent itself is pleasure, and therefore the passions of pleasure are changeable and slippery, and infected with the poison, as it were, of
corrupting enticements, therefore it is clear that Adam, deceived by the desire of
pleasure, withdrew from the commandment of God and from the enjoyment of
grace. How then is pleasure, which alone deprived us of Paradise, able to recall
us to Paradise? (CSEL 82.241–242)[14]

There is no reason to believe that the two followers were advocating a life
dedicated to riotous pleasure seeking, but Ambrose rejected any attempt to
criticize the practice of asceticism:

What then do these people want, who try to pervert those whom the apostle acquired, whom Christ redeemed by his own blood, when they assert that the baptized ought not to apply themselves to the disciplines of the virtues; that carous-
ings and an abundance of pleasures will hinder them not at all; that those who
miss out on them are foolish; that virgins ought to marry and bear children; that
likewise widows should repeat what they once painfully experienced in combination with a man; and that those who refuse to repeat intercourse are in the
wrong, even if they could restrain themselves? (Letter 63.23; CSEL 82.247–
248)

Jerome's response to Jovinian was even more virulent than that of the
others; in fact, it was quite scurrilous, and some of the supporters of asceticism tried to suppress publication of his letter (Letter 49.2). Jerome said that
"the defilement of marriage is not washed away by the blood of martyrdom"
(*Against Jovinian* 1.26), "that if it is good not to touch a woman, it is bad to
touch one" (1.7). As Peter Brown recapitulates, Jerome asserted

that even first marriages were regrettable, if pardonable, capitulations to the
flesh, and that second marriages were only one step away from the brothel. He
went on to suggest that priests were holy only in so far as they possessed the purity of virgins. The married clergy were mere raw recruits in the army of the
church, brought in because of a temporary shortage of battle-hardened veterans
of lifelong celibacy.[15]

This attack on Jovinian seemed suspiciously like an attack on married life
itself, on the whole process of reproduction. But if so, was not this an attack
on creation itself, on the text of Genesis where God had said, "Be fruitful
and multiply"? With this rejection of marriage, was the attack not dange-
rously like Manichaeism or the extreme ascetics attacked by Clement of Alexandria or the Messalians? To combat such a suggestion, Ambrose, albeit
hesitatingly, and Augustine began to read the text of Genesis in a more literal
fashion. Elizabeth Clark follows the development in Augustine as he groped
toward such an understanding and its implications for a comprehension of
human sexual relations. Clark dates Book 9 of Augustine's commentary on
Genesis to not long after 401:

Augustine's more literal interpretation of the Eden story emerges clearly in
Book IX of *De Genesi*. He reminds his readers that he intends to deal with real
events, interpreted not allegorically but according to their proper sense. In his
new exegesis of Adam and Eve's relationship in Eden, he accomplished his goal.
In fact the detailed position that Augustine sets forth in this book is the very one
he expounds several years later, in the heat of the Pelagian controversy.
Augustine writes in *De Genesi* IX that Adam and Eve would have reproduced in
Eden even if they had remained sinless. Although they had animal bodies, they
did not feel the appetite of carnal pleasure. They could have commanded their
organs of reproduction in the same way that they commanded other bodily
parts, such as their feet. They would have conceived offspring without experi-
encing bodily passion. And Eve would have given birth without pain.[16]

This notion of having a body and yet not feeling carnal pleasure is reminiscent of Hilary's statements about the body of Christ suffering, yet not feeling
pain. Augustine maintained the view (noted in Origen) that the body of Jesus
is exempt from sin, even from original sin, because the body does not come
about as the result of sexual union. Augustine thus walked a tight line:
Against the Manichees and the extreme ascetics he had to maintain that creation and marriage are good, but he also maintained the superiority of virginity to the married state. Church leaders in the eastern Roman Empire had
had to debate extreme ascetics and those who denied free will; Augustine
had to fight against those who felt they could maintain a holy church and
those who emphasized the goodness of marriage. Augustine answered that
humans live in a sinful world and that sin is handed on by procreation. As he
stated trenchantly in a sermon preached against the Pelagians, "Therefore let
no one deceive us. Scripture is clear, the authority is most fundamental, the
faith the most catholic: all born are damned; no one is freed unless reborn"
(Sermon 294.16; PL 38.1345). For Augustine, a major transition had taken
place from the original, completely good creation of humans and the state in
which they now found themselves. In answer to the objection that everyone
experiences some kind of passion, Augustine argued that Adam's life cannot
be reasoned from humankind's present state. Augustine contended that the
word *nature* can be used in two different senses: to describe humans as created in the beginning without sin and to designate humans after the expulsion from Eden (*Retractions* 1.9.3, 1.14.6).

> If, however, nature had not been dishonored by sin, God forbid that we should
> think that there would have been marriages in Paradise such that in them the re-
> productive organs would be activated to produce offspring by lustful passion,
> and not by the command of the will—just as the foot to walk, the hand to work,
> and the tongue to speak. Nor, as now is the case, would the wholeness of virgin-
> ity be corrupted to conceive offspring by the power of a disorderly passion, but
> it would follow the command of the calmest love, and thus there would be no
> pain, no blood from the virgin when she has intercourse, just as there would

also be no groan of the mother when she gives birth. But these things are not believed, because they are not experienced in this state of mortality. The reason is that a nature, changed by a defect into the worse, does not uncover an example of that original purity. (*On the Grace of Christ and on Original Sin* 2.40)

Human nature as currently experienced, then, is no real basis for judging what human nature really is. Augustine's image of what Adam originally was like parallels his image of what a society at peace should be like—the tranquility of order. Every person should know his or her place and obey superiors and command inferiors.

> Therefore the peace of the body is the ordered arrangement of the parts; the peace of the irrational soul is the ordered repose of the desires; the peace of the rational soul is the ordered agreement of knowledge and action; the peace of body and soul is the ordered life and health of the one enlivening it; the peace between mortal man and God is the ordered obedience, in faith, under the eternal law; peace between men is the ordered agreement of mind with mind; the peace of a home is the ordered agreement about commanding and obeying among those who live together; the peace of a city is the ordered agreement about commanding and obeying among the citizens; the peace of the Heavenly City is the most ordered and most united fellowship in the enjoyment of God, and of themselves in God; the peace of the whole universe is the tranquility of order. Order is the arrangement of things equal and unequal which bestows to each its own proper place. (*City of God* 19.13)

Where there is disorder there is no peace, and we can see how for Augustine obedience plays a major role—that of children to parents, of wives to husbands, of citizens to the state authorities. Within the human frame as currently constituted, Augustine found no peace. As Book 10 of the *Confessions* shows, Augustine had difficulty controlling all his numerous desires. He was acutely aware of day-to-day sufferings—not only of fraud and moral injustices but also of the ravages of wars and pirate incursions—acutely aware that this world is not at peace and perfect. How, then, could this world have been purposely created by a perfect God? Origen's answer concerning an original creation of rational creatures was closed to Augustine, and so he suggested that human life in Eden would have been perfect with no pain, suffering, or injustice. This was Augustine's answer to the Manichees and to those who thought like them: This creation is indeed good as formed by its creator. In answering the Donatists, however, Augustine stressed the sinfulness of all humans and upheld the validity of baptism independently of the conscious state of the minister or the recipient. These two responses seemed to go in opposite directions, for why would baptism be necessary for infants if the creation is good?

The Debate with Pelagius. The Pelagian controversy grew out of a hearing involving a follower of the monk Pelagius at a council in Carthage:

The bishop Aurelius said: "Let the following be read aloud." It was read aloud that the sin of Adam did harm to him alone, and not to the human race. When it had been read aloud, Caelestius said: "I said that about the transmission of sin I was uncertain, but only insofar as I was in agreement with someone to whom God had given the grace of knowledge, because I heard different opinions from those who indeed have been appointed presbyters in the Catholic Church." The deacon Paulinus said: "Tell us their names." Caelestius said: "The holy presbyter Rufinus in Rome, who lived with the holy Pammachius. I heard him say that there is no transmission of sin." The deacon Paulinus said: "Is there any other person?" Caelestius said: "I heard many say [this]." The deacon Paulinus said: "Tell us their names." Caelestius said: "Is not one priest sufficient for you?" Later on in another place the bishop Aurelius said: "Let the rest of the document be read." It was read aloud that infants who are born are in the same condition that Adam was before the transgression. They read to the end of the small document which had previously been inserted. The bishop Aurelius said: "Have you at any time, Caelestius, taught, as the deacon Paulinus says, that infants who are born are in the same condition that Adam was before his transgression?" Caelestius said: "Let him explain what the expression is 'before the transgression.'" The deacon Paulinus then said: "Do you deny that you taught this? It is one of two things: let him either deny that he taught this, or let him now condemn it." Caelestius said: "I already said, Let him explain how he employs the expression 'before the transgression.'" The deacon Paulinus then said: "Deny that you taught these things." The bishop Aurelius said: "I ask what I can deduce from this man's obstinacy. I say that Adam, as established in Paradise, is said to have been made immortal at first, i.e., before, but after through the transgression he became liable to decay. Do you say this, brother Paulinus?" "I say this, my lord," said the deacon Paulinus. The bishop Aurelius said: "The deacon Paulinus wants to know whether infants who are about to be baptized here and now are certainly the same as before the transgression of Adam, or whether an infant certainly acquires the guilt of transgression from the same origin of sin from which it is born?" The deacon Paulinus said: "Let him deny whether he taught this, or not." Caelestius said: "I have already said about the transmission of sin that I have heard many appointed in the Catholic Church refute this and others affirm it, although this is a subject for research, but not a heresy. I have always maintained that infants need baptism, and ought to be baptized. What else does he want to know?" (*On Grace and on Original Sin* 2.3)

Here we catch a glimpse of different Christian networks in Italy. Paulinus was a deacon of Ambrose of Milan; Caelestius was influenced by the teaching of Rufinus of Syria in the eastern Roman Empire. These two networks had different answers to heated questions. Are infants infected with sin, guilty of sin, or only punished for the sin of Adam? In contrast to Augustine, and in accordance with a well-established Christian tradition, Pelagius held that humans are no different from Adam, that they are not born as sinners since to sin requires the exercise of free will, but that humans choose to be good or evil. Adam provided a bad example to the rest of the race; that was all. There is no cataclysmic difference between the present human condition and that in Eden. Augustine was horrified. How could this miserable existence come from God?

> Would it please you [Julian] that we should place [in paradise] chaste men and women who struggle against sexual desire; pregnant women, who are vomiting, not wanting food, pale; other women giving birth to not fully developed offspring in premature delivery; others groaning and howling as they give birth; as for those just born they are all crying and then laughing; later they talk and speak incorrectly; afterward they are in school to learn their letters, weeping aloud under lashes, whips and switches. There are a variety of punishments meted out to suit the varieties of dispositions: above all, innumerable diseases, assaults of demons, and attacks of wild beasts, by which some are tormented, and others killed. Those indeed who are healthy are brought up under uncertain events by the care of their pitiable parents. Would there also inevitably be [in paradise] bereavements and sorrow and grief with aching hearts for loved ones? But it would take too long to run through all the evils in which this life abounds, nor are these any sins. (*Contra secundam Juliani responsionem opus imperfectum* 3.154; CSEL 85.1.459)

Would his opponent, Julian of Eclanum, "fill this Paradise of the most honorable and auspicious delight calamitously and indecently with the funerals of dead men and the torments of the dying?" (*Contra secundam Juliani responsionem opus imperfectum* 6.41; PL 45.1608). We can hear echoes in these words of an old man of over seventy who had lost many friends, someone who had always been keenly sensitive to bereavement. Salvation was to be a return to the Eden/paradise of God's original plan:

> As happy therefore as [Adam and Eve] were as they neither were troubled by disturbances in their souls nor suffered any bodily ailments, so the whole of human society would have been happy if the first parents had not committed the evil which was passed on to posterity and no one of their progeny had committed a sin which reaped condemnation. This happiness would have remained until, through the blessing in these words "Be fruitful and multiply," the number of predestined saints would have been reached. Then would have been given that other greater happiness, which was given to the blessed angels, so that there would be a secure certitude that no one would sin and no one would die. Such would have been the life of the saints after no experience of toil, pain or death, as life will be after all these things, when the resurrection of the dead returns with the incorruptibility of bodies. (*City of God* 14.10)

Augustine wanted a life where friends could converse forever and not be interrupted by distance, death, or deceit; he wanted to find a "full peace" (*City of God* 19.9–11). The only way he could reconcile present human suffering existence with the notion of a perfect creator God was through the idea that this present life is a punishment for sin. This is the same answer of-

fered by Origen, but worked out differently. All humans somehow participate in that first sin of Adam. They are not just being punished for the sin of
one man, for that would imply injustice on God's part. Rather, all humans
are guilty of rebellion against God, of upsetting God's perfectly ordered universe. Whereas Pelagius and his followers had argued that babies are born
without sin, that their baptism is simply an initiation into the church's life,
Augustine claimed that babies are baptized because they are sinners. But
how could babies be sinners? Augustine asserted that this original sin is
handed on through the very process of conception, but when pressed, he
pled ignorance on exactly how human souls can contract sin: He could not
hold that the soul is a body but had difficulties with the notion of preexistent
souls entering bodies.[17] Nevertheless, this notion of a transmitted sin was essential to Augustine's answer to the problem of suffering: "This is the Catholic view which shows a just God in so many and so great punishments and
torments of infants" (*Contra secundam Juliani responsionem opus imperfectum* 2.22).

For Augustine, this controversy went to the very heart of the Christian belief:

> But what is under consideration are two men, by one of whom we were sold un-
> der sin, by the other we were redeemed from sins, by one we were thrown into
> death, by the other we are freed into life, because the former destroyed us in
> himself by doing his own will rather than the will of him by whom he was cre-
> ated, while the latter has saved us in himself by not doing His own will but the
> will of Him who sent Him. The Christian faith properly consists in the relation
> of these two men. (*On Grace and on Original Sin* 2.28)

Thus, all humans, even infants, are guilty and can be justly punished by God
to eternal damnation, even if for infants Augustine was sure that God would
be exceedingly mild in the extent of his eternal punishment. Such a doctrine
led inexorably to the notion that humans can be saved only through a gra-
cious action of God. Augustine had originally thought that humans can of
their own free will first believe, but he came to see that as an error:

> By this testimony [of Cyprian and of 1 Cor. 4:7] especially was I refuted, since I
> likewise had been in error, thinking that the faith by which we believe in God
> was not a gift of God, but that it was in us from ourselves, and that through it
> we obtained the gifts of God, by which we may live with restraint and righ-
> teously and piously in this world. For I used to think that faith was not preceded
> by God's grace, so that through it what we asked for our own advantage was
> given to us, except that we would be unable to believe if the proclamation of
> truth did not precede; but I used to be of the opinion that it belonged to us and
> was in us from ourselves to assent to the Gospel when it was preached to us.
> Some small works of mine which were written before my episcopacy contain a
> fair amount of this error of mine. (*Predestination of the Saints* 7)

Here we can see to what extent Augustine had gone in seeing the vitiation of human nature as a result of Adam's disobedience—it cannot love correctly as it is so impaired.

CONCLUSION

Christian leaders in both the east and the west were concerned about how to explain the suffering and injustice in this world. In contrast to Greek thinkers, who were content with the idea that the further away we were from the perfect One, the less perfect we would be, Christian leaders insisted that the work of God must, in the words of Genesis 1, be very good indeed. But such an insistence on God's goodness only highlighted the problem more: From where did human pain and suffering come? Christian leaders maintained the goodness and justice of God but put the responsibility for the flawed character of the cosmos on the free decision of Adam. Life in Eden had been very different from present human existence. Human experience of pain and suffering was not brought about by the good creator; it was not part of his original plan. All mainstream Christian leaders agreed on this point. Where they differed was in emphasis—was this life remedial training, or was it just punishment? Was it a school or a prison?

Suggestions for Further Reading

Brown, Peter L. *Augustine of Hippo: A Biography.* Berkeley and Los Angeles: University of California Press, 1969.

_____. *Religion and Society in the Age of St. Augustine.* New York: Harper and Row, 1972.

Clark, Elizabeth A. *The Origenist Controversy: The Cultural Construction of an Early Christian Debate.* Princeton: Princeton University Press, 1992.

Pagels, Elaine H. *Adam, Eve, and the Serpent.* New York: Vintage, 1989.

Rees, B. R. *The Letters of Pelagius and His Followers.* Woodbridge, England: Boydell, 1991.

_____. *Pelagius: A Reluctant Heretic.* Woodbridge: Boydell, 1988.

Rousselle, Aline. *Porneia: On Desire and the Body in Antiquity.* Oxford: Blackwell, 1988.

❧ SEVEN ☙

"Neither Male nor Female"

THE EARLY CHRISTIANS HAD ACCEPTED as their God the creator God of Genesis and had appropriated the story of Adam and Eve in Genesis 2–3 to explain how suffering and injustice had come into the world and why this world needed the redeemer Jesus. One aspect of the Genesis story that is still left to examine is the statement in Genesis 1:27: "God created the human: male and female he created it."

WOMEN AND LEADERSHIP ROLES

It was Saint Paul who made the magnificent sweeping statement, "There is no longer Jew or Greek, there is no longer slave or free, there is no longer male and female; for all of you are one in Christ Jesus" (Gal. 3:28). But it was also Paul, in a remarkably contorted argument, who recommended that Christian women follow normal dress codes, for "the husband is the head of his wife" (1 Cor. 11:3). He praised a woman, Junia, for her actions as an apostle (Rom. 16:7), and yet his writings contain a passage, disputed as to its authenticity but nevertheless present, that orders women to be silent in church and forbids them to speak (1 Cor. 14:33a–35). This tradition of the silencing of women is even more prominent in later letters attributed to Paul, such as 1 and 2 Timothy:

> I desire, then, that in every place the men should pray, lifting up holy hands without anger or argument; also that the women should dress themselves modestly and decently in suitable clothing, not with their hair braided, or with gold, pearls, or expensive clothes, but with good works, as is proper for women who profess reverence for God. Let a woman learn in silence with full submission. I permit no woman to teach or to have authority over a man; she is to keep silent. For Adam was formed first, then Eve; and Adam was not deceived, but the woman was deceived and became a transgressor. Yet she will be saved through childbearing, provided they continue in faith and love and holiness, with modesty. (1 Tim. 2:8–15)

In these texts there is no mention of a new creature through Christ, but of the continuation of the old Genesis story. Yet the position of writings such as

1 Timothy was challenged by other Christian texts circulating in the second century, for example, the *Acts of Paul and Thecla*.[1] This remarkable story was translated and circulated widely so that Thecla became one of the most popular names for Christian women. Some scholars argue that it was written by a woman, whereas others counter that Tertullian (*On Baptism* 17) claimed that it was written by a presbyter in Asia Minor, and, anyhow, say these scholars, males could have created female heroes. Whoever wrote it, what is most striking is not simply that Thecla, a woman, is the hero of the story, but that there is a pervasive opposition between male and female throughout the work. When Thecla is condemned to die in the arena, the women of the city cry out in opposition; when Thecla is brought into the arena, the men cry out for her death, but the women oppose it. When a bear attacks her, a lioness defends her; when a lion runs against her, the lioness and the lion perish together; when Thecla is tied to bulls and their testicles heated, a flame around her saves her. The sexual symbolism is intense. Finally Thecla is released and she teaches and preaches. Her sexuality has overcome male domination.

Now it is always unwise to jump too quickly from rhetorical strategies to sociological realities, but we can say that the author of this piece structured the narrative along gender lines and identified the Christian side with the female. In a male-dominated society such as the Greco-Roman, this is to identify with the weak and oppressed, the side least likely to win, the underdog. Sometimes in early Christian writings women are praised as leaders, as more intelligent than the founders of mainstream Christianity. The *Gospel of Mary* presents a narrative set just after the risen Jesus has appeared to his disciples and then departed. The disciples are depicted as grieving and are consoled by Mary. Peter asks her, as one whom Jesus loved above all other women, to tell them the words that Jesus spoke to her but not to them. She does so, but when she finishes speaking, Andrew speaks and says:

> "Say what you (wish to say) about what she has said. I at least do not believe that the Savior said this. For certainly these teachings are strange ideas." Peter answered and spoke concerning these same things. He questioned them about the Savior: "Did he really speak privately with a woman (and) not openly to us? Are we to turn about and all listen to her? Did he prefer her to us?"
>
> Then Mary wept and said to Peter, "My brother Peter, what do you think? Do you think that I thought this up myself in my heart, or that I am lying about the Savior?" Levi answered and said to Peter, "Peter, you have always been hot-tempered. Now I see you contending against the woman like the adversaries. But if the Savior made her worthy, who are you indeed to reject her? Surely the Savior knows her very well. That is why he loved her more than us." (*Gospel of Mary* 17–18)[2]

Again, we are dealing with authors who knew how to use gender symbolism to suggest the victory of the underdog.

Women and Liturgy

Before the rise to power of Constantine, women's voices generally were silent, although they may have been the majority of Christians. During the persecution of 303, at Cirta in North Africa an inventory was made of what was present in the house where the Christians used to meet: sixteen men's tunics, thirty-eight veils, eighty-two ladies' tunics, and forty-seven pairs of female slippers (*Gesta apud Zenophilum;* CSEL 26.186–197).[3] Earlier, around 250, Pope Cornelius of Rome had stated that more than fifteen hundred widows and persons in distress were being supported by the church at Rome (Eusebius *Ecclesiastical History* 6.43.11). But to recover what they were doing and thinking as Christians is almost impossible.

One area in which we can glimpse a struggle going on is that of the place of women in the liturgy. In the third century, Bishop Dionysius of Alexandria wrote to a brother bishop stating that menstruating Christian women could not participate in the Eucharist (PG 10.1281, 1284). Such an admonition already implied that women could not be in leadership positions in the Christian communities. Whatever the position of deaconess may have been in the early church, in the third-century *Didascalia apostolorum* the ministry of deaconesses was geared solely to women. This document is especially concerned with separating men and women: Men and women were not to use the same baths, if at all possible.[4] This same separation is found in rituals: A woman deacon was to anoint newly baptized women and to instruct them how to remain "in purity and holiness" (*Didascalia apostolorum* 16; Lagarde 71).

> You will choose from all the people those who appear well behaved to you and you will appoint them as deacons: a man for the carrying out of many necessary thing, a woman to care for the women. For there are houses where you cannot send deacons near the women on account of the unbelievers, and so you will send deaconesses. The office of deaconess is necessary for many other things also: first of all, whenever the women go down into the water [of baptism], those who go down into the water ought to be anointed with the oil of anointing by one of the deaconesses. ... It is necessary for a deaconess to enter the houses of unbelievers where there are believing women, and to care for those who are sick and to supply them with whatever they need. ... Let a woman rather be assiduous in the service of women, and a male deacon in the service of men. (*Didascalia apostolorum* 16; Lagarde 71–72)

Women in this document are excluded from teaching (*Didascalia apostolorum* 15; Lagarde 63–64) and from priestly duties. There are hints, in fact, that official regulations may not have been universally recognized. Giorgio Otranto points to a decree of Pope Gelasius from 494 in which the pope complained that women were exercising liturgical functions that properly pertained to the male sex, and Otranto opens up the question of whether the term *presbytera* found on some inscriptions is only honorific and means "the wife of a presbyter" or whether it in fact means "priestess."[5] Cyprian, bishop of Carthage, received a letter from a fellow bishop of Asia Minor who complained of the actions of a woman who was ecstatically filled and prophesied in the 230s. The bishop stated that she dared "to pretend that she sanctified the bread and celebrated the Eucharist with the invocation which should not be despised, to offer the Sacrifice to the Lord without the solemn obligation of the usual proclamation; she also dared to baptize many by using the usual and legitimate words of inquiry, so that nothing might appear to be different from the pattern found in the Church" (Letter 75.10).

Again, in some areas, Christian women may have developed their own liturgical actions. Irenaeus of Lyons, writing toward the end of the second century, sarcastically described a group centered around a man called Marcus:

> Pretending to consecrate cups mixed with wine, he [Marcus] prolongs greatly the word of invocation, and makes [the cups] reappear rosy red, so that that Grace, who is from beyond the cosmos, appears to shed her own blood into that cup by means of his invocation. Those present greatly desire to taste that drink so that that Grace, who has been summoned by that impostor, might pour into them. Again, handing to the women cups of mixed wine, he enjoins them to consecrate them in his presence. When this has been done, he himself brings another cup larger than the one over which the deceived woman consecrated, and empties the smaller one consecrated by the woman into the one prepared by himself, saying these words as he does so: "May that Grace who is before all things, incomprehensible and ineffable, fill your inner person, and increase in you knowledge of her, implanting the mustard seed in good soil (Mark 4:31; Luke 8:8). (*Against Heresies* 1.13.2)

The fourth-century heresy-hunter Epiphanius went to great lengths to argue against a practice he saw as abnormal: "For it is told how some women there in Arabia from the region of Thrace, produced this empty-headed notion: they consecrate a kind of bread-loaf in the name of the ever-Virgin, they assemble together, and they try in the name of the holy Virgin to do something extraordinary, they attempt an unlawful and blasphemous deed: to perform in her name the sacred rites by women" (*Panarion* 78.23). In these two groups, the savior figure was seen as feminine—the female Grace and the ever-Virgin: Women looked to a female figure for salvation.

Epiphanius also reported the rituals of followers of Quintilla and Priscilla:

> They bring forward many groundless testimonies, giving hommage to Eve because she was the first to eat of the tree of knowledge. They also assert that the sister of Moses was a prophetess as a testimony for the women appointed by them to the clergy, and they also say that the four daughters of Philip used to prophesy. Often in their assembly seven virgins carrying lamps enter in, dressed in white no less, to prophesy to the people. By exhibiting some kind of inspira-

tion to the people present, they work deception and they bring it about that they all lament as leading toward the weeping for repentance, shedding tears and bewailing by their gestures human life. There are among them women bishops, women priests, and the rest. They say that it makes no difference, "for in Christ Jesus there is neither male nor female" (Gal. 3:28). (*Panarion* 49.2–6)

Here there are references to the heroines of the Hebrew Scriptures as well as to the female figures of the Christian Scriptures, such as Philip's daughters (Acts of the Apostles 21:8–9), and the description of the seven spirits that are before the throne of God in the Book of Revelation may have functioned as a model for their ritual procession (Revelation 1:4–5:20). In a society so concerned about separating men and women, we may wonder what other religious rituals arose among women.

The Male Norm

One theme that does emerge in this androcentric society, even in writings that seem to come from women, is that of the metamorphosis of a woman into a man. In the *Acts of Paul and Thecla,* Thecla, after enduring the trials imposed on her, "sewed her *chiton* into a cloak like a man's" and headed off in search of Paul (*Acts of Paul and Thecla* 40). In the one text we have from this period, most probably written by a woman, the diary of the martyr Vibia Perpetua who died in 202 in Carthage, Perpetua's final dream is that she has to fight against an Egyptian in the theater. As they prepare for the fight, "my clothes were stripped off, and suddenly I was a man." As such, she overcomes the Egyptian (*The Martyrdom of Saints Perpetua and Felicitas* 10). In the description of the martyrdom of Blandina at Lyons in Gaul in 177, Blandina also is transformed: "Now Blandina was hung on the gallows and placed as food for the wild beasts that were brought in. She hung in such a way that a cross-shape could be seen, and, by her vigorous prayer, she caused great eagerness in those who were contending, because in their conflict and with their outward eyes they saw by means of their sister the one who was crucified for them" (Eusebius *Ecclesiastical History* 5.1.41). When Blandina finally dies, the crowd acknowledges that never had a woman endured so many terrible sufferings.

This theme of the transformation of female into male—succinctly formulated in the Gospel of Thomas 114 that every female who will make herself male shall enter the kingdom of Heaven—becomes prominent in later lives and sayings of women saints. In the beautiful and chilling story of Pelagia the harlot, the former prostitute Pelagia disappears from sight, and soon afterward news is heard of a monk Pelagius who has shut himself up in a cell closed in on every side with but one little window in the wall through which to converse to visitors. His fame increases, but at his death when his body is to be anointed, it is discovered that Pelagius was indeed Pelagia. The people cry out, "Glory to You, Lord Christ, who have hidden many treasures on the earth, not only male, but also female" (PL 73.670). As the desert mother Sarah said, "In sex I am a woman, but not in mind." And she rebuked some of the brethren by saying, "It is I who am a man, you who are women" (PL 73.925). When Theodoret, bishop of Cyrrhus, was ending his *History of the Monks of Syria* in the mid-fifth century, he introduced three stories about women monastics this way: "After recording the way of life of the noblest men, I think it useful to mention also women who have wrestled no less, if not more. For they are worthy of still greater praise, since it fell to their lot to have a weaker nature, but they showed the same eagerness as the men and freed their sex from its ancestral disgrace" (29.1; PG 82.1489).

Even then women had to try harder. Theodoret was quite explicit that virtue is a quality of mind, not body: Nature does not separate "virtue into male and female nor divide the religious life into two species. For such a difference belongs to bodies, not to souls. 'For in Christ Jesus,' according to the divine apostle, 'there is neither male nor female'" (*History of the Monks of Syria* 30; PG 82.1493).

Women as Eve's Daughters

By the time of Theodoret, this distinction of equal in mind, different in body had become standard and fairly commonplace; it allowed church leaders to admit and to praise the exploits of women, while finding a way, because of their sex, to exclude them from public positions in the church. The misogynistic attitudes of most male Christian leaders have been well documented by Rosemary Ruether and Elizabeth Clark.[6] Tertullian revealed all of his inhibitions when he addressed a female audience: "*You* are the entrance for the Devil; *you* are the one who unsealed that tree; *you* are the first who abandoned the divine law; *you* are the one who persuaded him whom the Devil was not strong enough to attack; *you* easily shattered the image of God, the man Adam; on account of *your* punishment, that is, death, even the Son of God had to die" (*On the Dress of Women* 1.1.2).

Church leaders consistently harked back to the Genesis story to prove the rightness of the subjection of woman and her inferiority. As John Chrysostom preached to his congregation:

> After the sin he said, "Your recourse shall be toward your husband and he shall rule over you." God said, "I made you equal in honor. You did not use your authority well: change to a subordinate position. You have not borne your liberty: receive slavery. You do not know how to rule and you have shown it in your attempt at government: become one of the ruled and recognize your husband as lord." "Your recourse shall be toward your husband and he shall rule over you." Note God's kindness here. So that when she heard the words, "He shall rule over you," she might not think that the power of the master would be burdensome, God mentions solicitude first by saying, "Your recourse shall be toward your husband," that is, "He will be your refuge, your haven, and your se-

curity. In all the terrors that come upon you, I grant you permission to have recourse to him and to take refuge in him." God united them not only in this way but also by their natural needs, throwing around them the chain of sexual desire like some kind of unbreakable bond. You see how sin brought in subordination, but our ingenious and wise God turned even these to our advantage.

Hear how Paul also speaks of this subordination, so that you may learn again the harmony between the Old and the New Covenants. He says, "Let the woman learn in silence, in all subordination." Do you see how he also subordinates the woman to the man? But wait, and you will hear the reason. "In all subordination," for, he says, "I do not allow a woman to teach." Why? For she taught Adam wrongly once and for all. "Nor to have authority over the man." Why, do you suppose? For she used her authority wrongly once and for all. "But to be in silence." But tell the cause also. [Paul] says, "For Adam was not deceived, but the woman was deceived and sinned." Therefore he made her come down from the professor's chair. (*Discourse 4 on Genesis; PG* 54.594–595)

We may wonder how the women listening could have agreed that God had been so ingeniously wise in his kindness. What we can say is that those women who tried to speak out or to assume leadership positions were later denounced. When Jerome made a list of heretics, they were all surrounded by women:

Since this is so, what do they want, those unhappy foolish women laden with sins, who are whirled around by every wind of doctrine, always learning and never coming to the knowledge of the truth? Or what do those associates of the women want, men with itching ears who do not know what they hear, what they say, who take up the oldest filth as if it were a new mixture, who, according to Ezekiel, plaster a wall without a proper mixture and, when the shower of truth comes, disintegrate? Simon Magus founded his heresy with the help of the harlot Helena. Nicolas of Antioch, that inventor of all uncleanness, led bands of women. Marcion sent ahead a woman to Rome to prepare souls to be deceived by him. Apelles had Philumena as an associate of his teachings. Montanus, the preacher of an unclean spirit, corrupted many churches through Prisca and Maximilla, women well born and rich, first by gold and then he defiled them by heresy. I will leave ancient times and come to more recent events. Arius to deceive the world first deceived the Emperor's sister. Donatus was helped throughout Africa by the wealth of Lucilla so that he might defile many unhappy people by his foul water [of baptism]. (Letter 133.4)

Jerome, with his own entourage of rich patronesses, had to be careful not to identify association with women as a sign of heresy, but he came reasonably close. For Jerome, women were the means by which heretics deceived believing men.

We know little about these women. The few sayings that have come down to us of the Christian prophetesses Maximilla and Priscilla have been so selectively chosen and edited that it is virtually impossible to know how they functioned and what the sum of their Christian message was.[7] Hippolytus alleged that their followers thought that "they had learned more through [these women] than from the law, and the prophets, and the Gospels" and that they magnified these women above the apostles (*Refutation of All Heresies* 8.19.1). Behind such biased reporting we can glimpse the powerful personalities of these women.

In the west, Ambrose of Milan seems to have emphasized the weakness of women: "Because Eve herself confessed her fault, a milder and more beneficial sentence followed, which condemned her error but did not rule out forgiveness, so that directed toward her husband she might serve him. First, so that going astray would not please her; secondly, so that, placed under the stronger vessel, she might not lead along her husband, but she would rather be ruled by his advice" (*On Paradise* 14.72). Augustine had no doubt about the inferiority of women:

> If Adam were already spiritual (in mind, not in body), how could he have believed what was said by the serpent, namely, that God prohibited them to eat of the fruit of that tree because he knew that if they did so, they would become as gods because they would be able to distinguish between good and evil? As if the creator would refuse to his creature so great a good! It would be extraordinary if a man endowed with a spiritual mind could believe this. Or, since the man himself could not believe this, was a woman added for this purpose, a woman who would be of limited intelligence and who perhaps would still live according to the perception of the flesh and not according to the consciousness of the mind? And is this why the apostle Paul does not ascribe to her the image of God? For Paul speaks in this way: "The man ought not to cover his head, since he is the image and glory of God, but the woman is the glory of man"—not that the mind of a woman cannot receive the same image, since he tells us that in grace there is neither male nor female. (*Literal Commentary on Genesis* 11.42)

Augustine distinguished between women in the natural state, wherein they clearly have inferior status, and the women in the state of grace, wherein they can (miraculously?) be equal to men.

Women as Benefactors

Alongside this general condemnation of the female sex as such, however, we find male leaders praising individual women who overcame the "frailty" of their sex: Jerome and John Chrysostom wrote admiring letters to women who were their supporters and benefactors;[8] Gregory of Nyssa wrote a eulogy on his sister, Macrina. As Anne Yarbrough shows, there was a remarkable development of asceticism among Roman women in the fourth century.[9] We are fortunate to possess the work of an aristocratic Roman matron, Faltonia Betitia Proba, written about 360. A poem on the creation of the world and the life of Jesus, it is a literary tour de force as it is composed entirely from a combination of excerpts of verses from Virgil.[10] A remarkable family of consular rank produced such women as Melania the Elder and her granddaughter Melania the Younger. These upper-class women of enormous wealth, and Chrysostom's friend Olympias, were clearly the exception to what most women could do. Although they could not be public church officials, they supported their male friends. When some of those whom Melania the Elder admired were banished from Egypt, she followed them and ministered to them from her private wealth. She built a monastery in Jerusalem, and for thirty-seven years at her own expense she assisted churches, monasteries, guesthouses, and prisons (Palladius *Lausiac History* 118; PL 73.1200). Her granddaughter followed in her footsteps. Olympias, too, gave to John Chrysostom for his holy church

> ten thousand pounds of gold, twenty thousand of silver, and all the holdings in realty belonging to her which lay in the provinces of Thrace, Galatia, Cappadocia Prima, and Bithynia; still more, the houses which belonged to her in the capital city: the one nearby the most holy cathedral, which is called "the house of Olympias," with the tribunary and the fully equipped bath, and all the buildings attached to the bath as well as a mill; the house in which she used to stay that belonged to her near the public baths of Constantius; another house of hers called "the house of Evander"; and all her suburban properties. (*Life of Olympias* 5)

This did not exhaust her wealth: She built a monastery and supported John Chrysostom in his exile. As her biographer writes, "For no place, no country, no desert, no island, no frontier land remained without a share in the gifts of this famous woman, but she assisted the churches with sacred ornaments and helped those living alone and in community, the poor, the prisons, and those in exile; in a word, she scattered her alms over the whole inhabited world" (*Life of Olympias* 13).[11]

These remarkable women found an outlet for their tremendous energies and talents, as well as their immense wealth, in the freedom that the ascetic life offered to them. In an age in which there was great danger in childbearing and the husband had complete legal control over the wife, the ascetic life offered opportunities for freedom and authority unknown to a married woman.[12] The experiences of Melania the Younger on this point are quite interesting. Married quite young to a leading Roman, Pinian, she bore two children, who both died. At this, she decided to follow the example of her grandmother because she had come to such a hatred of marriage (Palladius *Lausiac History* 119; PL 73.1202).

Although the ascetic life offered some individuals freedom, Elizabeth Castelli rightly points out that it theoretically still kept women second-class citizens.[13] Women could support male leaders financially, and they could lead outstanding lives and so influence by example, but they could not be public leaders or officiate in the public liturgy. They had a very definite place in Christian society, held to be naturally subordinate to males.

THE FEMININE GOD

The preceding two chapters discussed how Christians articulated their view of the divine world and its interaction with the human world through the mediation of the God-man, Jesus Christ. What is remarkable about this articulation are the options not explored. Although in so many other religions of the Mediterranean world a triad of divine persons was often seen in family terms—father, mother, son—male Christian theologians, except for the Gnostics, were silent about a father and mother generating a son and described rather a motherless Word. It is extremely risky to attempt to correlate any connection between the gender of the priest/priestess and that of the god/goddess, but we cannot help wondering what the Christian worldview would have been if women had been leaders in the Christian communities. If Christians in North Africa had been more attuned to the feminine in religion, would they have been less likely to agree with Augustine that a baby is a sinner, perhaps more likely to insist on the bringing of children into the kingdom of God? Would they have interpreted Genesis 2–3 differently from Augustine? Is it no accident that Augustine of Hippo, with his checkered sexual past, had located the first evidence of human's sinful condition in Adam's inability to control the erection of his penis—"so that whatever causes shame in that disobedience of the members about which those who after their sin covered these members with the fig tree leaves blushed with shame" (*On Grace and on Original Sin* 2.39; see also 2.41)—while his opponent, Julian of Eclanum, had had a happy married life? Although Augustine argued strenuously that marriage is not evil, he still did not give it a ringing recommendation—celibacy is clearly better. If women had been leaders in the Christian communities, it probably would have been harder for a rapprochement between Christians and the ruling class to have taken place, for a women-led movement would have appeared radical and subversive.

This is not to say simply that if there had been more women leaders in the Christian movement, things would have been different. Besides the fact that we have so little data, the very complexity of the notion of gender itself prohibits certainty; educational, social, economic, and even ecological factors enter into the social construction of gender. Some women were extreme ascetics, and the perils of birthing in late antiquity were real and imminent and might have encouraged women to renounce marriage and adopt a stance against procreation. The point is to suggest options not taken in the Christian articulation of the divine and remember that the discussions and debates that led to the formulation of a Christian worldview were done by male Christian leaders.

Yet even in such a male-dominated society that had but one masculine deity, even if three-personed, images of the feminine were still used to describe how this God interacts with humans.[14] Clement of Alexandria stated, "God

Himself is love; and through love he became feminine/was seen by us. Insofar as He is ineffable He is Father; insofar as he has compassion toward us He became Mother. The Father by loving became feminine; and the great sign of this is He whom He begot of Himself; and the fruit brought forth by love is love" (*The Salvation of the Rich Man* 37). Note the difficulty in the first sentence: Should the translation be "was seen," as the majority of manuscripts read, or "became feminine"? I suspect that the latter was the more original and that later editors were unhappy with this formulation and changed the word.

Clement spent a long time defending the image of Christians as children who feed on the milk of Christ (*Christ the Educator* 1.6), and in the concluding hymn of this treatise wrote, "O Jesus Christ, heavenly milk from the sweet breasts of the bride, expressed from the favors of your wisdom, the infants, reared with tender lips, are filled with the tender spirit from the nipple of the Word" (3.12.101; GCS 12.292). Ephrem of Edessa also used this imagery of God. In hymns on the nativity, Ephrem wrote, "He was exalted, yet He sucked the milk of Mary, and all creatures suck of His goodness, i.e., He is the Breast of Life which is the Breath of Life; the dead suck from His life and live. ... When indeed he was sucking the milk of Mary, He was suckling life to all. When he was lying on His mother's bosom, in His bosom all creatures were lying" (Hymn 4.149–154). "The Baby that I bear bears me, says Mary" (Hymn 17.1).[15] For Augustine, God is both father and mother to the children of God. In commenting on Psalm 27:10 (in the Latin translation Psalm 26:18), Augustine wrote, "*Because my father and my mother have forsaken me.* He made himself a child to God; he made him father, he made him mother. A father because he put together, because he calls, because he orders, because he rules; a mother because he caresses, because he nourishes, because he gives milk, because he embraces. *My father and my mother have forsaken me; but the Lord has taken me up* both to rule and to nourish" (*Enarratio in Ps.* 26.2.18; CCL 38.164).

Such feminine imagery of the divine is certainly drawn from the richness of the Hebrew Scriptures. In Isaiah 49:15, in response to a complaint that the Lord has forsaken Zion, the prophet has God declare, "Can a woman forget her sucking child, that she should have no compassion on the son of her womb? Even these may forget, yet I will not forget you." The figure of Wisdom as developed in the later Jewish writings is a feminine figure, "the mother of fair love" (Sirach 24:24), whose delight it is to play with the children of men (Prov. 8:31). Christ is identified with such a figure in the Christian Scriptures, as, for example, at 1 Corinthians 1:30, and 1 Peter 2:2 urges its readers to long, like newborn babes, for pure spiritual milk. The continued use of such imagery in the early Church thus derives from its use in the Bible but still does not explain why such imagery remained important. Much still has to be done in analyzing why particular male church leaders used such language.[16] Somehow, for the early Christian male leaders to talk of a loving, caring God, they had to use feminine language about that God; that God has to be feminine. Kari Børresen shows how this language of woman as mother in fact perpetuates the stereotypes of a male-dominated society,[17] as exemplified in the preceding quotation from Augustine where the male role is to rule, the female to nourish. Yet even in such a culture, if the divinity is truly to be a divinity for humans, it must in some way reflect the characteristics of all humans, that is, both male and female. Such a view is, of course, to turn around the saying of Paul that in Christ Jesus there is "neither male nor female" (Gal. 3:28) and to assert that the Christian God must be both male and female.

Suggestions for Further Reading

Clark, Elizabeth A. *Ascetic Piety and Women's Faith: Essays on Late Ancient Christianity.* Lewiston, N.Y.: Mellen, 1986.

_____. *Jerome, Chrysostom, and Friends: Essays and Translations.* New York: Mellen, 1979.

_____. *Women in the Early Church.* Wilmington, Dela.: Glazier, 1983.

Kraemer, Ross Shepard. *Her Share of the Blessings: Women's Religions Among Pagans, Jews, and Christians in the Greco-Roman World.* New York: Oxford University Press, 1992.

_____. *Maenads, Martyrs, Matrons, Monastics: Sourcebook on Women's Religions in the Greco-Roman World.* Philadelphia: Fortress, 1988.

Torjesen, Karen Jo. *When Women Were Priests.* San Francisco: Harper, 1993.

Conclusion

THIS BOOK HAS EXPLORED THE BIRTH of a worldview and how this worldview differentiated itself from its forebears. The spectrum of positions that could be included under the umbrella called Christianity was as wide then as it is today; there was no *one* Christian answer to questions of sex, of how to deal with governments, of who should be Christian ministers. But by the end of the fourth century, the Christians had their own public meeting places with their own rituals and observances and their own hierarchical organization, their own canon of holy writings, their own history, with its heroes the martyrs as well as the appropriated history of the Hebrew Scriptures. But some themes emerged that dominated the later history of Christianity as well as raised questions that remain troubling today.

Although some monks in Egypt in the late 390s may have roused a ruckus and railed against their bishop for teaching that God is incorporeal, Augustine of Hippo in his *Confessions* related his spiritual journey as a movement from believing that nothing can exist except bodies to a realization that God and the mind are not corporeal but spiritual substances. Augustine attributed this shift to his reading of some of the Platonists, presumably Plotinus and Porphyry. Augustine articulated what was the mainstream theological position of Christianity—that is, that there is a division in humans between mind and body that has its macrocosmic analog in the division between creator and created. The leaders of the Christian church were clearly influenced in this regard by their classical education. Yet as we saw in Chapter 5, they also rejected any attempt to minimize the gulf between creator and creature, to posit an intermediary figure below God but above creatures. The relationships among Father, Son, and Holy Spirit were to be internal to the deity, not external; yet the created world was to be redeemed as the body was to be resurrected.

The most distinctive feature of early Christianity was the role of its founder Jesus as the new Adam. He ushers in a new creation, and so this present realm must be seen as flawed and in need of change. Such an attitude can lead to total rejection of this world, to attempts to leave it by voluntary martyrdom, to denunciations of sexual intercourse as epitomizing the continuation of this world. In all this discussion of worldview, I have noted how frequently the text of Genesis 1–3 was used as a springboard for Christian reflection. It emerged in the debate over whether the Christian God was to be identified with the God of Genesis as well as in the question of how a good god could have allowed a world in which there is suffering. The Hebrew Scriptures could not be, and were not, ignored in the articulation of the Christian worldview; indeed they were highly influential in the formulation of such a worldview. The image of Christianity as a new creation was a powerful one and was honed to explain the Christian's relationship to the divine world, to this created world, and to its history.

These ideas were hammered out in the midst of a thriving Mediterranean community. The great eastern church leader Basil of Caesarea had listened to the lectures of the pagan rhetor Libanius in Constantinople, had spent five years studying in Athens under Platonic philosophers, and was friends in Caesarea with the pagan philosophers Eustathius and Maximus. Augustine came across the works of the Platonists because he was one of a budding circle of intellectuals eager to read the newly translated Plotinus. Christians attended the games and the gladiatorial spectacles as well as the civic festivities. In many towns Jews and Christians rubbed shoulders; for example, in Antioch Christians attended the celebrations of Rosh Hashanah and Sukkoth. Christianity defined itself in a pluralistic world, and its self-definition must be seen in terms of what groups Christians were distancing themselves from. Much changed in the fifth and sixth centuries. As Augustine lay dying, the Vandals were besieging Hippo. In the west, the barbarian invasions brought about the erosion of the educational system. In the eastern empire, the Academy at Athens, the last center of pagan intellectual life, was closed in 529 and adherents of paganism forced underground. Even though Homer, Plato, and Aristotle would continue to be read in the east, there was no longer an ongoing debate with a vital pagan intellectual life. The exclusion of pagans from municipal offices and positions in the imperial bureaucracy[1] as well as the increasing legislation against the Jews rapidly placed Christianity in a position of dominance vis-à-vis its former rivals. Positions that had been staked out in lively contest now reigned without opposition. The words of John Chrysostom spoken originally against a Judaism of equal strength could become instruments of oppression against a weak minority. As the world changed, so, too, did the Christians.

The worldview the Christians had forged for themselves in these early centuries was not challenged. Only when new ways of reading the Bible emerged in the eighteenth century,[2] only when the theory of evolution questioned the origin of humanity and when the notion of a cosmos as a closed unity was replaced by that of an expanding universe billions of years old, and only when the Christian religion was once again confronted with strong, vital "pagan" religious traditions in Africa, India, and elsewhere would the fundamental Christian view of the structure of the world require new paradigms and the reason for injustice and suffering, new answers.

Abbreviations

ANRW	*Aufstieg und Niedergang der römischen Welt,* ed. W. Haase and H. Temporini (Berlin: de Gruyter, 1972–)
CCL	*Corpus Christianorum,* Series Latina (Turnhout: Brepols, 1953–)
CJust	Codex Justinianus
CSEL	*Corpus Scriptorum Ecclesiasticorum Latinorum* (Vienna: Gerodi, etc., 1866–)
CTheod	Codex Theodosianus
GCS	*Die Griechischen Christlichen Schriftsteller der ersten drei Jahrhunderte* (Leipzig: Hinrichs, 1899–)
LCL	Loeb Classical Library
PG	*Patrologia Graeca,* ed. Jacques-Paul Migne (Paris: Migne, 1857–1866)
PL	*Patrologia Latina,* ed. Jacques-Paul Migne (Paris: Migne, 1844–1865)
PS	*Patrologia Syriaca* (Paris: Fermin-Didot, 1894–)

Notes

Introduction

1. Smart, *Worldviews.*
2. Brown, *The Body and Society;* Clark, *The Origenist Controversy.*
3. Newman, *An Essay on the Development of Christian Doctrine;* Pelikan, *The Emergence of the Catholic Tradition.*
4. Geertz, *The Interpretation of Cultures,* pp. 90, 98–188.
5. Fox, *Pagans and Christians,* pp. 214–241.
6. See Doran, *The Lives of Simeon Stylites.*

Chapter 1

1. Musurillo, *The Acts of the Christian Martyrs,* pp. 86–89.
2. The classic discussion remains de Sainte-Croix, "Why Were the Early Christians Persecuted?"
3. See the collection of documents in Swift, *The Early Fathers;* and Helgeland, "Christians in the Roman Army."
4. See Grabar, *Early Christian Art.*
5. Fox, *Pagans and Christians,* pp. 265–335, 585–592.
6. Frend, *The Rise of Christianity,* pp. 440–463.
7. An excellent bibliography is Barnes, *Constantine and Eusebius.*
8. See also the instructions given for the building of the Holy Sepulchre Church in Jerusalem at 3.31.
9. A translation is found in Rusch, *The Trinitarian Controversy,* pp. 57–60.
10. In *The Fathers of the Church* 26, it is Letter 60. In the numbering of the *Nicene and Post-Nicene Fathers,* it is Letter 20.19.
11. Letter 2 in *The Fathers of the Church* 26; Letter 40 in *Nicene and Post-Nicene Fathers.*
12. Letter 41 in *Nicene and Post-Nicene Fathers;* Letter 62 in *The Fathers of the Church.*
13. Letter 51 in *Nicene and Post-Nicene Fathers;* Letter 3 in *Fathers of the Church.*
14. The text translated is that edited by Ziegler, *Iuli firmici materni.*
15. In *Nicene and Post-Nicene Fathers* 4.21.
16. An older translation is found in *Nicene and Post-Nicene Fathers* 20.414–417.
17. Letter 17.13 in *Nicene and Post-Nicene Fathers;* Letter 7 in *Fathers of the Church.*
18. Letter 18.8 in *Nicene and Post-Nicene Fathers;* Letter 8 in *Fathers of the Church.*
19. See the discussion in Fowden, "Bishops and Temples," p. 70.

20. The Donatist schism broke out in North Africa after the persecutions of 303–305 and divided the African church through the fourth and early fifth centuries. The schism arose from the question of how those who had lapsed during the persecution were to be treated.

21. Markus, *Saeculum,* pp. 133–153.

22. Ibid., p. 43.

23. Ibid., p. 125.

24. This is most sensitively portrayed in Brown, *Augustine of Hippo,* particularly in c.17.

25. Markus, *Saeculum,* p. 71.

26. Brown, *Augustine of Hippo,* p. 324.

Chapter 2

1. See the comments on Frag. 12 by Robinson in Heraclitus, *Fragments.* See also Frags. 30.31a, b., 49a, 84a, 91a.

2. See also *Theaetetus* 160d; Aristotle *Metaphysics* 3.1010a14.

3. The fragments have been edited by Gallop: Parmenides of Elea, *Fragments.*

4. The theory of Xenocrates is found in a discussion in one of Plutarch's dialogues, *On the Obsolescence of Oracles* 416C–E.

5. The text is found in Calcidius's commentary on Plato *Timaeus* c299. I have used the edition of the fragments edited by des Places: Numenius, *Fragments,* p. 98 (Frag. 52).

6. See Dillon, *The Middle Platonists,* p. 46.

7. Armstong, "Plotinus," p. 243.

8. Ibid., p. 223.

9. Brashler and Dirkse, "The Prayer of Thanksgiving."

10. This text forms part of what is called the Hermetic corpus. The texts are edited and brilliantly commented on by Festugière, *La revelation d'Hermes Trismegiste.* A stimulating recent study is that of Fowden, *The Egyptian Hermes.*

11. This topic has been thoroughly explored by Wilken, *The Christians as the Romans Saw Them.*

12. I have used the edition by Helmreich: Galen, *De usu partium.* I have indicated the page in Helmreich's text. The fragments of Galen on Jews and Christians have been collected by Walzer, *Galen on Jews and Christians.*

13. Again, this writing of Porphyry is known only because cited by the Christian Augustine in order to refute it (Letter 102.8). The power of Porphyry's argument can be grasped from the fact that Augustine wrote to refute it one hundred years after Porphyry's death.

Chapter 3

1. See the description in Sanders, *Judaism.*

2. Archaeological and inscription evidence is conveniently gathered together by Millar, "Judaism in the Diaspora," vol. 3, part 1, pp. 1–86.

3. For a full discussion, see Kraeling, *The Synagogue.*

4. Just exactly what these terms mean is a vexed question. See the discussion and bibliography in Schürer, *The History of the Jewish People,* vol. 3, part 1, pp. 150–176.

5. See the discussion in Stern, *Greek and Latin Authors,* vol. 2, pp. 349–353.
6. See ibid., vol. 2, p. 110.
7. Petigliani, "A Rare Look."
8. Brooten, *Women Leaders in the Ancient Synagogues;* Kraemer, *Her Share of the Blessings,* pp. 93–127.
9. Meeks, *The Moral World of the First Christians,* p. 83.
10. This legislation has been conveniently collected by Linder, *The Jews in Roman Imperial Legislation.*
11. Bachrach, "The Jewish Community," p. 402.
12. See Jones, *The Later Roman Empire,* vol. 2, p. 738.
13. Ibid., vol. 2, p. 748.
14. Bachrach, "The Jewish Community," p. 421.
15. See Avi-Yonah, *The Jews Under Roman and Byzantine Rule,* pp. 198–204.

Chapter 4

1. A classic expression of this remains Berger and Luckmann, *The Social Construction of Reality.* An excellent application to early Christianity is Meeks, *The Moral World of the First Christians.*
2. Testimonies to these groups are conveniently collected in Klijn and Reinink, *Patristic Evidence for Jewish-Christian Sects.*
3. See Drijvers, "Marcionism in Syria."
4. I have used the translation of Layton, *The Gnostic Scriptures.*
5. The intimacy of the teacher-pupil relationship has been explored by Neymeyr, *Die christlichen Lehrer in zweiten Jahrhundert;* and Valantasis, *Spiritual Guides of the Third Century.*
6. Kraeling, *The Christian Building.* On the whole question of the meeting places of early Christians, see the excellent study by White, *Building God's House in the Roman World.*
7. Layton, *The Gnostic Scriptures,* p. 267.
8. Layton, *The Gnostic Scriptures,* pp. 234–235 (Frag. C).
9. I have used the translation found in Walzer, *Galen on Jews and Christians,* p. 15.
10. Brown, *The Body and Society,* p. 6.
11. Fox, *Pagans and Christians,* pp. 373–374.
12. This section of the *Acts of Peter* is quoted in the letter of Ps. Titus *De dispositione sanctimonii,* and is found on p. 50 of the edition by de Bruyne, "Epistula titi."

Chapter 5

1. See the discussion of Celsus in Chapter 2.
2. Williams, *Arius,* pp. 121–122.
3. Ibid., pp. 134–135.
4. Ibid., p. 143.
5. See the full discussion of this debate in Clark, *The Origenist Controversy.*
6. MacMullen, *Changes in the Roman Empire,* p. 275.
7. Williams, *Arius.*
8. Hanson, *The Search,* p. 9.

9. The text is found in Gelasius, *History of the Council of Nicea* 3; PG 85.1348C. Hanson, *The Search*, p. 9.

10. Hanson, *The Search*, p. 112.

11. *Homily* 22.3, as found in Richard, *Asterii sophistae.*

12. From the letter of Auxentius, found in the scholia to the Council of Aquileia. I have translated the text as found in CCL 87.160.

13. See the discussion in Williams, *Arius,* pp. 215–229, on the philosophic background for the rejection by Arius of the notion of the Son's participation in the Father.

14. See ibid., pp. 181–198, on the notion of time before creation.

15. Hanson, *The Search*, pp. 181–202, esp. pp. 184–185.

16. Ibid., p. 424.

17. Stead, *Divine Substance,* pp. 260–261.

18. Hanson, *The Search*, p. 441.

19. Ibid., p. 426.

20. See Hanson, *The Search*, pp. 287–288.

21. Ibid., p. 292.

22. Hanson, *The Search*, pp. 690–691.

23. The translation is by Fitzgerald: Homer, *The Odyssey*, pp. 4–7.

24. I have translated the text in the edition of Bonnet, *Acta apostolorum apocrypha* 2.1, a reprint of the original edition of 1898.

25. See Brown, *The Community of the Beloved Disciple.*

26. The fragments are collected in Lietzmann, *Apollinaris von Laodicea und seine Schule.*

27. Letter to the bishops of Diocaesarea II (Lietzmann) 256; dated ca. 375.

28. "Favor" translates *eudokia* (cf. Luke 2:14). The last phrase "a good opinion" (*eu dokein*) plays on this word.

29. Brown, "The Rise and Function of the Holy Man," p. 100. See also Brown, *The Making of Late Antiquity.*

Chapter 6

1. Rudolph, *Gnosis,* pp. 91–92.

2. See Louth, "Messalianism and Pelagianism."

3. For a full account of their history, see Lieu, *Manichaeism.*

4. For a full discussion of this literature, see Collins, *The Apocalyptic Imagination.*

5. See Clark, *The Origenist Controversy.*

6. See the edition of these baptismal homilies in Chrysostome, *Huit catecheses baptismales inedites.*

7. Frend, *The Rise of Christianity,* p. 347.

8. Brown, *The Body and Society,* p. 20.

9. See ibid., pp. 346–347.

10. On Cyprian, see Letter 64.5 (CSEL 3.2.720–721); on Ambrose, see *On Paradise* 6.31 (CSEL 32.1.288), and *On Abraham* 2.11.84 (CSEL 32.1.635); on Ambrosiaster, see *Questions on the Old and New Testament* 81a (PL 35.2278).

11. Brown, *Augustine of Hippo,* p. 148.

12. Clark, *Ascetic Piety and Women's Faith,* pp. 353–385.

13. Brown, *The Body and Society,* pp. 358–359.

14. There the number given is 14 in the letters outside the collection; in the *Nicene and Post-Nicene Fathers* the letter is found as 63, and the quotation is from 63.13–14.

15. Brown, *The Body and Society,* 377, quoting *Against Jovinian* 1.13, 15, 34.

16. Clark, *Ascetic Piety and Women's Faith,* pp. 370–371.

17. In his *Retractions,* Augustine wrote concerning this question, "Then I did not know, and I do not know now" (*Retract* 1.1.3). See Preuss, *Eloquence and Ignorance.* Jerome also slowly began to see the problems involved in this question. See Clark, *The Origenist Controversy,* pp. 222–223.

Chapter 7

1. See MacDonald, *The Legend and the Apostle.*

2. As translated in Robinson, *The Nag Hammadi Library,* p. 473.

3. An English translation is found in Stevenson, *A New Eusebius,* pp. 287–289.

4. *Didascalia apostolorum* 3. The Syriac text is found in Lagarde, *Didascalia apostolorum,* p. 9; the Latin text is in Connoly, *Didascalia apostolorum,* p. 27.

5. Otranto, "Notes on the Female Priesthood"; quoted in Rossi, "Priesthood, Precedent, and Prejudice," pp. 80–88.

6. Ruether, "Misogynism and Virginal Feminism"; Clark, *Women in the Early Church.*

7. These sayings can be found collected in the excellent sourcebook by Kraemer, *Maenads, Martyrs, Matrons, Monastics,* pp. 224–230.

8. Clark, *Jerome, Chrysostom, and Friends.*

9. Yarbrough, "Christianization in the Fourth Century."

10. Clark and Hatch, *The Golden Bough, the Oaken Cross.*

11. I have translated the text as edited by Malingrey: Jean Chrysostome, *Lettres a Olympias.*

12. See Ruether, "Mothers of the Church"; Clark, *Ascetic Piety and Women's Faith,* pp. 175–208; and Kraemer, "The Conversion of Women."

13. Castelli, "Virginity and Its Meaning."

14. A fuller discussion of this issue is found in Bradley, "Patristic Background of the Motherhood Similitude"; and Børresen, "L'Usage patristique."

15. I have translated the text from the edition of Beck, *Des heiligen Ephraem des Syrers.* In *The Nicene and Post-Nicene Fathers* the hymns are numbered 3 and 12, respectively.

16. The model for such work is that done on Cistercian monastic use of the imagery by Bynum, *Jesus as Mother.*

17. Børresen, "L'Usage patristique," pp. 206, 217–219.

Conclusion

1. CTheod 16.5.42 (on November 14, 408); CTheod 16.10.21 (on December 7, 416).

2. See Frei, *The Eclipse of Biblical Narrative.*

Bibliography

Armstrong, Arthur H. "Plotinus." In *The Cambridge History of Later Greek and Early Medieval Philosophy*. London: Cambridge University Press, 1967.

———. ed. *The Cambridge History of Later Greek and Early Medieval Philosophy*. Cambridge: Cambridge University Press, 1967.

———. *Classical Mediterranean Spirituality: Egyptian, Greek, Roman*. New York: Crossroad, 1986.

Avi-Yonah, Michael. *The Jews Under Roman and Byzantine Rule*. New York: Schocken, 1976.

Bachrach, Bernard S. "The Jewish Community of the Later Roman Empire as Seen in the *Codex Theodonaius*." In *"To See Ourselves as Others See Us": Christians, Jews, and "Others" in Later Antiquity*, ed. Jacob Neusner and Ernest S. Frerichs. Chico, Calif.: Scholars, 1985.

Barnes, Timothy D. *Constantine and Eusebius*. Cambridge, Mass.: Harvard University Press, 1981.

———. *Early Christianity and the Roman Empire*. London: Variorum, 1984.

Beck, Edmund. *Des heiligen Ephraem des Syrers Hymnen de Nativitate*. Louvain: Secretariat du Corpus SCO, 1959.

Berger, Peter L., and Thomas Luckmann. *The Social Construction of Reality: A Treatise in the Sociology of Knowledge*. Garden City, N.Y.: Doubleday, 1966.

Blumenthal, Henry J., and Robert A. Markus. *Neoplatonism and Early Christian Thought: Essays in Honour of A. H. Armstrong*. London: Variorum, 1981.

Bonnet, Maximilian. *Acta apostolorum apocrypha*. Hildesheim: Olms, 1959.

Børresen, Kari Elisabeth. "L'Usage patristique de metaphores feminines dans le discourse de Dieu." *Revue théologique de Louvain* 13 (1982): 205–220.

Bradley, Ritamary. "Patristic Background of the Motherhood Similitude in Julian of Norwich." *Christian Scholar's Review* 8 (1978): 101–113.

Brashler, James, and Peter A. Dirkse, trans. "The Prayer of Thanksgiving." In *The Nag Hammadi Library*, ed. James. M. Robinson. San Francisco: Harper and Row, 1977.

Brooten, Bernadette J. *Women Leaders in the Ancient Synagogues*. Chico, Calif.: Scholars, 1972.

Brown, Peter R. L. *Augustine of Hippo*. Berkeley and Los Angeles: University of California Press, 1967.

———. *The Body and Society: Men, Women, and Sexual Renunciation in Early Christianity*. New York: Columbia University Press, 1988.

———. *The Making of Late Antiquity*. Cambridge, Mass.: Harvard University Press, 1978.

———. *Power and Persuasion in Late Antiquity: Towards a Christian Empire*. Madison: University of Wisconsin Press, 1992.

_____. *Religion and Society in the Age of Saint Augustine.* New York: Harper, 1972.
_____. "The Rise and Function of the Holy Man in Late Antiquity." *Journal of Roman Studies* 51 (1971): 80–101.
_____. *The World of Late Antiquity, A.D. 150–750.* New York: Harcourt Brace Jovanovich, 1971.
Brown, Raymond. *The Community of the Beloved Disciple.* New York: Paulist, 1979.
Bynum, Caroline Walker. *Jesus as Mother: Studies in the Spirituality of the High Middle Ages.* Berkeley and Los Angeles: University of California Press, 1982.
Cadoux, Cecil John. *The Early Church and the World.* Edinburgh: Clark, 1925.
Castelli, Elizabeth. "Virginity and Its Meaning for Women's Sexuality in Early Christianity." *Journal of Feminist Studies in Religion* 2 (1982): 61–88.
Chrysostome, Jean. *Huit catécheses baptismales inedites.* Edited by Antoine Wenger. Paris: du Cerf. 1957.
_____. *Lettres à Olympias et vie anonyme d'Olympias.* Edited by Anne-Marie Malingrey. Sources Chrétiennes 13bis. Paris: du Cerf, 1968.
Clark, Elizabeth A., *Ascetic Piety and Women's Faith: Essays on Late Ancient Christianity.* Lewiston, N.Y.: Mellen, 1986.
_____. *Jerome, Chrysostom, and Friends: Essays and Translations.* New York: Mellen, 1979.
_____. *The Origenist Controversy: The Cultural Construction of an Early Christian Debate.* Princeton: Princeton University Press, 1992.
_____. *Women in the Early Church.* Wilmington, Dela.: Glazier, 1983.
Clark Elizabeth A., and Diane F. Hatch. *The Golden Bough, the Oaken Cross: The Virgilian Canto of Faltonia Betitia Proba.* Chico, Calif.: Scholars, 1981.
Collins, John J. *The Apocalyptic Imagination.* New York: Crossroad, 1989.
Connoly, R. Hugh. *Didascalia apostolorum.* Oxford: Clarendon, 1929.
De Bruyne, Donatien. "Epistula titi, discipuli Pauli, de dispositione sanctimonii." *Revue Benedictine* 37 (1925): 47–72.
De Sainte-Croix, Geoffrey Ernest Maurice. "Why Were the Early Christians Persecuted?" *Past and Present* 26 (1963): 6–38.
Dillon, John. *The Middle Platonists: 80 B.C. to A.D. 220.* Ithaca: Cornell University Press, 1977.
Doran, Robert. *The Lives of Simeon Stylites.* Kalamazoo, Mich.: Cistercian, 1992.
Drijvers, Hans J.W. "Marcionism in Syria: Principles, Problems, Polemics." *Second Century* 6 (1987–1988): 153–172.
Droge, Arthur J. *Homer or Moses? Early Christian Interpretation of the History of Culture.* Tübingen: Mohr, 1989.
Feldman, Louis H. *Jew and Gentile in the Ancient World: Attitudes and Interactions from Alexander to Justinian.* Princeton: Princeton University Press, 1993.
Festugière, Andre Jean. *La révélation d'Hermes Trismegeste.* 4 vols. Paris: Lecoffre, 1944–1954.
Fowden, Garth. "Bishops and Temples in the Eastern Roman Empire, A.D. 320–435." *Journal of Theological Studies* 29 (1978): 53–78.
_____. *The Egyptian Hermes: A Historical Approach to the Late Pagan Mind.* Cambridge: Cambridge University Press, 1986.
Fox, Robin Lane. *Pagans and Christians.* New York: Knopf, 1987.

Frei, Hans. *The Eclipse of Biblical Narrative: A Study in Eighteenth and Nineteenth Century Hermeneutics.* New Haven: Yale University Press, 1974.

Frend, W.H.C. *Martyrdom and Persecution in the Early Church.* Oxford: Blackwell, 1965.

_____. *The Rise of Christianity.* Philadelphia: Westminster. 1987.

Gager, John G. *The Origins of Anti-Semitism: Attitudes Toward Judaism in Pagan and Christian Antiquity.* New York: Oxford University Press, 1983.

Galen. *De usu partium.* Edited by Georg Helmreich. Leipzig: Teubner, 1907–1909.

Geertz, Clifford. *The Interpretation of Cultures.* New York: Basic, 1973.

Goodenough, Erwin R. *Jewish Symbols in the Greco-Roman Period.* 13 vols. New York: Pantheon, 1953–1968.

Grabar, Andre. *Early Christian Art.* New York: Odyssey, 1968.

Grant, Robert McQueen. *Gods and the One God.* Philadelphia: Westminster, 1986.

Greer, Rowan A., and James L. Kugel. *Early Biblical Interpretation.* Philadelphia: Westminster, 1986.

Gregg, Robert C., and Dennis E. Groh. *Early Arianism: A View of Salvation.* Philadelphia: Fortress, 1981.

Hanson, Richard Patrick Crosland. *The Search for the Christian Doctrine of God.* Edinburgh: Clark, 1988.

Helgeland, John. "Christians in the Roman Army, A.D. 173–337." *ANRW* 2.23.1, 724–834.

Heraclitus. *Fragments: A Text and Translation with a Commentary by T. M. Robinson.* Toronto: University of Toronto Press, 1987.

Homer. *The Odyssey.* Translated by Robert Fitzgerald. Garden City, N.Y.: Doubleday, 1963.

Jones, Arnold Hugh Martin. *The Later Roman Empire, 284–602.* Oxford: Blackwell, 1964.

Kannengiesser, Charles. *Arius and Athanasius: Two Alexandrian Theologians.* Brookfield, Vt.: Gower, 1991.

Kannengiesser, Charles, and William L. Petersen. *Origen of Alexandria: His World and His Legacy.* Notre Dame, Ind.: University of Notre Dame Press, 1988.

Kelly, John Norman Davidson. *Early Christian Creeds.* London: Longman, 1972.

_____. *Early Christian Doctrines.* San Francisco: Harper and Row, 1978.

Klijn, Albertus Frederik Johannes, and G. J. Reinink. *Patristic Evidence for Jewish-Christian Sects.* Leiden: Brill, 1973.

Kraeling, Carl Hermann. *The Synagogue.* New York: Ktav, 1979.

_____. *The Christian Building.* New Haven: Dura-Europos Publications, 1967.

Kraemer, Ross S. "The Conversion of Women to Ascetic Forms of Christianity." *Signs* 6 (1980–1981): 298–307.

_____. *Her Share of the Blessings: Women's Religions Among Pagans, Jews, and Christians in the Greco-Roman World.* New York: Oxford University Press, 1992.

_____. *Maenads, Martyrs, Matrons, Monastics: Sourcebook on Women's Religions in the Greco-Roman World.* Philadelphia: Fortress, 1988.

Lagarde, Paul de. *Didascalia apostolorum.* Göttingen: Becker and Eidner, 1911.

Layton, Bentley. *The Gnostic Scriptures.* Garden City, N.Y.: Doubleday, 1987.

Lietzmann, Hans. *Apollinaris von Laodicea und seine Schule.* Tübingen: Mohr, 1904.

Lieu, Samuel N.C. *Manichaeism in the Later Roman Empire and Medieval China: A Historical Survey.* Manchester: Manchester University Press, 1985.

Linder, Amnon. *The Jews in Roman Imperial Legislation.* Detroit: Wayne State University Press, 1987.

Long, Anthony A., and David N. Sedley. *The Hellenistic Philosophers.* Cambridge: Cambridge University Press, 1987.

Louth, Andrew. "Messalianism and Pelagianism." *Studia Patristica* 17 (1982): 127–135.

MacDonald, Dennis R. *The Legend and the Apostle: The Battle for Paul in Story and Canon.* Philadelphia: Westminster, 1983.

MacMullen, Ramsey. *Changes in the Roman Empire.* Princeton: Princeton University Press, 1990.

Markus, Robert A. *Saeculum: History and Society in the Theology of St. Augustine.* Cambridge: Cambridge University Press, 1988.

Meeks, Wayne A. *The Moral World of the First Christians.* Philadelphia: Westminster, 1980.

Millar, Fergus. "Judaism in the Diaspora: Gentiles and Judaism." In *The History of the Jewish People in the Age of Jesus Christ (175 B.C.–A.D.135)*, by Emil Schürer. Rev. ed. 3 vols. in 4. Edinburgh: Clark, 1973–1987.

Musurillo, Herbert. *The Acts of the Christian Martyrs.* Oxford: Clarendon, 1972.

Neusner, Jacob, and Ernest S. Frerichs. *"To See Ourselves as Others See Us": Christians, Jews, and "Others" in Late Antiquity.* Chico, Calif.: Scholars, 1985.

Newman, John Henry. *An Essay on the Development of Christian Doctrine.* London: Pickering, 1881.

Neymayr, Ulrich. *Die christlichen Lehrer in zweiten Jahrhundert.* Leiden: Brill, 1981.

Numenius. *Fragments.* Edited by E. des Places. Paris: Les Belles Lettres, 1973.

Pagels, Elaine H. *Adam, Eve, and the Serpent.* New York: Vintage, 1989.

Parmenides of Elea. *Fragments: A Text and Translation with an Introduction by David Gallop.* Toronto: University of Toronto Press, 1984.

Pelikan, Jaroslav J. *The Christian Tradition: A History of the Development of Doctrine. Vol. I, The Emergence of the Catholic Tradition (100–600).* Chicago: University of Chicago Press, 1971.

Petigliani, Tetizia. "A Rare Look at the Jewish Catacombs of Rome." *Biblical Archaeology Review* 6 (1980): 32–43.

Preuss, Mary C. *Eloquence and Ignorance in Augustine's "On the Nature and Origin of the Soul."* Atlanta: Scholars, 1985.

Rees, Brinley Roderick. *The Letters of Pelagius and His Followers.* Woodbridge, England: Boydell, 1991.

————. *Pelagius: A Reluctant Heretic.* Woodbridge, England: Boydell, 1988.

Richard, Marcel, ed. *Asterii sophistae: Commentariorum in Psalmos quae supersunt.* Oslo: Brogger, 1956.

Robinson, James M., ed. *The Nag Hammadi Library.* San Francisco: Harper and Row, 1977.

Rossi, Mary Ann. "Priesthood, Precedent, and Prejudice: On Recovering the Women Priests of Early Christianity." *Journal of Feminist Studies in Religion* 7 (1991): 73–94.

Rousselle, Aline. *Porneia: On Desire and the Body in Antiquity.* Oxford: Blackwell, 1988.

Rudolph, Kurt. *Gnosis: The Nature and History of Gnosticism.* San Francisco: Harper and Row, 1987.

Ruether, Rosemary Radford. *Faith and Fratricide: The Theological Roots of Anti-Semitism.* New York: Seabury, 1974.

———. "Misogynism and Virginal Feminism in the Fathers of the Church." In *Religion and Sexism: Images of Women in the Jewish and Christian Tradition,* ed. Rosemary Radford Ruether. New York: Simon and Schuster, 1974.

———. "Mothers of the Church: Ascetic Women in the Late Patristic Age." In *Women of Spirit: Female Leadership in the Jewish and Christian Traditions,* ed. Rosemary Radford Ruether and Eleanor McLaughlin. New York: Simon and Schuster, 1979.

———. ed. *Religion and Sexism: Images of Women in the Jewish and Christian Traditions.* New York: Simon and Schuster, 1974.

Ruether, Rosemary Radford, and Eleanor McLaughlin, eds. *Women of Spirit: Female Leadership in the Jewish and Christian Traditions.* New York: Simon and Schuster, 1979.

Rusch, William G., ed. and trans. *The Trinitarian Controversy.* Philadelphia: Fortress, 1980.

Sanders, Ed P. *Judaism: Practice and Belief, 63 B.C.E.–66 C.E.* Philadelphia: Trinity Press International, 1992.

Schürer, Emil. *The History of the Jewish People in the Age of Jesus Christ (175 B.C.–A.D. 135),* ed. Geza Vermes and Fergus Millar. Rev. ed. 3 vols. in 4. Edinburgh: Clark, 1973–1987.

Segal, Alan F. *Rebecca's Children: Judaism and Christianity in the Roman World.* Cambridge, Mass.: Harvard University Press, 1986.

Shanks, Herschel, ed. *Christianity and Rabbinic Judaism: A Parallel History of Their Origins and Early Development.* Washington, D.C.: Biblical Archeology Society, 1992.

Smart, Ninian. *Worldviews: Crosscultural Explorations of Human Beliefs.* New York: Scribner's, 1983.

Stead, Christopher. *Divine Substance.* Oxford: Clarendon, 1977.

———. *Substance and Illusion in the Christian Fathers.* London: Variorum, 1988.

Stern, Menahem. *Greek and Latin Authors on Jews and Judaism.* 3 vols. Jerusalem: Israel Academy of Sciences and Humanities, 1974–1984.

Stevenson, James. *A New Eusebius: Documents Illustrative of the History of the Church to A.D. 337.* New York: Macmillan, 1957.

Swift, Louis J. *The Early Fathers on War and Military Service.* Wilmington, Del.: Glazier, 1983.

Torjesen, Karen Jo. *When Women Were Priests.* San Francisco: Harper, 1993.

Valantasis, Richard. *Spiritual Guides of the Third Century.* Minneapolis: Fortress, 1991.

Walzer, Richard, comp. and trans. *Galen on Jews and Christians.* London: Oxford University Press, 1949.

White, L. Michael. *Building God's House in the Roman World: Architectural Adaptation Among Pagans, Jews, and Christians*. Baltimore: Johns Hopkins University Press, 1990.

Wilken, Robert L. *The Christians as the Romans Saw Them*. New Haven: Yale University Press, 1984.

———. *John Chrysostom and the Jews: Rhetoric and Reality in the Late Fourth Century*. Berkeley and Los Angeles: University of California Press, 1983.

———. *The Land Called Holy: Palestine in Christian History and Thought*. New Haven: Yale University Press, 1992.

Williams, Rowan. *Arius: Heresy and Tradition*. London: Darton, Longman and Todd, 1987.

Winslow, Donald F. *The Dynamics of Salvation: A Study in Gregory of Nazianzus*. Cambridge, Mass.: Philadelphia Patristic Foundation, 1979.

Yarbrough, Anne. "Christianization in the Fourth Century: The Example of Roman Woman." *Church History* 45 (1976): 149–165.

Young, Frances M. *From Nicaea to Chalcedon: A Guide to Literature and Its Background*. Philadelphia: Fortress, 1983.

Ziegler, Konrat, ed. *Iuli Firmici Materni v c de errore profanarum religionum*. Leipzig: Teubner, 1907.

About the Book and Author

Every religion represents a worldview, an account of human beings and their place in the world, of birth and death, of pain and suffering, of wealth and poverty, of injustice and war. At the dawn of the Christian era, the first Christian intellectuals wrestled with these questions, and in *Birth of a Worldview,* Robert Doran tells the story of how they worked to make their world comprehensible.

Amid much internal strife, amid the competing worldviews of Hellenistic paganism and early Judaism, figures from Justin Martyr to Saint Augustine hammered out what became the worldview that dominated thought in the Christian West for a millennium. By illuminating the varieties of views within the early church and the rich cultural environment in which these views were contested, Doran reveals a fascinating process that might well have turned out dramatically differently. In this high-stakes game, heretics were simply the losers.

Among the many riches of this book are the review of the role of women, the documentation of the vitality and influence of Jewish intellectual thought, and the continuing impact of Greek intellectual thought during Christianity's formative years. In addition, Doran's generous and effective use of long passages from a wide range of original sources gives his account a freshness and authenticity not to be found in other accounts of this period.

Birth of a Worldview is a breakthrough study of the first Christian intellectuals. Scholarly and engaging throughout, it will attract a wide range of scholars, students, and general readers in religious studies and ancient history.

Robert Doran is professor of religion at Amherst College. He is the author of *Temple Propaganda: The Purpose and Character of 2 Maccabees; The Lives of Simeon Stylites;* and many articles on the early Christian church.

Index

importance of, 115
and original sin, 124, 127–129, 130
Bardaisan, 119
bar Kosiba, Simon, 51
bar Kosiba revolt, 51–52, 57
Basil of Caesarea
  influences on, 158
  and Jesus/God relationship, 104–105, 108
Bible. *See* Christian Scriptures
Blandina, 149
Body, 79–80. *See also* Sexuality
Book of Proverbs, 86
Børresen, Kari, 156
Brown, Peter, 28, 80, 113–114, 136

Caecilian of Carthage, 132
Caelestius, 140
Caesar, Julius, 54
Caligula, Gaius, 55
Callistus of Rome, Pope, 90
Cappadocians, 104–105, 121–123
Carpocrates, 88
Carthage, 132
Cassian, John, 126–127
Cassianus, Julius, 116–117
Castelli, Elizabeth, 153
Celibacy. *See* Virginity/celibacy
Celsus, 48, 56, 85
Cerinthus, 88
Change, 33–34, 40
Christianity
  and alienation, 65
  and God/Jesus relationship, 85–114
  Hebrew Scriptures and defining, 66–78, 83, 157–158
  human nature and original sin, 115–143
  influence of Greek philosophy on, 31–33, 35–36, 37, 157–158
  lifestyle prescriptions, 78–83
  pagans on, 47–49
  and relations with Jews, 56–58, 61–63
  and relations with Roman Empire, 9–28

study methodologies for, 2–7
and women, 145–156
Christian Scriptures
  and Arian debate, 97, 100
  on civic relations, 10
  interpretations of Christ and apostleship, 5–6
  and mustard-seed fallacy, 2–3
  and Origen, 96
  and terminology, 99
  and Valentinians, 70–71, 87
  and women/femininity, 145–146, 149, 155
  See also Genesis
Christian writings
  early Christianity and authoritative, 70
  treatment of Judaism, 57, 58, 61–63
  and women, 146–156
  See also Christianity; *specific authors*
Chrysostom of Antioch, Saint John
  and anti-Judaism, 62
  and newborns, 125
  on sin and marriage, 119, 120, 126
  and women, 150–151, 152, 153
Church-state issues
  Augustine on, 27–28
  Eusebius and monarchy, 14
  and Roman Empire after Constantine, 14–18
  See also Roman Empire
Cicero, 19, 54
Circumcision, 61
City of God (Augustine), 26, 28
Civic affairs
  Christianity and involvement in, 11–12
  and Jews in Roman Empire, 59–60
  See also Political culture
Clark, Elizabeth, 136, 137–138, 150
Claudius, 55
Cleanthes, 35
Clementine Recognitions, 5
Clement of Alexandria, 74, 78
  and femininity in the divine, 154–155
  on marriage, 81, 116–117, 126
  on sin and newborns, 123–124

Lifestyle
  Christian ritual, 78–79. *See also*
    Liturgy, Christian
  and Christian sexuality, 79–83. *See
    also* Sexuality
Liturgies, Roman, 59–60
Liturgy, Christian
  baptism, 115, 124, 127–129, 130,
    139
  the Eucharist, 78–79
  and women, 147–149
Logos
  Athanasius and impassibility of, 100–
    102
  and Justin Martyr, 75
  as mediator, 88–98, 99
  as mind of Jesus, 108–109
  and Platonism, 42, 86
  in Stoic cosmology, 35–36
  and two natures of Jesus, 109–113
  Valentinians on, 86–87
Longinus, 32
Lucifer of Calaris, 15

Mani, 117
Manichees, 19, 117, 134, 135
Marcion, 67–68
Markus, Robert A., 25
Marriage
  Christian defense of, 116–117, 118,
    125–126, 131
  Greco-Roman society and Christian
    rejection of, 80–83
  See also Sexuality
Martial, 55
Martyrdom, 10
Martyrdom of Isaiah, 57
Mary
  and Arian controversy, 111
Mathematics
  and Platonic cosmology, 40–41
Maximilla, 151–152
Melania the Elder, 152–153
Melania the Younger, 153
Melito of Sardis, 58, 89
Messalians, 117
Methodius of Olympus, 96, 97

Milan, 16
Military service, 11
Mind
  and Jesus/God relationship, 85
  and Platonism, 37–38, 42–44
Mishnah, 52
Monarchians, 89–90
Monotheism, 78
Mosaic Law
  and Christians, 66–67, 74, 76, 83
  See also Hebrew Scriptures
Moses
  Justin Martyr on, 75
  See also Mosaic Law
Mustard-seed fallacy, 2–6

Narcissus, 45
Nerva, 55
Nestorius of Constantinople, Bishop,
  109, 111
Nicene Creed, 14
Nicenes, 16
Noetus, 89
North Africa, 128, 132
Nous. *See* Mind
Numenius, 42, 47

Odysseus, 45
Odyssey (Homer), 73, 105–106
Olympias, 153
On the Parts of the Human Body
  (Galen), 47
Order
  and Augustine, 139
  and Greek cosmology, 33, 34, 44
Origen, 58
  and civic involvement, 11
  and Hebrew Scriptures, 74, 75–77
  and incorporeal God, 35
  and Jesus/God relationship, 90, 92–
    96
  and original sin, 121, 127–128
  and Platonism, 78
Ossius of Cordova, 15
Otranto, Giorgio, 147–148
Ousia, 98–99, 102, 103–105

Ovid, 54

Paganism
  and the divine in human form, 105–
    106
  and divine knowledge, 46
  post-Constantine assault on, 18–23,
    158
  view of Christianity and Judaism, 47–
    49
Palestinian Talmud, 51
Parables
  and Augustine on forceful
    conversion, 25
  and Christian treatment of Judaism,
    57
  mustard-seed, 2–3
  and Valentinus on Jesus, 71
  See also Christian Scriptures; Hebrew
    Scriptures
Parmenides of Elea, 33, 34, 40
Paul
  on civic relations, 10
  imagery and the body, 80
  interpretation of apostleship, 5
  Marcion and rejection of Hebrew
    Scriptures, 67, 68
  Stoic influences, 37
  and women, 145, 151
Paulinus, 140
Pelagia, 149–150
Pelagian controversy, 139–141
Pelagius, 140–141
Perfect Discourse, 46
Perpetua, Vibia, 149
Persecution
  early Christian, 9–10, 11, 147
  and Jews, 158. *See also* Jews
  of paganists, 21–22, 158
Peter, 10
Philo of Alexandria, 56, 63
  and Jewish settlement during
    Diaspora, 52
  and Logos, 85–86
  and Platonism, 3, 73
  on two levels of existence, 38–39

Plato
  cosmology, 37–41, 42
  and human difference, 118
  influence of, 32
  on private cults, 19
  See also Platonism
Platonism
  and Augustine, 133, 157, 158
  cosmology, 34, 37–46, 75
  influence on Christianity, 47–49, 71,
    78, 157–158
  mind and body in, 85
  Philo and, 3, 73
Pliny, 78–79, 86
Plotinus
  cosmology of, 42–46
  and incorporeal mind, 85
  influence of, 32–33, 69, 157
Plutarch, 41–42
Pneuma, 35, 36
Political culture
  and development of Christian
    thought, 3–4, 158
  and women's role, 154
  See also Roman Empire
Polycarp of Smyrna, Bishop, 9
Pompey the Great, 54
Porphyry
  and Augustine, 157, 162(n13)
  criticism of Christianity, 49
  Life of Plotinus, 32, 72–73
  on the mind, 85
Posidonius of Apamea, 31–32, 34
Praxeas, 89
Predestination, 71. *See also* Free will
Priscilla, 148–149, 151–152
Proba, Faltonia Betitia, 152
Prophecy, Christian, 74–75
Prudentius, 22–23
Ptolemy, 73–74, 87

Quintilla, 148–149
Qumran Covenanters, 56, 63

Redemption
  and Arian debate, 97–98, 101–102